Nathanael West

Nathanael West:
An Interpretative Study

by James F. Light

Second Edition

Northwestern University Press
Evanston   1971

James F. Light is Bernhard Professor and Chairman of the English Department of the University of Bridgeport.

For Amy and Rowena

Acknowledgments

A BOOK SUCH AS THIS is a collaboration of many people. The most important of my collaborators, without whose aid the work could not have been written, are the numerous friends and acquaintances of Nathanael West who shared their knowledge of him with me. Especially I must express my appreciation to such close friends of West as Miss Josephine Herbst, Mr. Philip Lukin, Mr. John Sanford, Dr. Saul Jarcho, and Mr. Jeremiah Mahoney, all of whom responded to my requests for biographical help with a generosity beyond rational expectation. Only slightly less am I indebted to other friends and acquaintances of West, among them Mr. Ira S. Robbins, Mr. Quentin Reynolds, Mr. Frank O. Hough, Mr. William A. Dyer, Professor I. J. Kapstein, Mr. John Monk, Mr. James T. Farrell, Mr. Edmund Wilson, Mr. Sidney Jarcho, Mr. Allan Seager, Mr. Nathan Asch, Mr. Malcolm Cowley, Mrs. Richard Pratt, Mr. Robert M. Coates, Mr. Edward Newhouse, Mr. Wells Root, Miss Jo Conway, Mr. William Faulkner, Mr. Whitney Bolton, Mr. Bennett Cerf, Mr. Charles A. Pearce, and Mr. Stuart McGowan. To Mr. Milton E. Noble, the Recorder of the College of Brown University, Mr. James R. Strawbridge, Recorder of Tufts University, and Mr. Walter Degnan, principal of De Witt Clinton High School, I owe thanks for providing me with certain facts about West's academic career.

It would be impossible to express fully my gratitude to Professor William White of Wayne State University, Mr. Richard Gehman, Mr. Cyril Schneider, and Mr. Herman Levart. Each of these men has contributed on his own to West scholarship; yet each generously placed at my disposal notes and letters which might have had professional value for him. In addition I should note my debt to Professor White for his exhaustive bibliography of West, published in Volume XI, pages 207–225, in the University of Virginia series *Studies in Bibliography*.

I am deeply grateful to my friends Jack Conroy, who first suggested that I might do such a book, and Professor David Owen of Syracuse University, who helped and encouraged me in the writing of the first draft of the manuscript. Professor Walter Rideout of the University of Wisconsin, Miss Karen Jensen of Northwestern University Press, and Mr. Malcolm Cowley read later drafts, and to them I am indebted for advice on both style and content. Conversations about West with my friends and students have helped me in numerous intangible ways. In this respect I am most indebted to Professor James R. Bash of Indiana State University, Professor Ed Cady of Indiana University, President Leonard Lief of Lehman College, Professor Walter Sutton of Syracuse University, and Professor Norman Silverstein of Queens College, New York.

To the corporation of Yaddo, and especially to Mrs. Elizabeth Ames, I owe my gratitude for a summer's stay at the Yaddo Artists' Colony, where the manuscript began to approach its final form. I am grateful to *American Quarterly*, *Contact*, *Prairie Schooner*, *College English*, and *Modern Fiction Studies* for allowing me to use material which, in somewhat different form, has appeared in their pages. To Miss Mary Day and Mrs. Svea Reuther, secretaries respectively of the English departments of Indiana State University and the University of Bridgeport, I am grateful for aid far beyond the call of duty. I am deeply appreciative of a grant from the Ford Foundation that partially subsidized the publication of the study.

The following copyright permissions have been generously granted:

Note

Parenthetical numbers in the text indicate page references to the Farrar, Straus and Cudahy edition of *The Dream Life of Balso Snell* and of *A Cool Million*, both in *The Complete Works of Nathanael West* (1957), and to the New Directions editions of *Miss Lonelyhearts* (n.d.) and *The Day of the Locust* (1950).

Contents

Foreword

WHEN *Nathanael West: An Interpretative Study* was first published in 1961, there were numerous critical essays upon West but no full-length study of the body of his work. As for the facts of his life, little information existed beyond the scanty data provided in Richard Gehman's introduction to the New Directions edition of *The Day of the Locust.* The intent of my study, as I stated in the original foreword, was "to emphasize . . . the interrelationship between West's life and his art, so that the work, basically, and the life, subordinately, may be seen a little more clearly."

Though some of my earlier critical attitudes have been modified or expanded and though the present study contains additional biographical information, my original purpose remains unchanged in this new edition.

Since the appearance of *Nathanael West* in 1961. West's reputation has grown. That fact is attested to not only by the continuing interpretations of his work appearing in scholarly journals but also by one lengthy monograph, two full-length critical studies, and a book-length biography. The monograph, written by Stanley Edgar Hyman and entitled *Nathanael West* (University of Minnesota Press, 1962), appeared as one of a series of pamphlets on American writers. Noting that he was indebted to *Nathanael West: an Interpretative Study* "for nearly all my biographical information," Mr. Hyman claims that West's genius was in finding "objective correlatives for our sickness and fears: our maimed and ambivalent sexuality, our terror of the idiot mass, our helpless empathy with suffering, our love perverted into sadism and masochism. West did this in convincing present-day forms of the great myths: the Quest, the Scapegoat, the Holy Fool, the Dance of Death." For Hyman, West's greatest book is *Miss Lonelyhearts*, which he claims is one of the three best books, along with *The Great Gatsby* and *The Sun Also Rises*, of the twentieth century. Less successful, for Hyman, is *The Day of the Locust*, which he feels "has no dramatic unity, and in comparison with *Miss Lonelyhearts* . . . has no moral core." Possibly the most controversial and debatable contention of Hyman's study is his discovery of a latent homosexuality and an Oedipal complex in the character of Miss Lonelyhearts. According to Hyman, the climactic scene of the novel, in which Doyle shoots Miss Lonelyhearts, "is of course a homosexual tableau—the men locked in embrace while the woman [Betty] stands helplessly by," and the "case history" of Miss Lonelyhearts can be conjectured in Freudian terms:

> Terrified of his stern religious father, identifying with his soft loving mother, the boy renounces his phallicism out of castration anxiety—a classic Oedipus complex. In these terms the Shrikes are Miss Lonelyhearts' Oedipal parents . . . the scene at the end of Miss Lonelyheart's date with Mary Shrike is horrifying and superb. Standing outside her apartment door, suddenly overcome with passion, he strips her naked under her fur coat while she keeps talking mindlessly of her mother's death, mumbling and repeating herself, so that Shrike will not hear their sudden silence and come out. Finally, Mary agrees to let Miss Lonelyhearts in if Shrike is not home, goes inside, and soon Shrike peers out the door, wearing only the top of his pajamas. It is the child's Oedipal vision perfectly dramatized: he can clutch at his mother's body but loses her each time to his more potent rival.

A more ambitious study is Victor Comerchero's volume *Nathanael West: The Ironic Prophet* (Syracuse, 1964). For Mr. Comerchero *The Dream Life of Balso Snell* foreshadows *Miss Lonelyhearts*, for both are "personal, psychological, and philosophical" novels, but *Miss Lonelyhearts* is by far the greater achievement. Similarly, claims Mr. Comerchero, *A Cool Million* prepares the way for *The Day of the Locust*, for both are primarily "social-psychological and political" novels, but *The Day* is by far the greater.

In his analysis of the novels Mr. Comerchero emphasizes the influence of Freud, the French surrealists and symbolists, and the concepts of the quest and the wasteland as filtered down to West through Jessie L. Weston's *From Ritual to Romance* and T. S. Eliot's *The Waste Land*. For Comerchero, West attempted to crystallize character "by using Freudian images as symbols or objective correlatives of a psychological state," and a good part of the "vague uneasiness" West induces in his audience is "due to our subliminal perception of this Freudian dimension." Under such an emphasis, in one of Mr. Comerchero's least convincing illustrations, Miss Lonelyhearts' religious conversion, at the end of *Miss Lonelyhearts,* becomes the fulfillment of a repressed castration complex: "What Miss Lonelyhearts really accepts is his castration. The religious conversion is really a conversion from latent to overt homosexuality." Approvingly, Comerchero then quotes Hyman's vision of the end of the novel as a "homosexual tableau," and adds: "Hyman has also noted that 'it is West's ultimate irony that the symbolic embrace they manage at the end is one penetrating the body of the other with a bullet.' "

In addition to emphasizing the Freudian influence, Comerchero documents West's indebtedness to the French surrealists and symbolists. The former, such as Breton, Eluard, Lautréamont, and Apollinaire, probably taught West that "the most cruel but most efficient way to overcome conventionalized or dramatized feelings was to make fun of them." From them also West may have learned to combine comedy and tragedy, and their influence helps to explain his obsession with the grotesque, his sense of despair and futility, and his perception of the horror and absurdity of the human condition. To such symbolists as Baudelaire and Rimbaud, according to Comerchero, West "probably owed his extraordinary inclination toward holocaust, toward a damned and sacrificed hero." From Baudelaire West may have especially gained his preoccupations with the concepts of the scapegoat and of apocalypse, and from him also West may have learned to blend "sordid realism and nightmarish fantasy" into a unique half-world.

Perhaps the most important influence of all, in Comerchero's view, is that of T. S. Eliot. From Eliot, says Comerchero, "West derived some of his symbolism—particularly that of the wasteland; and his vision of the contemporary scene seems to have differed little from Eliot's except for a suggested solution: West had none." To make his case Comerchero claims that, in *Miss Lonelyhearts*, "The echoes from Eliot's *Waste Land* have . . . suggested that the novel is a moving modernization of the Grail legend." Comerchero then draws innumerable parallels, some of them perceptive and others farfetched, between Miss Lonelyhearts' mythic "quest" and the quest for the grail as it is treated in Eliot's (and West's) source, *From Ritual to Romance.* For Comerchero, one example of the parallels (though, I feel, a dubious one) is that between Weston's description of a nature ritual, involving an Old Man who appears as a vegetation spirit, and West's chapter "Miss Lonelyhearts and the Clean Old Man." For Comerchero, the parallels here "are ingenious but unmistakable." This Comerchero notes:

> Miss Lonelyhearts and Ned Gates, alias Havelock Ellis and Krafft-Ebing (obvious surrogates for the doctor [mentioned in a footnote by Miss Weston as one of the common figures in a vegetation ritual]), encounter a "clean old man" who, as a homosexual, is not only a "defunct Vegetation Spirit" but one who will serve to suggest his female counterpart [also mentioned by Miss Weston as participating in the ceremonial] as well. In his avowed purpose "to help," *i.e.*, to revitalize the old man, Miss Lonelyhearts' behavior parallels an early preliterary version of the Gawain variant. . . .
> Is it too ugly to see the old man as a Christ figure? Perhaps ugly, but quite probable. Not only does he

"love mankind," but like the Fisher King, he is sick, unvital, and literally, because of his sickness, sterile.

Possibly the most original and, in some ways, the most dubious portion of Mr. Comerchero's study is his contention that there is such a cumulative character as "Westian man" and this "collective man . . . has been created in West's own image." This character is sexually incompetent, totally entrapped, endlessly suffering, and possessed of an unconscious death wish. For those critics who might accept the concept of a "Westian hero" (or victim) but who balk at identifying that creature with West himself, Comerchero asserts that West made a "complex attempt" to disguise his psyche by keeping his self-portrait "muffled and ambiguous," but the revelation, despite West's constant masks, exists for perceptive readers to discover.

A more limited, and certainly less daring, study than Comerchero's is Randall Reid's *The Fiction of Nathanael West: No Redeemer, No Promised Land.* In his introduction Mr. Reid notes that "A critical study of Nathanael West is hardly a novelty," and he then adds: "West is routinely cited as a precursor of literary trends, his name is sure to be dropped in any discussion of the grotesque, and book reviewers automatically compare new Hollywood novels with *The Day of the Locust. Miss Lonelyhearts* has even undergone that ceremony which, in some literary circles, constitutes ritual initiation—two recent critics have detected in it a case of repressed homosexuality." For Reid, then, there is no longer any possibility that West's work will be forgotten; instead, he sees the danger that the art will be "taken for granted." Reid thus emphasizes the uniqueness of West's art as art. In doing so he concentrates upon the sources, literary and otherwise, upon which West drew, and he emphasizes the significance of satire and parody as primary devices which West used to express his pessimistic conviction that, for modern man, there is "no redeemer, no promised land." To Reid, West's art defies categorization, for though West is a "formal writer who made deliberate use of conventions," he is also an experimentalist who deserves to be remembered as "one of the more interesting innovators" of the twentieth century. Thus West is "a curious figure. He repudiated social realism but focused on sociological themes, dismissed psychological novels but was an acute literary psychologist, laughed at art but was a conscious and dedicated artist. He was a dandy with proletarian sympathies, a comic writer who specialized in unfunny jokes."

In his discussion of the novels of West, Reid is impressive in his analysis of the use of scatology as a comic conceit in *The Dream Life of Balso Snell* and in the documentation of his thesis that what *Balso* "means" is "that a good many fashionable ideas and stanzas have been made ridiculous through parody." In minimizing the thematic conflict in the book between spirit and flesh, and as a consequence ignoring the serious intent of the farce, parody, and satire which dominate the tone of the book, Reid does, however, do some injustice, or so it seems to me, to the novel.

Possibly Reid's best chapter is that on *Miss Lonelyhearts*. There, drawing in great fullness on West's sources, Reid concretely illustrates West's indebtedness to William James; to Dostoevsky's *Crime and Punishment;* to Huxley's *Antic Hay;* to the symbolist French poets (especially in their hallucinatory images and compressed language); and to the ritual theater, the comic-strip novel, and the concept of the waste land (though Reid claims that *Miss Lonelyhearts'* "psychology owes far more to regenerative myths than to Freud and far more to ascetic or apocalyptic Christianity than to Jessie L. Weston"). In the chapter, Reid also indicts, by close reading, the Hyman-Comerchero reading of an Oedipal complex and latent homosexuality in Miss Lonelyhearts. Quoting the "case history" of Miss Lonelyhearts as constructed by Hyman, Reid notes that, despite its plausibleness, the history

> contains a disconcerting number of inventions, misstatements, and omissions. From the novel, we know only that Miss Lonelyhearts' father was a minister, not that he was stern or loud-voiced or that Miss Lonelyhearts was terrified of him. The only evidence that Miss Lonelyhearts even had a mother—hard or soft, loving or cruel—is the fact of his own existence. Further, Miss Lonelyhearts is not "suddenly overcome with passion." Instead, he is trying "to work this spark [of desire] into a flame," (p. 91) trying "desperately to keep the spark alive" (p. 92). Mary is so far from being the object—maternal or otherwise —of his desire that his sexual response is an effort of the will, not a passionate act. Her "tantalizing breast" fails to tantalize. And the case history ignores the connivance of the Shrikes in the comedy enacted, a comedy in which Miss Lonelyhearts is perhaps the most passive and innocent party. The comedy's chief author is, of course, Shrike himself.

Of the "homosexual tableau" on which the novel ends, Reid comments:

> Again, this is persuasive until one reads the novel. The embrace is "symbolic" enough, but it is hardly suggestive of homosexuality. Doyle shouts a warning, but Miss Lonelyhearts "did not understand the cripple's shout and heard it as a cry for help from Desperate, Harold S., Catholic-mother, Brokenhearted, Broad-shoulders, Sick-of-it-all, Disillusioned-

with-tubercular-husband. He was running to succor them with love (p. 212)." Miss Lonelyhearts has clearly lost all sense of particular identity. The object of his embrace has neither sex nor substance. It is an abstraction, a compound illusion projected upon a real person whom Miss Lonelyhearts barely recognizes. And Doyle, the other party to the "homosexual tableau," tries to escape the embrace and also tries to get rid of the gun. It is the entry of the "helpless" Betty, "cutting off his escape," which leads to the grotesque accident of Miss Lonelyhearts' death.

The most significant contribution to biographical knowledge of West is Jay Martin's *Nathanael West: the Art of his Life* (Farrar, Straus and Giroux, 1970). Done with the cooperation of Mr. and Mrs. S. J. Perelman, the literary executors of the West estate, the book does not greatly alter general understanding of West's character (though it does, by its facts, refute much of Comerchero's conception of a "Westian man" created in West's own image). The book does, however, correct numerous errors of earlier biographical sources, and it also adds a host of details that help to eliminate some of the mystery from West's life but still leaves what Mr. Martin calls a "myth [which] has become part of our modern history." By this accumulation of facts —especially about the women in West's life—Martin makes West into a more rounded human being than the skeleton constructed in earlier studies, which were done without the aid, and often despite the hostility, of the Perelmans. In drawing his portrait, Martin emphasizes the divided character of West, especially the qualities of his tough intellectualism as opposed to his tender sensitivity toward people, and contrasts the dualism which left him devoted to the spirit of the twenties (skepticism, artistic experimentation, aestheticism) and yet drawn to the spirit of the thirties (less concerned with art than life and strongly devoted to commitment and social reform). Martin further claims that West was unable to relate closely to any one person—save, possibly, for his sister Laura and his friend Perelman—but that he had "an enormous capacity to understand and identify with mass life in general." If Martin is correct, it might well follow, as Martin claims, that "What may have begun as a personal incapacity, then, he turned brilliantly into a triumph of art. . . . West's perception of the fact and implications of the birth of mass man and his ability to give his understanding form in fiction constituted his interest for his contemporaries, and explains his special fascination for us."

The weaknesses of Mr. Martin's study are possibly the flaws of high ambitions and good intentions. Because of the former his book is a long one, which is padded with the historical milieu and which devotes excessive attention to such minor writings as West's unpublished stories and plays and his trivial screenplays. Because of his noble intentions, Martin indulges in rhetoric that might well be challenged even by some dedicated Westians. Of a group of unpublished stories, Martin claims: "West's tales are not stories in the ordinary sense; for he set out in them to define form and character anew." Of the little magazine *Contact*, which West co-edited with William Carlos Williams for the three issues of its existence, Martin claims: "Viewed historically . . . *Contact* was to be the culmination of two decades of little-magazine publishing." Of West's work as a whole, Martin insists: "One of West's great achievements had been in writing a series of anti-novels in which is summarized the history of the twentieth-century poetic imagination, from symbolism through surrealism and super-realism." Such claims reveal a critic who has fallen in love with his subject —and numerous major critics do now seem to agree that

though West may not be a novelist of the stature of Faulkner and Hemingway, he is more than merely a significant
minor artist—but they also seem somewhat extravagant and
even inappropriate as judgments on a writer who despised
romantic rhetoric and who used words, as Malcolm Cowley
has claimed, so precisely and with such condensation that
his books read like telegrams sent to distant lands.

Despite the irony implicit in such rhetoric, it is good to
see, at last, a comprehensive biographical study of a writer
who served both as a seismograph for his time and a prophet
of ours. As I indicated in the Foreword to my own earlier
study, that book was not and could not be such a study. Its
justification still remains the attempt to show the relationship between West's work and life. In addition, as I earlier
stated, "I have tried to show the most important influences
on his [West's] mind and art. The theme of the Quest,
which I feel is biographically relevant, runs through each
analysis of the novels, but the analyses themselves are less
examples of archetypal or psychological criticism than attempts at explaining the text adequately."

Nathanael West

1 *The College Years*

In February of 1922, at the age of eighteen, Nathan Weinstein, later to become known as the novelist Nathanael West, matriculated at Brown University. The road he traveled to Brown is a curious and perplexing one.

Born in New York on October 17, 1903, Weinstein, or West, was the only son of Jewish immigrant parents, Max Weinstein and Anna Wallenstein* Weinstein. His early

---

* Anna (originally Chana-Mindel Leizerovna Wallenstein) and Max (originally Mordecai Weinstein) were both immigrants from the Russian province of Lithuania. In this territory, where Germanic

schooling, in which he made an indifferent record, came in Manhattan grammar schools, first P.S. 81 on 119th Street, and then, for grades seven and eight, P.S. 186. After graduation in 1917, West entered De Witt Clinton High, a large school with an excellent academic reputation. West's irregular attendance—in one term alone he had 38 absences—continued a habit and reflected an attitude that West had revealed in elementary school, and he quickly became one of the weakest students enrolled. The school's passing grade was 60; West's marks, each representing a half-year's work in the subject, were as follows: English 70, 50, 40, 80, 70, 70. Latin 60, 40. Spanish 60, 30. History 80, 65. Elementary Biology 75, 60. Chemistry 60, 30, 60. Algebra 40, 60, 20, 60. Geometry 40, 40. Elocution 70, 60, 85, 75, 0, 0.[1] Although there were both a school newspaper and a literature and art magazine, *The Magpie,* Weinstein, or West, took no part in these or any other extracurricular activities. Something of a dreamer, lackadaisical and easygoing, he soon acquired the ironic nickname of Pep. No one at De Witt Clinton was greatly surprised when West left school in June, 1920, without graduating.

By the time he left De Witt Clinton, West had passed, though barely, in enough subjects to have gained nine college entrance units. Since college entrance requirements, at least in most Eastern colleges of any merit, demand a mini-

influences were strong, Lazar Wallenstein (Anna's father) and Nachman Weinstein (Max's father) worked together in the construction business. Though the families were friendly, Lazar Wallenstein was considerably more affluent in Lithuania than was Nachman Weinstein, and Nachman and his five sons—Jacob, Julius, Charles, Max, and Abraham—were employed as builders, primarily carpenters and stonemasons, by Lazar Wallenstein. With the policy of Russification begun around 1881 by Alexander III, the freedoms of both Jews and Germans in Lithuania were restricted, and beginning in 1887, with the migration of Julius Weinstein, the two families aided each other in seeking a new land and new hopes in America.

mum of fifteen college entrance units, it seemed unlikely
that West would soon gain entrance to a worthy college.

A year after he left De Witt Clinton, however, West
managed to enter Tufts University. There, in September,
1921, West was accepted as a candidate for the "B.S. Arts"
degree. His acceptance was based on a De Witt Clinton
transcript which showed him as having earned, solely at
De Witt Clinton, fifteen and one-half college entrance units
as follows: Latin, three; Physics, one; Modern History, one;
Free Hand Drawing, one-half; Biology, one; Chemistry,
one; and eight units unspecified but distributed among Elementary English, Elementary Language (Spanish), American History, Elementary Algebra, and Plane Geometry.[2]
The glaring discrepancies between the records of West's
academic work at De Witt Clinton High School and the
records of the work for which West was given credit at
Tufts University are explainable by a simple fact: that West
falsified his De Witt Clinton transcript and added six credits to his academic record. His matriculation at Tufts, however, had not altered his dislike for class attendance, and on
November 25, 1921—after receiving failing marks in all his
courses—he was advised to withdraw from the university.
This he did, and in February, 1922, enrolled at Brown University as a transfer student from Tufts.

In enrolling at Brown University, West used the name
Nathan Weinstein, a name slightly different from Nathaniel
Weinstein, which he had used when he enrolled at Tufts.
The consequences of this slight difference in name were
rather astonishing. The reason for the strange results was
that at Tufts there had been enrolled another Nathan Wein-
stein, an entirely different person from the future Nathanael
West. This namesake of the future novelist had been born
in June, 1899. He had prepared for college at English High
School in Boston, had attended Harvard Dental school from

5

1917 to 1919, and had then, in February, 1920, entered Tufts University. (The future Nathanael West had of course been born in New York and was attending high school there from September, 1917, to June, 1920.) The Boston Nathan Weinstein withdrew from Tufts in June, 1921. By that time, this namesake of the future novelist had done work for which Tufts had given him sixty hours of college credit: forty-seven gained at Tufts and thirteen at Harvard Dental School. When the future Nathanael West entered Tufts, he enrolled as Nathaniel Weinstein (the spelling is correct), but when, a few months later, he enrolled at Brown, he used the name Nathan Weinstein. From this slight change in name, apparently, there occurred a result that may have been planned, but possibly was accidental: the college credits earned by the Boston Nathan Weinstein were credited by Brown University to the record of the New York Nathan Weinstein. This credit windfall was not made official until March, 1922, at which time Brown University evaluated the credits earned by the Boston Nathan Weinstein at Harvard Dental School and Tufts University. The evaluation lowered the earned credits slightly, but the New York Nathan Weinstein (or Nathanael West) still retained fifty-seven college credits earned by another man. Some of these credits—in Chemistry, Biology, Physics, and Economics—were in areas required in most colleges, and the acquisition of credits in these subjects, all of them uncongenial to West's mentality, undoubtedly helped West to stay in college and made it possible for him to graduate in two and a half years.[3]

Despite this credit windfall, it could not, to an objective observer, have seemed likely that West would do well enough to remain long at an institution with such high academic standards as Brown. Looking beneath the obvious, however, that same observer might have found some reason

6

to believe that West's career at Brown might turn out better than his previous academic endeavors. For one thing West's parents were highly intelligent. Though the intelligence on the paternal side was directed primarily toward acquiring money, this was counterbalanced by the inheritance from the maternal, or Wallenstein, branch of the family. As the linguistic accomplishments of Anna Weinstein's sister, Susanna Wallenstein, would suggest, the Wallensteins were accustomed to high educational standards: Susanna was skilled in Russian, French, German, and Yiddish, and knew Latin, Greek, Hebrew, and Polish moderately well. Another of Anna's sisters, Pauline Wallenstein, and two brothers, Saul and Samuel, though not blessed with exceptional talent, showed strong artistic inclinations. More to the point, West's own parents had great respect, almost reverence, for education. For each of their children, but most of all for their son, they wished at least a college degree.

In addition West himself, during adolescence, had shown a mental, artistic temperament rather than a physical, acquisitive one. Fond of outdoor life (the family habitually spent summers in the country) and addicted to dreams of sports heroics, he was still more withdrawn, reticent, and bookish than most boys. A thin, ungainly child, lacking in vigor, "pepper," and real athletic ability, he seemed out of place at Camp Paradox, where he spent a number of summers. There he was "a quiet chap and not much of a mixer."[4] As Art Editor of the camp newspaper he printed his own cartoons to satirize the conventional values and idealized figures of the campers. Yet as the camp dreamer, he often seemed in another world. Once while he was playing baseball:

A long fly was heading straight for Pep . . . the ball hit Pep on the head and rolled away for a homer. He'd been standing there mooning about this Dusty Evsky.

7

. . . He wasn't Nate after that, not to anybody. He was Pep.[5]

As a child West loved playing with toy soldiers, and in his teens he spent many hours learning military lore. Most of all, though, words and names had magic for him. John Sanford remembers a day in Harlem in which

> you were standing on a grass island in Seventh Avenue, and a bus came along, and he [West] astounded you by reeling off its name: De Dion Bouton. And staring in wonderment and envy and admiration you said: "Gee, Nate, how j'ever find that out?" and he said, "Well, I'll tell you, Julie. I ast the driver." And then a second bus passed by, and he named that too: Metallurgique.[6]

Usually when West was at home, he was reading, and he so disliked interruptions that he trained his bull terrier to bite anyone who came into the room while he was reading. He knew German—as did the entire family—but preferred to read in English. By the time he was ten he had begun Tolstoy; at thirteen he had read much of Russian literature. The work of Dostoevsky, in particular, made a lasting impression, and quite possibly the Russian's presentation of the superman philosophy impressed West's youthful mind with dreams of being above the standards and restrictions of the common herd. At this time, too, West was reading *Madame Bovary*, which he admired greatly. Apparently, however, the art of Flaubert made West feel conscious of the limitations of American writers, for in the margin of *Madame Bovary* he noted his estimate of American writing: "No good Americans." Perhaps he had the greatest respect for Henry James, though he deplored James's stylistic convolutions and artificialities of language.*

---

* West's parents often gave their children leather-bound sets of English and Russian authors; West received presents of the writings of

Such literary precocity implied that there was more in West, unconventional and disturbing though it might be, than any school had yet uncovered. The task of Brown would be to challenge the mind without stifling the imagination of a man worthy of its trouble.

At the time Brown was a small Ivy League institution of around twelve hundred students. Its campus was not unattractive, though the factory-brick architecture of its buildings was often derided by unsympathetic observers from Harvard and Princeton and Yale. The Sophomore class, of which West became a member in February, 1922, numbered approximately two hundred. About half of the class were active in campus affairs, while the other half commuted from Providence and nearby towns.

A picture of West during his college period shows a thin, sensitive face, protruding ears, and hair parted in the middle and combed toward the sides. The gentle, quietly smiling eyes are dominant, and arrest attention even in a photograph. How he appeared to his contemporaries is suggested by Philip Lukin, West's roommate during most of his career at Brown. Recalling his first impressions, Lukin writes that West was

> a typical college type of the sophisticated variety. He was meticulously clothed in the then current fashion which meant Brooks Brothers suits, argyle socks, Whitehouse and Hardy brogues, Brooks shirts and ties and Herbert Johnson or Lock and Co. hats. One might assume that he was a dandy when it came to clothes and one would assume that this was an attempt to compensate for his lack of other [attractive] physical attributes.[7]

Tolstoy, Turgenev, Dostoevsky, Chekhov, Thackeray, Dickens, Shakespeare, Hardy, Balzac, and de Maupassant, as well as a number of the novels of Horatio Alger.

Another close friend, Jeremiah Mahoney, adds that West and his friend Brae Rafferty

> made a quaint looking pair. Both were slender; both had sallow, rather coarse and faintly blemished skin, prominent noses, long heads, and a taste for similar clothing—the homburg, the funereal overcoat, the Brooks suit. Together, strolling down College Hill, they resembled a couple of well-heeled mortuary assistants.[8]

Despite his quaint appearance, West was well liked in college. Two incidents recalled by his friend Quentin Reynolds reveal his affable nature. One summer West persuaded Reynolds that he should properly condition himself for football. Since West's father was a contractor, the proper kind of a job was readily available, and West and Reynolds spent their vacation lugging bricks.

> Most of the laborers on the construction job were Italian or Irish. It used to amaze me to see how Pep endeared himself to these ignorant and rather rough characters. They never knew that he was the Boss's son; they just liked him. He had a knack for drawing them out and he had a wonderful knack for listening. Most college kids in the 1920's were strictly non-listeners. Pep was one of the few who would listen, and when he talked, he talked their language—the language of the Bronx where he too had grown up.[9]

Reynolds also remembers an incident involving West and a giant Texan who played on the Brown football team. The Texan was an amiable soul when sober, but when he was drinking, it was something else again. On one of his sprees he came across the 130-pound West and gave him a vicious beating. This so aroused the student body that a meeting was called. A proposal to tar and feather the Texan was being seriously considered when West walked into the meeting. Then, as Reynolds tells the story,

> "Leave him to me," Pep told us solemnly. "I have already challenged him to a fair fight."
> This shocked us. Pep couldn't fight his way out of a charlotte russe, the Texan was the strongest man in college.
> "I have made just one condition," Pep Weinstein said with a straight (if bandaged) face. "He must get down to my weight."[10]

Thanks to West's satiric, gentle nature, the ugly spirit of the meeting dissolved itself in laughter.

On his qualities of likableness and gentleness West's friends are agreed, just as most of them remember him as "gracious, reserved, almost shy."[11] However, West was not always forbearing. Once a Jewish classmate—an obnoxious boy, prone to introduce himself by announcing "My name is ———. My father is a judge"—tried to force his way into the rather close-knit group of West and his friends. When West rebuffed him, his denunciation of the group, "The cream of the Jews and the scum of the Irish," gave West and his friends more amusement than annoyance.[12] An incident recalled by Frank O. Hough shows even better that West could, if annoyed enough, be other than gentle.

> Because Pep was tall and gangling, some people were inclined to think of him as a weakling, which was far from the case. . . . One night a few months after graduation a bunch of us in New York were heading for a party, crowded into a taxicab. I was sitting in the front seat with the driver when I heard my wife in back let out a shriek. Instantly Pep ordered the cab to the curb and leaped out dragging another character by the neck, then proceeded to beat the living day-

lights out of him. Why? Because he had made an indecent pass at my wife.[13]

To West, Brown campus life was many things. One area was athletics. According to Quentin Reynolds, West had great respect for athletic heroes and "especially liked my roommate Roy Eisenberg (our quarterback), a first-rate player even though he only weighed about 140 pounds. Nat admired his terrific guts on the field."[14] Although he participated in no collegiate sport (he was swiftly cut when he tried out for the baseball team), West was a loyal follower of the Brown teams. Dressed in sartorial splendor, and with pocket flasks filled, Lukin and West would cheer frantically during the games and hold lengthy post-mortems afterwards. In this vicarious living and reliving of great moments on the playing field, West recalls his contemporaries F. Scott Fitzgerald and Ernest Hemingway. Most likely West had occasional dreams of glory similar to those of Fitzgerald:

> "Once upon a time" (I tell myself) "they needed a quarterback at Princeton, and they had nobody and were in despair. The head coach noticed me kicking and passing on the side of the field, and he cried: 'Who is *that* man—why haven't we noticed *him* before?' The under coach answered, 'He hasn't been out,' and the response was: 'Bring him to me.'
> ". . . we go to the day of the Yale game. I weigh only one hundred and thirty-five, so they save me until the third quarter, with the score—"
> —But it's no use—I have used that dream of a defeated dream to induce sleep for almost twenty years, but it has worn thin at last.[15]

Possibly West also saw in athletics a world of classic order, one of perfect control in which rules were followed and the best man really won; and possibly he would have sympathized with Hemingway's need for, and consequent worship of, such a simplified universe:

> [An] analyst once wrote me [Hemingway], What did
> I learn from psychoanalysts? I answered, Very little
> but hope they learned as much as they were able to
> understand from my published works. You never saw
> a counter-puncher who was punchy. Never lead
> against a hitter unless you can outhit him. Crowd a
> boxer, and take everything he has, to get inside. Duck
> a swing. Block a hook. And counter a jab with every-
> thing you own. Papa's delivery of hard-learned facts
> of life.[16]

A second thing that West found at Brown was a life of the hard-drinking, hard-petting, adolescent Bohemian in the Scott Fitzgerald tradition. Exemplifying it were Larry Schumann, the rich friend with the $600 raccoon coat and the $500 monthly allowance, and Thomas Bernard Farrell, Jr., a barber's son and a brilliant student who made quite a success at Brown as the college bootlegger. "Tom kept his fancy clothes in [West's and Lukin's] room and went home . . . in the clothes his parents provided for him."[17] Lukin, Rafferty, Mahoney, West, and John Kazanjian comprised what was christened by West the "Hanseatic League," and they so frequently found their way down the Hill to Joe Schmedley's, a small all-men's restaurant, that they

> became habitues, had—almost but not quite—our own
> table, our own favorite antique waiter; and each of
> us felt, I think now, that the ritual somehow had
> distinguished us as a discriminating group of young
> gentlemen—a touching bit of naiveté, since the
> clientele was made up of traveling men, gamblers,
> prize fighters, members of the Providence Steamroller
> football team, sporting life in general. After dinner

we frequently resorted to a movie, either to relax or to mock at what the common man was relishing those days—a kind of intellectual élite, perhaps, descending from our ivory tower to sample and reject the cloying sweets of the public fare.[18]

Usually the "Hanseatic League" laughed during the tragic scenes and wept during the comic ones, reactions which drew irritated shushings from other patrons. Then West and Mahoney changed their tactics and affected

to be greatly moved. On one occasion, we cried over the movie "Ramona." Our sophisticated friends were shocked, didn't know whether we were serious or not, and weren't told. This incident, minor as it is, illustrates the mock-serious character of much of his [West's] behavior. . . . Pep welcomed new ideas as he welcomed new sensations, and he certainly enjoyed piquing complacency of any kind, especially intellectual complacency.[19]

Often the League went to Federal Hill, the Italian district, where the attraction was the saloons that, despite prohibition, never thought of closing. Occasionally the League met close friends such as Frank O. Hough, John Monk, Hobart Haskins, Quentin Reynolds, and Paul Brown. Brown was an envied figure because he "could drink liquor without tasting it . . . he had a trick of opening his gullet so that the liquor would pour directly into his stomach."[20] On Federal Hill, beer and wine washed down Italian bread and pork chops and hot peppers and meat balls. Prices were low, fifteen cents for a sandwich, the same for a giant schooner of beer, and the sessions were long, sometimes lasting from two in the afternoon until midnight. The beer was what the students called "needle beer," a frightening mixture of near-beer and something stronger that ranged from alcohol to ether; it is not surprising that at times the group "did get very drunk."[21]

Often the League wandered to the dances for which Brown was famous. The more elaborate of these were wild, hard-drinking affairs, characterized by a vast amount of petting (an activity in no way hampered by a Brown custom in which the girls removed their girdles before dances) and by wanton juvenile destructiveness (the havoc wrought by the class of 1924's Junior Prom was such that the Providence Biltmore barred all future Junior Proms from its property). There were also tea-dances and Saturday night dances held in halls near the campus; and attendance at these could be supplemented by visits to the Arcadia, a public ballroom. Pick-up dancing was the rule here, and West especially favored the Arcadia because he could find plenty of partners, toward whom he alternated between shyness and brashness. Whether or not he qualified as a "snake," a rug cutter of the twenties, is a moot point: Lukin remembers him as an excellent dancer, his cousin, Saul Jarcho, as just average. In Mahoney's view

> As a dancer, as in all his movements, he was clumsy-graceful, coltish. He once brought back from New York a simple triangular dance step and a clumsily cramped way of holding the left arm, and spent hours demonstrating its complexity to a host of neophytes. The thing could have been learned in two seconds, but he convinced everyone of its difficulty and soon it became the fashionable posture at college dances. Here, if nowhere else, he left his mark on his contemporaries.[22]

Add to West's ambition to be a snake that he played the banjo—fairly well, according to Jarcho—and it appears that he was trying hard to be "collegiate" (as that term was understood in the twenties), and, what's more, he was succeeding almost to the point of caricature. He was aided in this enterprise by a handsome allowance. According to Lukin, West received weekly spending money of $22 over and above his traveling expenses, tuition, room, and clothes. "This was for the 1920's a most substantial sum. My own allowance, and my father was a rather successful physician, was $12 a week under similar terms."[23] Quentin Reynolds also remembers that West received an allowance considerably higher than his friends, and that he was "amazingly generous" with it.[24] Other friends, throughout West's life, have made similar comments about his generosity.

Fraternity life and politics were a third important part of the world at Brown, and in some ways West's involvement in those activities illuminates what he was in college and what he later became as man and writer. West was extremely attracted to fraternity life. Reynolds recollects that West "spent a lot of time at my fraternity house—Delta Tau Delta—and everyone liked him."[25] Similarly West was popular at Hough's fraternity, "the snootiest and most anti-Semitic fraternity on the campus,"[26] and he spent considerable time talking and drinking with Hough's fraternity brothers. According to Hough, West was "welcome at any house on the campus; many's the time I woke in the morning to find him snoring beside me in my absent roommate's bed."[27]

With his own roommate, Philip Lukin, West often talked of fraternities. Lukin himself had no wish to join a fraternity, but West had. It was a strong desire, reminiscent of Scott Fitzgerald's desperate urge to belong to one of the better eating clubs at Princeton, and West often returned to the subject. Occasionally he would tick off the list of Brown fraternities and decide upon those he might be willing to join, for he was insistent that he would only join one of the better fraternities. If he had made such a fraternity,

Lukin surmises, West "would have become completely immersed in middle-class snobbishness as expressed in such fraternity groups and been content with his lot, gone back to New York . . . and never written a line."[28]

West made none of the Brown fraternities and for a very simple reason. Brown, at the time, had no fraternities that accepted Jews. To such friends as Reynolds and Hough, West appeared unperturbed: "Jews were not admitted to fraternities then, but this never bothered Nat."[29] To Lukin, West expressed what was probably his real feeling, and Lukin surmises that the exclusion of West from the Brown fraternities generated deep-seated and long-lasting bitterness, so that

> the West of later years is a mystery to me in terms of the Pep Weinstein of college years. There is an almost complete antithesis. I can only trace it through what must be the hidden resentment at what seemed to be the rejections of college years.[30]

Probably the exclusion brought West forcefully to the knowledge that he was both a Jew and an outsider. In childhood he had not had to live close to those perceptions. His parents had tended to worship *Lamdanuth* (learning) rather than *Chassiduth* (piety) and conceived of themselves less as Jews than as Russians, less as Russians than as Germans, and less as Germans than as Americans—but as Americans (especially the Wallensteins) of aristocratic rather than peasant ancestry. Now, in college, West learned the terrible ambiguity of being an "assimilated" American Jew. On one hand he was friendly with the Brown fraternities, for "nobody ever thought of Pep as being Jewish anyhow."[31] Yet, he was not a "brother" of the fraternity members.

In such a position West, like other second-generation Jews, could strive to be either more "Jewish" or less "Jewish," or he could remain as "Jewish" as he was. West, either consciously or subconsciously, chose to become less "Jewish." In college this desire is implied by the vast amount of time West spent in his classes writing in his notebook the name Nathan von Wallenstein Weinstein,[32] a pastime which not only suggests boredom and romanticism but even more is indicative of a discontent with the self. Just as revelatory is the fact that in college West avoided a certain kind of Jew, the insistently "Jewish" Jew whom West satirized as a type in his first novel, and had nothing to do with organized Jewish activities on campus. After college, West more consciously rejected much of his ancestral heritage. This rejection is evidenced not only in his change of name but even more in his writing. Although he never attended Hebrew schools (but did memorize parts of the Torah and did attend, with his family, the annual high holiday ceremonies presided over by Rabbi Robert Harris at the German Temple Israel), West must have been acquainted with Hebraic lore. But this rich world is almost completely excluded from his work. About the only identifiable Jews in his writings are the following: A Jew who shouts, "I'm a Jew! I'm a Jew!" (p. 8) to flaunt his Jewishness, and the "sensitive young Jews who adore culture" (p. 30), referred to in passing in *Balso Snell;* a crooked lawyer named Goldstein, out to fleece and fleece alone, portrayed in a one-chapter sketch in *A Cool Million;* two characters, undoubtedly Jews, in a short story illustrative of Hollywood greed and venality; and a race-track tout, the dwarf Abe Kusich, who is treated in depth in West's last novel and who represents the fullest extremity of human suffering. Generally, the Semites are summed up by Balso Snell when he says they "are like to a man sitting in a cloaca to the eyes, and whose brows touch heaven" (p. 8). Either particularly or generally, the portrait is so unflattering that several critics have complained of West's anti-Semitism.

From a rejection of "Jewishness," according to psychologists and sociologists, two results will probably follow. One is the need for acceptance and approval by a new group. The other is anxiety and insecurity because of the fear that acceptance may be withheld. Those Jews who desire, and attempt, complete assimilation are caught in a terrible dilemma. The noted sociologist Stonequist comments:

> They are the Jews who have given up, in whole or in part, the Messianic mission and so have lost the inner security which that belief has given to the traditional Jew. They are divided in their social allegiance, drawn forward by the Gentile world but uncertain of its hospitality, restrained by sentiments of loyalty to the Jewish world but repelled by its restrictions. They are self conscious and feel inferior because their social status is in question. They are the partly assimilated, the partly accepted, the real Wandering Jews, at home neither in the ghetto nor in the world outside the ghetto.[33]

In college, West's urge toward fine, tasteful, essentially conformist clothing, as well as his constant and excessive generosity, show his need for approval. Even his shyness, like his quiet voice, would have been regarded, in the Ivy League circles of the period, as a mark of breeding, one opposed to "brashness," and would have helped West win approval in non-Jewish circles. In addition, West's occasional confusion when with strangers and his trembling hands when he was ill at ease in a social situation suggest the state of his mind at certain times. Most illuminating, however, is West's attraction to, and exclusion from, the fraternities of Brown throughout his college career.

The life at Brown in the twenties was more than athletics, adolescent bohemianism, and fraternity snobbishness. A fourth part of West's campus life, even if it was spiced at times with adolescent high-jinks, was the academic and intellectual. William Herbert Perry Faunce, the eloquent and modernist Baptist theologian, was well into his thirty-year tenure as President of Brown, and his stirring advocacy of a liberal education for undergraduates, as well as his sympathy for modern science, set the tone for the college. Brown had a lively faculty, and the English department at this time was particularly distinguished. Among its members were William Hastings, the noted Shakespearean scholar; Lindsay Todd Damon, the editor of the Lake English classics; young and provocative Percy Marks, whose sensational novel of "flaming youth," *The Plastic Age,* was a current best seller; and the beloved Ben Clough, whose overflowing classes listened raptly to his squeaky, tinny voice, and who could make literature exciting and alive even to athletes.

The liveliness of the faculty had its counterpart in the student body. Among West's intimates were S. J. Perelman, Quentin Reynolds, Frank O. Hough, and I. J. Kapstein. Perelman was drawing the cartoons that gained him a reputation in college humor magazines and exhibiting the sharp wit that has placed him in the front rank of American humorists. Reynolds, prominent on the staff of the Brown *Jug,* the college humor magazine, was also dabbling in theatrical activities, playing football, swimming on the varsity, boxing his way to a collegiate championship, and, in his spare time, thinking of a career as a writer. Frank O. Hough, though failing to please Professor Clough in an advanced writing course, was learning the craftsmanship that later enabled him to write his panoramic historical novels. I. J. Kapstein, a future professor at Brown, was not only writing his own sensitive poetry and short stories, but also helping to build

Casements into one of the most notable literary magazines ever born on a campus.

While these men were far too gifted to be typical of the Brown student body, they suggest a prevailing atmosphere in which it was "neither shameful nor *declassé* to be interested in the things of the mind. The leaders of the campus were not ashamed to be so interested and thus the rest, of course, would not be."[34] No doubt the literary and social ferment of the time aided this mood, but another factor was the presence on the campus of many returned veterans. "Unlike the World War II veterans," says William A. Dyer, Jr., who was later to become general manager of the Indianapolis *Star and News*, "these boys were not disillusioned or cynical. Far from it. They were men of the world, who had been to Paris perhaps not very far beyond—and had seen life."[35] At any rate, West responded to this intellectual climate. It was true that he made a poor start at Brown academically, and eventually had to repeat four of his courses: Introduction to the Study of Literature, Greek Civilization 15, Psychology and Ethics, and the second term of the History of Medieval and Modern Europe. It was equally true, however, that after the first term West began to acclimate himself; soon he was one of Professor Clough's "fat cats. . . . I suspect that Ben was one of the first to suspect his (Pep's) writing talent."[36] Lukin remembers that West did well in Professor Fithian's cram course for seniors, in algebra, a course required for graduation. Fithian taught algebraic principles in terms of probabilities in cards and dice, and West thought highly of the course, as did, for obvious reasons, many of the prominent campus gamblers.

But West's enthusiasm for class work was sporadic. Usually he was content to draw satirical sketches (much in the manner of Beardsley and Beerbohm), to doodle images of emaciated, suffering martyrs (much in the style of Roualt), and to write over and over, in various ornate styles, the name Nathan von Wallenstein Weinstein. One course of which he must have approved was given by Professor Courtney Langdon; its purpose, according to Frank O. Hough, was to keep the football team eligible. Professor Langdon, who held an endowed chair and liked to make references to the "puny administration," was tremendously popular; his popularity was probably not altogether unrelated to his boast that he had never, in his entire teaching career, failed a student.

> His conventional opening lecture went approximately as follows: "Gentlemen, this is reputed to be a snap course; this semester I propose to make it snappier than ever. All I ask is that those of you who prefer to read the newspaper occupy the back row, so that those who are interested can hear what I have to say." As I recall, Pep and Quent [Reynolds] took him at his word and sat in the back reading the newspaper. Both passed.[37]

As a rule, West was happy to settle for the "gentleman's mark" of C, and there were times when he did not do even that well. On one occasion, when he was totally unprepared for an exam in a course given by Percy Marks, he yielded to temptation and cribbed from Lukin, who was a consistent A student. The cheating was pretty blatant—even the errors were identical—and Marks called the two men before him. West was quite fearful of the outcome of the investigation, primarily because he felt he had let his parents down. According to Lukin:

> Pep was on college discipline due to over-cutting and would have been dismissed for this infraction [and] I assumed the blame. . . . In the course of settling up this cribbing matter, in which I accepted dismissal from the course, I had to be interviewed by Dean Otis Randall. At one point during the interview Dean

Randall turned to me and said, "Tell me something, Mr. Lukin. Does Mr. Weinstein take dope?" I mention this as an example of the impression that Pep gave some of the faculty people who did not know him well. He was vague and apparently, according to their way of thinking, not too much on the ball and was given to flights of fancy in his non-curriculum scribbling and conversation which apparently gave the impression that he might be under the influence of narcotics.[38]

Apparently Dean Randall was not alone among the faculty in his impression of West. Professor Clough recalls meeting West outside of class only once, and then West seemed vague and confused, as if he had been drinking.

Still, in spite of his indifferent class work, the things of the mind were dominant in West's life at Brown. The college bull sessions, the wide-ranging and undisciplined reading, the experiments in writing—these were his most effective instructors. In bull sessions West tended toward flighty, even disconnected, ramblings, but his ability to quote verbatim and at length from his reading made him an impressive conversationalist. He exhibited a fascinatingly original mind and a preoccupation with the bizarre: for example, his conception of St. Puce, a flea later to reappear in *Balso Snell* as the sole inhabitant of the body of our Lord:

He roamed the forest of God's chest and crossed the hill of his abdomen. He measured and sounded that fathomless well, the Navel of our Lord. He explored and charted every crevasse, ridge and cavern of Christ's body. From notes taken during his travels he later wrote his great work, *A Geography of Our Lord*. (p. 12)

The thread of imagery concerned with smells and bodily orifices which often ran through West's talk suggests to

Jeremiah Mahoney that "he was fascinated by the ironic contrast between his suppurating animal body . . . and the dandiacal way he dressed, acted, and thought as one of the high world."[39] Constantly, too, he attacked set values, no matter where they appeared, but he did it without bitterness, "not as a cynic, but as a mental acrobat."[40]

In bull sessions or at the teas at which West occasionally was host, the basic subjects were those which always have preoccupied literary-minded undergraduates: sex and art and religion. (Politics almost never entered in.) There were the smutty jokes and the campus amatory gossip; there were the endless debates over the virtues of free love and, the burning question of the twenties, a sexual double standard. Probably reflecting his reading in such writers as Huysmans, Machen, and Baudelaire, West was contemptuous of womankind: Odo of Cluny's reference to the female as a *saccus stercoris* was one of his favorite comments. He was also unshakably conservative in his defense of the sexual double standard. When the talk turned to art and the artist's life, topics might range from Mencken and Nathan and the *Smart Set* to Celtic mysticism to Verlaine and Rimbaud. The recent campus lectures of "AE," Padraic Colum, and James Stephens were discussed and rediscussed, and Arthur Symons' pronunciamentos on symbolism were hotly argued. When the talk swung to religion, such matters as whether God existed—or man, either—were probed and resolved, and reconsidered and anew resolved. Sometimes religious discussions evoked experiments in magic, often drawn from Eliphas Lévi's book, *Les Dogmes et Rituel de Haute Magie;* at other times they soared to questionings of the mystical experience. In this connection, there is a story which, while probably apocryphal, may have been heard by such administrators as Dean Randall; it is said that West, wishing to "plumb all human experience . . . tried smoking opium.

The pay-off being that it made him so violently ill he then and there gave up any ambition to become a dope addict."[41] There was a strong interest in Catholicism among the students at this time, and West occasionally contributed to the bull sessions some of the lore that he had accumulated from his considerable reading in the lives of the saints. Like many such readers he had gained a thorough knowledge of the mystical experience, but he read, and discussed what he read, with skepticism, not so much for spiritual inspiration as for "the perversities and oddities in the medieval Catholic writers."[42]

Gossip about the faculty and students also figured in the talk, and though this was largely ephemeral one incident deserves mention. The great local literary event of West's time at Brown was the publication of Percy Marks's novel, *The Plastic Age*. Few of West's circle thought much of the book, but despite its conventional form, imagery, and ideas, it *had been* written by a faculty member, it *was* about college life, it let the students feel that they were living in the forefront of the Jazz Age, and above all it provided a new and provocative pastime: spotting connections between Brown and the college in the novel. For example, the book began with a satiric comment on the American habit of building colleges on hills, and Brown was located on College Hill. It became a game among the students to find correspondences between fictional characters and campus personalities, and reflections of actual happenings in fictional events. The book's indictment of fraternity rushing, anti-intellectualism, and racial discrimination had local as well as universal parallels, while the suggestion of a literary renaissance at the fictional college set a number of Brown's literary lights to preening their feathers. The wild poker game and the cold-deck artist who presided at it echoed reality, as did the dramatization of a bacchanalian dance:

> Again the music, again the tom-tom of the drums.
> On and on for hours. A man "passed out cold" and
> had to be carried from the gymnasium. A girl got
> a "laughing jag" and shrieked with idiotic laughter.
> . . . On and on, the constant rhythmic wailing of the
> fiddles, syncopated passion screaming with lust, the
> drums, horribly primitive; drunken embraces. . . .[43]

Discussions of the book and of Marks's later novel *Martha* consisted primarily of scornful indictments of their romantic falsifications. No doubt it was discussion of this kind which gave rise to the idea for the travesty of *The Plastic Age* and *Martha* presented by the senior class in 1924 as the St. Patrick's Day show. Typically, these annual shows consisted of brief skits satirizing campus events and characters, and featured a chorus line of the hairiest and most gargantuan football players, bewigged and clad in scanty female costumes. Typically, too, the St. Patrick's Day show was a communal creation, born in a fever of disorganized activity. The 1924 production, a three-act musical farce titled *The Plastered Duchess*, differed from the standard model in that there was real talent among its creators. Hough, West, John Monk, and (probably) Quentin Reynolds did most of the writing; Lukin played a slave girl and Reynolds a duchess; and S. J. Perelman painted a weird, surrealist backdrop which later was torn up to provide souvenirs. Legend has it that faculty members were forbidden to attend, but that Professor Ben Brown, who hid in the balcony, managed to see the entire performance.

The show was one of the bawdiest ever staged at Brown, and as one consequence university officials permanently banned future St. Patrick's Day shows. Two lines from its hit song are an adequate summary of the production's intellectual content:

Red-hot Martha, red-hot Martha—
Pull your bloomers down!

Both the acting and the audience reaction were largely influenced by alcohol. One scene called for Lukin to bow to the duchess, but it proved too great an assignment; he clutched at Reynolds and both fell down. "Whereupon," recalls Lukin, "the duchess in all her dignity announced, 'You're drunk, you bastard.' "[44] This was quite true, and seemed funny at the time; but the aftermath was not so funny. West, Frank Hough remembers, "fortunately passed out during the second act, but the whole thing got so out of hand—so raw and crude—that Quent and I expected momentarily to be fired from college."[45]

In bull sessions West talked, something he seldom did in class, and tested his mentality against his peers; in his reading he tested his mentality against the great and near-great as revealed in their writing. For his class work, his reading consisted of Greek and Roman literature; French literature, his strongest academic subject; the material assigned for survey courses in English literature; depth reading of literature in such specific courses as Lyric Poetry, Modern English Drama, and Browning; philosophy, especially ethical and religious philosophy; and history. He read deeply in all these areas except history, which was his weakest subject, but he did not confine himself to works related to his studies. According to one classmate, West had the largest personal library of any Brown man at that time, and with his typical generosity he was constantly loaning or giving books to his friends.[46] As often as not when he should have been reading for his classes, he was deep in Dostoevsky or Cabell or Mencken. His tastes were catholic, ranging from *Smart Set* to *Droll Stories* to *Pilgrim's Progress,* and he retained what he read to an impressive degree. I. J. Kapstein remembers that the minor writers most important to West were such bizarre and exotic ones as Arthur Machen, Edgar Saltus, Max Beerbohm, and Anatole France, all of whom were then close to the hearts of campus aspirants to literary fame. Of these, Machen was the writer West read most closely. Machen's *The Hill of Dreams* was published in its American edition in 1923, and that "Robinson Crusoe" of the soul, with its themes of the artist's loneliness, solitude, and separation from mankind, probably touched upon the youthful romanticism of West. Even the artist's revulsion from the common man and everyday suburbia, "the only hell that a vulgar age could conceive or make, an inferno created not by Dante but by the jerry-builder,"[47] reflected the desire, which West may have shared, for an artistic aristocracy. Probably the tricky end of *The Hill*, in which the "artist" is revealed to be insane and his "work" dissolves into hopelessly illegible scribblings, appealed forcefully to West's latent pessimism as well as his love of the bizarre.

In addition to these minor writers, Cabell and Huysmans impressed West greatly, and their influence, notably Huysman's imaginative use of the sense of smell and Cabell's mockery of man's dream worlds, is apparent in West's first novel. Huysman's treatment of the black mass, which he develops most fully in his novel about Satanism, *Là Bas*, fascinated West: he was aroused by magic, the blacker the better, wherever he found it. The strangeness of the lives and the imagery of the writings of Verlaine and Rimbaud also excited West tremendously.[48]

More important to him than any of these, however, were Flaubert, Dostoevsky, and Joyce: a sure indication that West possessed a fund of solid literary sense despite his predilection for the Flaubertian riots of color in *Salammbô*, the violence and grotesqueries of *The Possessed*, and the experimental technique of Joyce. On the other hand, he disliked "middle-of-the-road realism . . . middle-class writers writing on the middle-class."[49] The novels of Sinclair Lewis and Theodore Dreiser, in particular, exemplified this kind of writing to West. Later in his life the publishing firm of Knopf, which took the lead in bringing out bulky editions of American realists and naturalists, became the symbol for West of what he contemptuously called "the long-winded Scandinavians."

West's interest in the realms of the mind manifested itself in the writing that he was already doing in college. Few of his friends took this activity very seriously. According to Jeremiah Mahoney, West's roommate Lukin was an exception:

> He sincerely felt, I think now, that Pep had great talent that should be exercised, not wasted. To me—and to Pep at the time—this concern bordered on the ludicrous. One of our games . . . was to sit around idly conversing in Pep's room while he scribbled away at something. Frequently when he finished, he would crumple up the paper and toss it toward the fireplace, whereupon sometime during the next five minutes Lukin would surreptitiously slide over, pick it up, and presumably store it away.[50]

Lukin himself, however, comments that though Mahoney's facts are right, the interpretation is wrong. According to Lukin, West was by nature sloppy, while he himself was tidy. That is the reason Lukin picked up after West, and while occasionally Lukin may have commented, "This is pretty good," or, "You ought to do something with this," his remarks were more in the way of courteous commonplaces than an awareness of West's genius. In addition Lukin comments that West himself took his writing very seriously.

He was consumed by the desire to write well and filled with "self-torture"—the word is Lukin's—by the compulsion to get his visions on paper.[51]

West's most notable extracurricular activity was his work for *Casements*, the Brown literary magazine, for which he drew the first cover design. Inspired by Keats's "Magic casements, opening on the foam of perilous seas," the design was, according to John Monk, an excellent one, the more remarkable because "I always marvelled that he could draw at all; my impression was that his hands shook perceptibly."[52] West also contributed to *Casements* an article, "Euripides —a Playwright," and a poem, "Death." While impressive as undergraduate performances, they reveal little of the talent of the later author. The poem reflects West's detestation of those "minor poets" whose chief subject matter is death, and in its concluding lines expresses West's antireligious attitude:

> Why must you disturb
> The mediocre mind to thought
> And scare more souls to God?[53]

The essay on Euripides shows a typical undergraduate with auctorial leanings parading his wide reading a trifle ostentatiously. West quotes with approval a current oracle among critics, James Huneker, reveals his fascination with the Dionysus legend (a fascination later echoed in *Balso Snell*), and shows more concern for the inspirational quality of the writing than for the content: "You cannot touch it [the *Bacchae*] anywhere without having the desire to write and never stop writing."[54] The most interesting part of the essay, because it foreshadows what West strives to achieve in his later work, is West's praise of Euripides' writing in its fusion of the satirist with the man of feeling. This fusion convinced West that Euripides was a great playwright.

West was also beginning to think of the materials that were to go into *Balso Snell*. The surname of a Brown baseball coach (one oblivious to West's athletic prowess) was Snell, and the name amused West because it was close to "smell." On several occasions during his last two years at college, West invented various adventures of a hero by that name. John Sanford, who was not at Brown but whom West often saw in New York, recalls that by 1924 West had told him virtually everything that was to be found in *Balso Snell*. In addition, West, probably subconsciously, was molding the *Balso* materials toward certain thematic concerns. The body-mind opposition fascinated him. As a young boy, he was undoubtedly wrestling with an eternal problem of youth: the breaking of the silver cord, the assertion of independence and manhood. As a youth who had read Nietzsche and Flaubert, Dostoevsky and Baudelaire, he was aware of his difference from ordinary humankind, and he was susceptible to certain ideas about the superman, above ordinary codes and laws. These superman concepts he would have to struggle with and conquer before he was fully human, but in college the ideas were attractive. John Sanford remembers that once West told him the story of a crippled beggar who asked the poet Baudelaire for alms. Baudelaire retorted, "I'm not poor enough to give alms," and gave him a kick in the face instead. Apparently West approved the action of Baudelaire, and for Sanford the approval indicated West's lack of love for the weak and helpless, his receptivity to Nietzschean ideas.[55]

An early use of the *Balso* materials was made by Quentin Reynolds in a speech on Spring Day of 1924. Reynolds had been elected Speaker for the occasion and appealed to West for help. Eventually West gave him a manuscript which proved to be a narrative of Balso Snell's pilgrimage into the bowels of the legendary Trojan Horse. Among the charac-

ters were St. Puce, the flea who lived under the armpit of
the Saviour, and Maloney the Aeropagite, who wanted to
emulate the agony of our Lord by crucifying himself with
thumbtacks. The speech, says Reynolds, was a resounding
success.

> English professors who had ignored me now looked
> at me speculatively. Had they all unknown been
> harboring a genius in their midst? Pep had sworn me
> to secrecy, but finally the pressure was too great; I
> told Ben Clough, our favorite professor, the truth, that
> Pep had written it all. Pep told Clough that I was
> lying, and he called upon Sid Perelman to back him
> up. Sid did so.[56]

The Brown Yearbook for 1924, attempting to sum up
West as a college personality, describes him as

> an easy-going genial fellow. . . . He passes his time
> in drawing exotic pictures, quoting strange and
> fanciful poetry, and endeavoring to uplift *Casements*.
> He seems a bit eccentric at times, a characteristic of all
> geniuses. . . . May his slogan always be *"Honi soit
> qui mal y pense."*[57]

Jeremiah Mahoney's summary goes deeper:

> When I knew him, Pep was very young, hardly more
> than a child really, but an extremely curious and
> disinterested one. The world of ideas was his toyshop.
> Like the rest of us, he had few sound bases of
> evaluation save his own whims and the romantic
> pseudo-sophistication common to the early twenties.
> He liked being an animal; he liked feeling like
> superman; he didn't really know then, perhaps, what
> it was to be human.[58]

It was this young animal who was scheduled to graduate
in June, 1924. At the last moment, however, there arose an

obstacle: he failed Professor Crosby's course in Modern Drama. Like many another undergraduate, before and after him, he struggled with his pride. Then, the struggle won (or lost), he pleaded that the mark be changed. Real or assumed, his contriteness moved the good professor; the E was transformed into a D. Soon afterward, with Lukin, Reynolds, and an anonymous theological student, he celebrated this forthcoming Ph.B. degree by getting gloriously drunk. The next morning, recalls Lukin, he and West awoke late and then sprinted, half-dressed, toward the graduation procession. In line, appropriately dressed at last, they marched ceremoniously toward the future. Among the onlookers were West's parents. Lukin remembers they seemed to glow with pleasure and pride and triumph. They well might have, for their son's graduation from Brown was no mean achievement. To have graduated in two and a half years was even more remarkable. In West's case, it showed a daring and inventive mentality, the mind of what Melville would have called an "original."

2 *The Dream of Art*

WITH THE END OF COLLEGE, West returned, officially polished and educated in halls of Ivy, to New York City. Six feet tall, with brown hair and brown eyes, he was suave, sardonic, and skeptical in manner. A rather shy man—though at times of excitement given to loquaciousness and to gesticulation—he was indolent and slow-moving physically but alert, imaginative, and exotic mentally. Though he was friendly now, as always, with ordinary people—as at ease with them as they were with him—and though he was now, as always, sympathetic toward the pain of those pathetic humans who were doomed to be bruised and wounded by life, he felt his own difference from such people, and that distinction he emphasized by the role he played as elegantly dressed dandy and aesthete.

Now, as always, West distrusted emotions, possibly because he felt that his own might betray him, and he repressed his own feelings and scorned people who publicly displayed theirs. When John Sanford, in a sentimental moment rare for him, once confessed to West how great an influence he had played in Sanford's life—Sanford had given up a career as a lawyer to gamble on a living as a writer—West squirmed in embarrassment and then cut the confession short by leaving the bus on which the two men were riding.

By the time West returned home his mother, who had been an elegant and beautiful young woman, once courted by the noted painter Maurice Stern, was even heavier and paler than she had been in West's childhood. She was settled even further into the role she had assumed after her marriage, that of a mother interested in food, cooking, and domestic comfort, absorbed in her family, and immersed in conventional dreams for the bourgeois success of her children; as one of West's friends commented, she was "the typical *Yiddische hausfrau*."[1] Hinda, West's sister, a year younger than he, seemed, despite the fact that she had been a graceful, fragile child, "to be headed for a repetition of the mother."[2] John Sanford remembers that in his childhood West had had numerous slight quarrels with his mother and Hinda, and now, despite his fondness for both of them, their personalities, as well as his mother's conventional dreams for him, occasionally annoyed him.

Always West's favorites in his family were his sister Loraine, or Laura, and his father Max. Slim and gangling, like her brother, Laura was an "easy-going savvy sort,"[3] with an alert, creative, and inquisitive mind. Though she was seven years younger than her brother, West increasingly turned to her for companionship and intellectual stimulation. The two spent innumerable hours together, alternately joking and exchanging ideas. With each passing year the two grew closer together, and the brother-sister relationship became staunchly loyal and protective on both sides.

West's father, Max Weinstein, was a short, energetic, hardworking man. Gentle, quiet-spoken, and unassuming, he was warmhearted and friendly. With several of his brothers, he had founded a contracting business soon after the family arrived in America, and, beginning with the erection of tenement houses on the lower East side, he progressed to the construction of six-story luxury apartment houses in uptown Manhattan as far as 157th Street. From the time of his immigration to America, Max conceived of himself as American rather than Jewish, and he emphasized his identification with his adopted country by some of the names he gave his buildings: Arizona, Colorado, Hudson, and Fulton. Like his wife, Max was absorbed in the education and success of his children, and, just as much as she, he was the product of a time when the Horatio Alger dream was vivid in the minds of innumerable Americans, especially recent immigrants, and when "success" was defined in simple, materialistic, middle-class stereotypes.

By 1925 the construction business was in financial difficulties—troubles which prefigured the future for the whole American economy—and West's father worried a good bit about his precarious credit. In addition, he had hurt his chest in an automobile accident. Undoubtedly, these facts explain the impression that Max made on John Sanford at about this time: "a sickly man, very thin, very pale, very quiet, and much dominated by [West's] mother."[4] Probably these realities also explain, in part, the pressure that the family, and especially West's father, exerted upon West to assist in the family enterprises. As best he could, West resisted these arguments. Though he worked for a time as a construction superintendent, he insisted—more by passive indifference to a commercial career than by outright hostility—that he wanted a chance to write. Not only that, he wanted the chance in Paris.

For over two years, the impasse continued. West's continued indifference to business affairs and his mother's persuasiveness—she persistently argued that West should have his chance—finally prevailed. At a family consultation in September, 1926, Max's brother Charles and his brother-in-law Saul—who, as yet, were relatively unaffected by the construction crisis—agreed to bear the cost of the journey. On October 13, he set sail for Europe.

For West, this was a victory, not so much over his family as over their desires for his future career. For him, the victory symbolized a break with the past. He would not be a plumber, a timekeeper, a bricklayer, or a salesman for real estate. He would not lie to himself and come to love his lie and believe it truth.

As if to certify his rebirth, he had already changed his name: on August 16, 1926, at the City Court of New York, he had legally become Nathanael West. No longer merely a gift to his parents (Nathan is Hebrew for gift), he was his own man. He was now an American of the twentieth century. If his origin was "Jewish"—and he had no shame in its being so but doubted that any blood line could truly be defined as Jewish—he was not immediately identifiable as such, not by his appearance, his accent (he despised such "Jewish" comedians as Fanny Brice), his profession, or his name. From this time on West used his new name for his artistic career (though he retained the name Weinstein for business purposes until 1932), and possibly he chose to be Nathanael, not Nathaniel, because somehow the former seemed distinctive, original, unique. Certainly when Julian Shapiro (who eventually became John Sanford) asked for suggestions about a possible change of name, West showed, somewhat like his creature Balso Snell, his American, and yet romantic, orientation: he advised Sanford to consider the name "Starbuck."

For West, Europe meant Paris. At Brown, according to one of West's interviewers, "Two movements split the campus literary renaissance, Catholic mysticism and French surrealism, and West played around with both of them. He has been teetering between the two since."[5] Probably it was his interest in surrealism, both in painting and writing, that led West to follow the host of young American expatriates to Paris.

The lure of Paris was, of course, an American phenomenon of the twenties. At first that promised land attracted all the sad young men scarred by World War I and its aftermath of cynical spoliation. By the time West got to Paris, however, the disillusionment which provided the initial impetus of expatriatism had largely run its course. By 1924 some American pilgrims went abroad because of the frustration of living in an America where the meaning and the values of art were slowly being smothered by Babbittry. But more often the pilgrimage had become merely the thing to do: the *wanderjahr* for the young intellectual or artist, the Bohemian summer vacation for the college student, the romantic fulfillment of the middle-aged tourist. These groups had neither been scarred nor made cynical by the war. They were just human beings, sometimes pretentious and full of fakery, who were drawn by the legend of Paris. Sometimes, too, they were attracted by a very practical fact: Paris at twenty-five francs to the dollar was considerably cheaper than hometown Bohemia. For all, Paris was educational, but it was a schoolroom that was full of dangers as well as wonders.

West was one of the *wanderjahr* expatriates. If he had been scarred, it was by something other than the war; if he was cynical, it was the conventional collegiate cynicism purveyed by Mencken. On the surface, he was a normal, likable young American to whom Paris was a wonderland come true. In it he thrived. Like some of the college crowd, he grew a beard, a flowing, reddish-brown one; like some of the fakes, he occasionally amused himself by posing and preening. Like many another writer living a conventional life in bourgeois hotels near Montparnasse, such as the Lutétia and the Libéria, he was both scornful of and attracted by the role-playing associated with the "artistic" life. In an unpublished story of expatriates in Paris, entitled in various versions "The Fake," "L'Affaire Beano," and "The Imposter," he noted:

> "In order to be an artist one has to live like one." We know now that this is nonsense, but in Paris in '25 and '26 we didn't know it. . . . To be recognized as artists, we were everything our enemies said we were.
>
> By the time I got to Paris, the business of being an artist had grown quite difficult. Aside from the fact that you were actually expected to create, the jury had been changed. It no longer consisted of the tourists and the folks back home, but of your fellow artists. They were the ones who decided on the authenticity of your madness. Long hair and a rapt look wouldn't get you to first base. You had to have something new on the ball. Even dirt and sandals and calling Sargent a lousy painter was not enough. You had to be an original. Things were a good deal less innocent than they had been, and more desperate.
>
> When I got to Montparnasse, all the obvious roles had either been dropped or were being played by

experts. But I made a lucky hit. Instead of trying for strangeness, I formalized and exaggerated the costume of a bond salesman. I wore carefully pressed Brooks Brothers clothing, sober but rich ties, and carried gloves and a tightly-rolled umbrella. My manners were elaborate and I professed great horror at the slightest breach of the conventional. It was a success. I was asked to all the parties.[6]

At times, or so he later romanticized, West and a friend acted another role. They lingered at the dock when a boat from America came in. Then, gracefully, they managed introductions to a couple of the more attractive, but obviously unattached and helpless, young American girls. From this point it was no long distance to the purpose of the stratagem: a free meal for the men, a guided tour of the heart of Parisian Bohemia for the girls.

These Bohemian pursuits were aspects of West's Paris, but more important to him were the artistic movements he found there. Dadaism and surrealism intrigued him most. The earlier, Dadaism, which had reached its peak by 1921, was one manifestation of the complete cynicism engendered by the war. Four words define, as well as it can be defined, the underlying spirit of Dada. These words are disgust, revolt, destruction, and despair. The key word is despair. The very name Dada, chosen at random out of a German-French dictionary by Tristan Tzara, the father of Dadaism, is the child's word for hobby or hobby horse, and the word suggests by its sound the helplessness of children, just as the Dadaists recognized the helplessness of their own protests against organized society. This hopelessness differentiates the tone of Dadaism from that of the optimistic movements of revolt in the nineteenth century. Philosophically, therefore, Tzara could assert, "Measured by the scale of eternity, any activity is futile."[7] Taken in full belief, such a doctrine could, and did, lead to frequent discussions of whether suicide would be the solution, the only solution, to man's knowledge of his own insignificance. Taken too seriously, such inquiries could even lead to suicide, as with Jacques Vaché, who, because of his cynicism, was almost a Dadaist saint. Although he wrote little, his definition of Dada humor remains acute: "a sense of the theatrical and joyless futility of everything, when one knows."[8]

Though still alive, Dadaism by 1927 had become less fashionable than the newer surrealist movement. Like Dadaism, surrealism was devoted to the ideal of artistic liberty, but surrealism had swerved from Dadaism's motifs of disgust and despair to an artistic attempt to discover a realm of reality beyond the physical. This *surréel* was deep within the inner life of man and could be discovered in dreams and fantasies. The function of the artist was merely to record the revelations, sometimes induced by drugs, of the subconscious, unreasoning mind.

In literature this theory initiated recordings of dreams and transcriptions of automatic writing. It also led to deliberate efforts to achieve startling word arrangements (an aspect carried over from Dadaist "poetry" written by taking words at random from a newspaper). Often the results were innumerable shocking images created in a verbal delirium: "The vice called surrealism," notes Louis Aragon, at one time among the foremost surrealists, "is the immoderate and passionate use of the drug which is the image."[9]

In painting, surrealism led to attempts to capture a dreamlike moment, unreal to the common vision but *surréel* in its truth. Often in his attempts to suggest the surrealistic, to perform psychoanalysis in paint, the artist painted clocks dreamily hanging in space or disembodied pelvic bones and crutches or upside-down figures or vermin or Coke bottles sprouting from human forms. Des Esseintes, the hero of Huysman's *A Rebours* and a fictional character that stimulated West, clearly foreshadows much of surrealistic painting. Des Esseintes likes such art as

> A head of a Merovingian style, resting against a bowl, a bearded man, at once resembling a Buddhist priest and an orator at a public reunion, touching the ball of a gigantic cannon with his fingers; a frightful spider revealing a human face in its body. The charcoal drawings went even farther into dream terrors. Here, an enormous die in which a sad eye winked; there, dry and arid landscapes, dusty plains, shifting ground, volcanic upheavals catching rebellious clouds, stagnant and livid skies.[10]

Obviously surrealism owes a good deal to Freud. Like Freudianism, it searched the frightful, unexplored caverns, the sexual fantasies, and the urges to self-destruction in man. At the same time, the surrealist, working as an investigator of the human mind, felt he was justified in inducing (and recording insofar as possible) the strange intangible forces lying at the depths of the rational man. The liberation of these forces was the undertaking of the explorer of the mind, whether poet or painter or analyst. Ideally, surrealistic art became not only a record of exploration but also "a magical invocation, an evocative magic or witchcraft whose creation and effect were both miraculous. . . . The poet then is the priest who causes the miracle by a magical use of words, by an incantation which he himself does not fully understand."[11] The magical, evocative quality which the artist can produce with language is ultimately inexplicable, but it may be partially achieved by the chance, "metaphysical" juncture of far distant realities, as, for instance, in Lautréamont's famed image of a sewing machine and an umbrella posed on a dissecting table; or the opening image of André Breton's *Fata Morgana:* "This morning the daughter of the mountain is holding on her knees an accordion of white bats"; or the wry, satiric image from Benjamin Péret's "Au bout du monde": "Stupid like sausages whose sauerkraut has already been eaten away"; or Michel Leiris's hallucinatory image of the sun in his "Marécage du sommeil":

> When the sun is but a drop of sweat
> a sound of bell
> the red pearl falling down a vertical needle.*

These movements of Dadaism and surrealism that confronted West were probably not wholly new to him. Before he reached Paris, he had read and been excited by a number of the French symbolists; he had been deeply affected by Flaubert's *The Temptation of St. Anthony*, with its sensory evocation of the saint's fantastic dream visions; he had read much in the supernatural, mytho-religious visions conjured up by Machen; and he had pondered, with many of his college friends, the philosophy of Saltus, with its constant indictment of the human condition and its continual assertion that perhaps suicide is the wisest solution to the immense and terrible affliction called life. In addition, West had already read Poe, who was as prominent an influence upon French surrealism as the earlier symbolists, and had probably

---

* The three translations are from Anna Balakian, *Surrealism: the Road to the Absolute* (New York, 1959), pp. 122, 126, and 125. The original French of each passage is as follows: (1) Ce matin la fille de la montagne tient sur ses genoux un accordéon de chauves-souris blanches (Breton); (2) Bêtes comme des saucisses dont la choucroute a déjà été mangée (Péret); (3) quand le soleil n'est plus qu'une goutte de sueur/ un son de cloche/ la perle rouge qui tombe le long d'une aiguille verticale (Leiris).

43

decided that the psychological intensity Poe believed attainable only in the short poem could also be attained in the short novel. Though all of this reading had influenced West, his period in Paris amid the turmoil of Dadaism and surrealism brought him closer to a definition of his ideas about life and art.

In West's first novel, *The Dream Life of Balso Snell,* the influence of Paris is strongly apparent. Even more, *Balso* reveals, as first novels often do, a considerable amount about its author. In the novel, a young man searches in brash, immature cynicism for a meaning in life. The protagonist, Balso Snell, first of all rejects Judaism: early in the novel he breaks away from an aggressive, talkative Jew who shouts, "I am a Jew! and whenever anything Jewish is mentioned, I find it necessary to say that I am a Jew. I'm a Jew. A Jew" (pp. 7–8). Later on the rejection is extended from Judaism to the Catholic religion specifically and the Christian mythology generally. In a satire permeated with disgust, St. Puce, a flea who lives upon Christ's body, is compared in his life and death and agony to Christ. West reduces the Immaculate Conception of Christ to absurdity by comparing it to another Immaculate Conception: "the subsequent actions of Saint Puce's life [after birth] lead me to believe that the egg was fertilized by a being whose wings were of feathers. Yes, I mean the Dove or Paraclete—the Sanctus Spiritus" (p. 11).

Above all, however, *Balso* is a rejection of the artistic, the rational, and the spiritual pretensions of man. In revealing man's ultimate phoniness, *Balso* emphasizes the illogic and confusion of man's dream life. At the same time, *Balso* asserts that the dream life reaffirms common everyday truths. This interest in the subconscious shows the influence of Freud (for West, the modern writer's Bullfinch), but it also reflects West's interest in James Joyce, surrealism, and the various experimental techniques of *Transition*, a magazine which West read avidly. The confused and surrealistic night-town scene in *Ulysses* may well have provided the initial inspiration for the novel. West's close friend I. J. Kapstein calls the *Walpurgisnacht* scene "the major influence on *The Dream Life*."[12]

The highly irrational dream adventures of Balso are presented in a style that is not only vulgarly humorous but also highly allusive. As in a dream, *Balso Snell* weirdly unreels: it has no plot of any sequential kind, characters are physically distorted and change their shapes magically, and the manifest meanings are but the index to the latent or disguised meanings. The tone of disgust which dominates the novel is apparent in the constant use of excremental images—"Written while smelling the moistened forefinger of my right hand" (p. 14), vulgar jokes—"A hand in the bush is worth two in the pocket" (p. 7), disagreeable physical images—"The intestine had burst through the stomach wall" (p. 7), and unpleasant words—"What a beautiful name for a girl! Hernia Hornstein! Paresis Pearlberg! Paranoia Puntz" (p. 7)!

The dream life of Balso begins when he enters the "Anus Mirabilis" of the original Trojan Horse, and his adventures end when he has the sexual climax of a wet dream. Between these two events, Balso meets a collection of dream grotesques; all of them, as he realizes midway through the novel, are "writers in search of an audience" (p. 37).

The first of these grotesques is a Jew who offers to guide Balso through the bowels of the wooden horse. Balso has just entered the lower intestine, and in its gloom has become depressed. To combat his mood, he sings a song:

> Round as the Anus
> Of a Bronze Horse

> Or the Tender Buttons
> Used by Horses for Ani
>
> · · ·
>
> Round and Ringing Full
> As the Mouth of a Brimming Goblet
> The Rust-Laden Holes
> In Our Lord's Feet
> Entertain the Jew-Driven Nails (pp. 4–5)

The gaiety of his song does not dispel Balso's gloom, and he thinks of the "Phoenix Excrementi, a race of men which he had invented" (p. 5). At the thought he trembles, and in the hope of attracting someone's attention he shouts a paean of praise to his surroundings. It is then that the Jewish guide appears. Soon Balso and the guide are arguing heatedly, and eventually the guide is taunted into haranguing Balso with a host of philosophic statements avowing the circularity, and the unity, of nature. Finally, Balso breaks the guide's hold on his collar and flees.

This first chapter indicates Balso's character, the character of the inhabitants of the wooden horse, and the basic theme of the novel. From the beginning one notes a conflict within Balso between the philosophies of monism (or idealism) and pluralism (or materialism). Balso's song, concerned with the eternal roundness of things, dramatizes the monistic yearnings of Balso for some Emersonian Over Soul or Nietzschean Primordial Unity. He is searching for the optimistic, transcendental view of existence, but the Baudelairean title he gives his song—"Anywhere Out of the World or A Voyage Through the Hole in the Mundane Millstone"—illustrates the cynicism with which Balso views the attempt to escape from the materialistic universe of multiplicity. Even if the transcendental view, uniting the multiplicity of matter into the oneness of spirit, is correct, it is also frightening. Though the Phoenix Excrementi, like the immortal bird and the oneness of spirit, are immortal, like the oneness of some Over Soul, they must "eat themselves, digest themselves, give birth to themselves by evacuating their own bowels" (p. 5).

Balso, who is torn between his yearnings to be a lyric poet and his inheritance as a citizen of a race of "inventors and perfectors of the automatic water-closet" (p. 6), cannot see only the visions of his transcendental guide. Where the tradition-oriented guide sees a glorious memorial of the past, the skeptical modernist in Balso sees decay. Typically, at one point, the guide sees a "beautiful Doric prostate gland," while Balso, looking at the same sight, sees only an "atrophied pile" (p. 6). Patriotically, Balso feels that these wonders of the ancient world cannot compare with the marvels of Grand Central Station.

Though veiled by vulgarity and a deliberate contempt for the weaknesses of readers, *Balso Snell* undoubtedly deals with one of the central themes of literature: the conflict between idealism and materialism. Balso is in part a realistic man, alive to the comfort that can be gained from the monistic and idealistic view of the universe, but too aware of the pragmatic foolishness of such a viewpoint to derive much solace from it. He cannot totally accept the philosophic idealism of the guide and, by implication, of the other inhabitants of the Trojan Horse.

To assure that the reader grasps these points, West repeats them in a variety of dramatic and satiric ways. The practical side of Balso and its difference from the character of the inhabitants of the Trojan Horse is reasserted in the second grotesque that Balso meets. Maloney the Aeropagite is a Catholic mystic, "a man, naked except for a derby in which thorns were sticking, who was attempting to crucify himself with thumb tacks" (pp. 9–10). In this mortification of the flesh Maloney feels he is emulating the great saints. The practical Balso is unmoved by such spiritual yearnings:

> I think you're morbid. . . . Take your eyes off your navel. Take your head from under your armpit. Stop sniffing mortality. Play games. Don't read so many books. Take cold showers. Eat more meat. (p. 3)

Continuing his peregrinations, Balso comes upon a third grotesque: John Gilson, a precocious eighth-grade student. He, like Maloney, yearns for the spiritual, but he is aware that the physical and the spiritual in man are natural antagonists. This complicated child is much concerned with the nature of reality, and has written a diary which Balso reads. It describes the pull of the spirit away from the man of physical sensations. This spiritual pull lures each man toward a false personality, one other than that of the natural man governed by simple cause and effect and basic physical drives. This spiritual pull attempts to substitute some Iago or Raskolnikov for mere honest John; and though John Gilson tries to cling to the simple physical man by smelling his own excrement, the attempt is unsuccessful. John assumes a false personality, a spiritualized cardboard nose, and in his diary writes a tale in the form of a journal. He writes this tale under the pseudonym of John Raskolnikov Gilson, and he calls it "The Making of a Fiend."

John Raskolnikov tells a fable about an unmotivated murder (Gide's *acte gratuit*). The basic source for the tale is *Crime and Punishment*, though there are echoes of Villiers de l'Isle Adam's short story, "Le Désir d' Etre un Homme," in which the actor Esprit Chaudral commits murder so that he may have a personality of his own unlike the roles he plays. West's fable, or Gilson's, begins with John Raskolnikov's childhood of spiritual Nietzschean longing. Raskolnikov is bedeviled by his imagination, a "wild beast that always cries for freedom" (p. 16). As an adult, Raskolnikov works in the philosophy department of the public library. There he is surrounded by books, and these constantly remind him of man's spiritual "fervors, deliriums, ambitions, dreams" (p. 17). At the same time, he lives by choice in a rooming house dominated by the noises and smells of sheer animality. Another of the roomers is an idiot, who exacerbates John Raskolnikov. In the nude, John seeks and kills the idiot. Later, he finds his body reacting like that of a girl, and when some sailors pass, he has an orgasm. After the murder, the memory of the deed gradually begins to grate upon the mind of Raskolnikov, who at the end of the tale is in the insane asylum.

This third section of the novel can also be interpreted as a conflict over basic reality, only now the struggle between the spirit and the flesh takes a more dramatic form. Considered in this way, the reason for the murder is the spiritual desire to attain complete freedom from the rational, restraining chains that determine a man's deeds just as an animal's actions are determined by physical drives. Thus the murder has no rational cause, for policemen would not "consider the shape and color of a man's throat, his laugh, or the fact that he does not wear a collar, reasonable motives for killing him" (p. 19).

But this is not the only cause for the murder. In Raskolnikov the imagination (or the spirit) is pent within walls of flesh and continually cries for freedom. When Raskolnikov murders the idiot, he does so to gain the victory of the spirit over the flesh. Dramatically, this is effective because the idiot —through his pink, fat throat, his filthiness, his toilet-like swallowing—has become the flesh in all its animal vulgarity.

The further implication is that Raskolnikov has not only murdered the animal flesh of another, but also has attempted the symbolic murder of the flesh within himself.

As an attempt, however, to gain lasting spirituality, the murder is a failure. Though the spiritual victory is present, the flesh, only fleetingly transcended, remains. After the murder there surges within Raskolnikov a very physical, animal fear. Even after the terror has subsided, the animal flesh remains. Raskolnikov feels a change of sex and caresses fictitious breasts "like a young girl who has suddenly become conscious of her body on a hot afternoon" (p. 22). Later on he has an orgasm which leaves him physically sick. The orgasm suggests that the murder itself is not a spiritual triumph at all, but instead is only the beginning of abnormal sexual satisfaction. One can hardly overlook the sexual implications of the murder: how Raskolnikov had undressed beforehand, and how he had gone to commit the murder with his sexual organs tight, like the genitals of a dog.

Now, Raskolnikov Gilson ends his tale, the murder (or the spiritual desire) exists within the animal flesh "like a piece of sand inside the shell of an oyster" (p. 22). Already this spiritual yearning, which like a deadly tumor will grow and grow, has left Raskolnikov in the "freedom" of insanity, waiting for the final ironic "freedom" of death. Only through these "freedoms" can Raskolnikov be loosed from the domination of the flesh, and even insanity offers only partial freedom.

This is quite a concept for a boy still in short pants, but in another literary effusion John Gilson (no longer Raskolnikov) makes much the same point. He sells Balso a pamphlet he has written, and in it he is again preoccupied with the conflict between flesh and spirit. The pamphlet begins with Gilson's receiving the news that his mistress, Saniette, has died. Gilson remembers how he had always played the actor with Saniette. At one time, in a hotel bedroom, he had beaten her. An angry clerk had come to the bedroom, but he had been pacified by mention of the names of such sadists as the Marquis de Sade and Gilles de Rais. Because Saniette is also persuaded that Gilson's beating of her gives evidence of his spirituality, she is able to bear another with placidity. The pamphlet ends with Gilson's diatribe against Saniette and the particular audience which she represents: "smart, sophisticated, sensitive yet hardboiled, art-loving frequenters of the little theatre" (p. 30). For this audience Gilson intends at some future date to write a play. After congratulating the patrons of his play for their preference of Art over physical pleasures, he would have them deluged by excrement from the ceiling. Then "if they so desire, the patrons of my art can gather in the customary charming groups and discuss the play" (p. 31).

It is plain that the pamphlet is an attack upon the spiritual desires of man. These, one infers, are mere rationalizations of physical drives. To illustrate the concept, Gilson portrays himself as a man of intellect and thereby allies himself with the mind, against the flesh. When Saniette dies, he has no feeling, and even his search for an emotion is done sardonically. Coldly Gilson perceives that, to attain sexual gratification, he has had to create a false, an actor, personality. In retrospect he is able to discern that all his "acting has but one purpose, the attraction of the female" (p. 26). He sees that physical gratification is the cause of all the so-called mental and spiritual qualities of man. Compulsively, then, the physically unattractive person must strive after the compensatory attainments, for the desire to procreate is so strong as to be unconquerable. This drive of the flesh is Freud's Id, the primitive self in all men. It is the "chauffeur" within Gilson, for, as he explains to Saniette, there are two men in his personality:

. . . myself and the chauffeur within me. This
chauffeur is very large and dresses in ugly, ready-made
clothing. His shoes . . . are covered with animal
ordure and chewing gum. . . .

The name of this chauffeur is The Desire to
Procreate.

He sits within me like a man in an automobile.
(p. 29)

With this concept in mind, the reason for Gilson's diatribe against art becomes clear. Those who would pretend
that artistic and spiritual achievement—books, religious systems, music, art—are anything but the result of a basic
physiological drive are self-deluded phonies: "art lovers and
book lovers, school teachers who adore the grass-eating
Shaw, sensitive young Jews who adore culture. . ." (p. 30).
To make such pretenders aware of the animal roots of their
existence, Gilson would pour loose excrement upon them.
Unfortunately, most of them would only continue in their
delusion.

Though the other adventures of Balso in his peregrinations through the Trojan Horse are both bizarre and humorous, they add little to this statement of the theme. At
one point, however, West emphasizes the underlying pathos
of the human condition. This piteousness is perceived by a
dream-creature of Balso named Beagle Hamlet Darwin, who
posits a kind of spiritual Darwinism. While the true Darwinism is based on conflict, the animalistic struggle for
physical survival, Beagle's spiritual Darwinism is based on
man's competition with such creatures of his own mind as
Dionysus (born three times) or Christ (born of a virgin).

This spiritual Darwinism is dramatized in a dream Balso
has (a dream within a dream, for the whole novel is a
dream-tale). The extremely confused and self-contradictory
sequence obviously satirizes the surrealistic recordings of

dream life. Balso dreams that he is in the lobby of Carnegie Hall. It is "crowded with the many beautiful girl-cripples who congregate there because Art is their only solace" (p. 37). Balso is attracted by their distorted bodies and declares his love to one of these surrealistic grotesques, a hydrocephalic hunchback named Janey Davenport. For a while Janey, desiring ideal rather than physical love, repulses Balso, but soon she promises him her body if he will kill Beagle Darwin, who, she claims, betrayed her. Before Balso can leave to perform this task, she insists that he read two letters from Beagle.

The first letter is a fictitious account of Janey's suicide. According to Beagle Darwin the suicide has been caused by the melancholy ruminations of a mind that is not content with a merely physical love but demands something more. The second letter relates Darwin's fabricated account of his reaction to the imaginary death of Janey. This fabrication, which he feels is required before he can meet his friends, must be suited to what the world expects of a grief-stricken lover. Eventually, he decides to act the part of mad Hamlet, and in this role Darwin prays to Dionysus, the son of Zeus:

> Who among us can boast that he was born three times, as was Dionysus? . . . Or who can say, like Christ, that he was born of a virgin? Or who can even claim to have been born as was Gargantua? Alas! none of us. (p. 55)

After this prayer, B. Hamlet Darwin sees truly the pathos of humanity. He pities man because he sees his tragic need to compete with such marvelous creatures as Gargantua and Christ; he blesses man as he realizes the tragedy of "the competition in which his hearers spent their lives, a competition that demanded their being more than animals" (p. 55). Thus, clownish and futile and pathetic, man ritualistically juggles the spiritual paraphernalia that is supposed to prove him more than a mere animal: "an Ivory Tower, a Still White Bird, The Holy Grail, The Nails, The Scourge, The Thorns, and a piece of The True Cross" (p. 56).

In his delusion man makes a pathetic picture, but at the same time, in his posing he makes an absurd one. By the final chapter, Balso has become a poseur; when he has an opportunity for sexual fulfillment, he and his beloved seize the moment to launch into stock seduction poetry. The chapter, the wittiest and bluntest of the novel, culminates, after some coyness, in sexual climax. The orgasm once again affirms the sole reality: the life of art, of the mind generally, is, like the original Trojan Horse, a thing of deceitfulness. In reality the artistic and spiritual approaches to life are only pretenses, ridiculous façades and disgusting rationalizations for the purpose of penetrating walls of flesh as the Trojan Horse penetrated the walls of Troy. The end of the quest, having passed Judaism, Christianity, Art, and Mind, comes in the total victory of the balls of Snell (representing his whole body), and this triumph of the flesh is symbolically made most apparent by the ultimate victory of death over such pretenses as art and mind and spirit. Balso's sexual union, like man's, has nothing spiritual about it; instead, copulation is similar "to the mechanics of decay. After death the body takes command. . . . So now, his body performed the evolutions of love with a like sureness" (p. 61). This complete victory of the body, and complete submission of the spirit, brings the only peace that man will ever find. It is the meaning of life, and it asserts there is no meaning; sheer absurdity is "the mystic doctrine, the purification, the syllable 'Om'" (p. 61). The language, as well as the revelation, mocks those who have found supernal meanings to justify life. Surrealistically this victory of the physical is affirmed in a poet's dream, revealed in a poet's climax, and true as dreams are true when they reveal what cannot face the light.

In the treatment of his theme, West proves himself a master of bizarre and fantastic imagery. It was no conventional mind that conceived of St. Puce, of the Trojan Horse as the spiritual disguises men use to attain sexual gratification, of Maloney the Aeropagite, of the Phoenix Excrementi, of the chauffeur within man, or of Samuel Perkins, whose only sensory impressions were gained through smell, but who, nevertheless, managed to build "from the odors of his wife's body an architecture and an aesthetic, a music and a mathematic" (p. 36).

West's humor, a wry laughter that is perhaps best compared with gallows humor, stems largely from these images of the bizarre. West, like his creation John Gilson, seems to feel that "I must laugh at myself, and if the laugh is 'bitter,' I must laugh at the laugh" (p. 27). This laughter at one's pain pervades the novel to such an extent that West would seem not only to be presenting the world of dreams but also to be implying that life itself is but a dream play, and all its players broken-hearted clowns:

> After all, aren't we all . . . aren't we all clowns?
> Of course, I know it's old stuff; but what difference
> does that make? Life *is* a stage; and *we* are clowns.
> What is more tragic than the role of clown? What
> more filled with the essentials of great art?—pity and
> irony. . . . Your wife has run away with the boarder,
> your son has killed a man, the baby has cancer. . . .
> The clowns down front are laughing, whistling,
> belching. . . . And you—you are back stage. . . .
> Slowly there filters through your clenched fingers the
> cries of your brother clowns. . . . soon you are out

front again doing your stuff, the same superb Beagle:
dancing, laughing, singing, *acting*. (p. 51)*

Balso Snell is an intriguing book for anyone interested in
Nathanael West, just as *This Side of Paradise* is important
for anyone who wishes to understand Scott Fitzgerald.
Balso is interesting, in one respect, because it is so psychologically revealing of its author. In fact, interpreting freely
and using Jung as an imaginative starting point, one might
find in it not only West's rejection of Judaism, but also his
rejection of the mother.† Equally fascinating are the youthful brashness and high spirits in which the author expresses
his cynical ideas. Ironically, the innocence and zest, the
adolescent buoyancy, considerably weaken the cynicism.
Most important of all, the book's attack upon art, spirit, and
mind is hilariously funny: *The New Yorker* called the
novel, on its republication in 1957, "a brilliantly insane Surrealist fantasy that tries very hard to mock Western culture
out of existence."[13]

A good part of the fascination that *Balso* holds for Westians is in the storehouse of materials it provides for West

---

* Of interest here is a comment from Colin Wilson's study of pessimism in modern art, *The Outsider* (Boston, 1956), p. 15: "What
can be said to characterize the Outsider is a sense of strangeness,
of unreality. . . . This is the sense of unreality, that can strike out
of a perfectly clear sky. . . . And once a man has seen it, the
world can never afterwards be quite the same straightforward
place. Barbusse has shown us that the Outsider is a man who cannot live in the comfortable, insulated world of the bourgeois, accepting what he sees and touches as reality. 'He sees too deep and
too much,' and what he sees is essentially chaos. . . . For the Outsider, the world is not rational, not orderly."
† Anyone interested in attempting such a Jungian analysis might
begin with Chapter VI, "The Battle for Deliverance from the
Mother," in Dr. C. G. Jung, *Psychology of the Unconscious* (New
York, 1916). Much might be done with Jung's discussion of the
horse, especially the Trojan Horse, as a maternal symbol: into it
man enters out of a wish to be reborn; from it he emerges not as
a child but as a man.

in his later novels. Occasionally phrases from *Balso* recur in later works; for instance, the idiot's masklike face in *Balso* reappears in the description of Harry Greener in *The Day of the Locust*. Characters are foreshadowed; Maloney the Aeropagite prefigures Miss Lonelyhearts, and Beagle Darwin foreshadows Shrike. Actions in later novels also echo actions in *Balso:* the laughter of the idiot and the opera basso in *Balso* prefigure the laughter of the Greeners and Tod Hackett in *The Day;* or, to cite another example, just as the idiot is murdered in *Balso*, the lamb in *Miss Lonelyhearts* is murdered in order to purge the animal flesh in man, and what is more, the murders are described in similar fashion.

Especially significant, however, are the ideas of *Balso* which recur, effectively and thoroughly dramatized, in West's later novels. The essential cause of Miss Lonelyhearts' despair is seen in *Balso*, for both heroes are questers, fruitlessly searching, one reverently, one cynically, for a central unity, an Over Soul, that will make the meaninglessness of multiplicity into the ultimate truth of some essential oneness. Balso searches through his song in praise of the circular. Miss Lonelyhearts' need for unity and order, so great as to border on insanity, forces him into trying constantly to balance and compose the multiplicity of the physical universe into static, ordered harmony. Like Balso, however, Miss Lonelyhearts must face the sad truth of man's dilemma: "Man has a tropism for order. . . . The physical world has a tropism for disorder" (p. 115). This kind of antagonism is but one manifestation of constant competition in West's world. This conflict may be simple Darwinistic strife. It may be the spiritual Darwinism postulated in *Balso* and fully dramatized in *Miss Lonelyhearts*, so that Miss Lonelyhearts cannot accept the purely physical man but instead must compete with Christ, attempt to *be* a modern Christ. Between different political systems, neither good, the conflict may, as in *A Cool Million,* grind to destruction the simple bumpkins, the Lemuel Pitkins, of the world. Or the hostile camps may be divided into actors and audience, one cheating, the other hating, as in *The Day.* Wherever one looks in the world of West, there is some kind of conflict, irreconcilable, insoluble, horrible.

Like *This Side of Paradise,* however, *Balso,* as a work of art, is weakened by the fact that it is not so much the book of a grown man as the book of a precocious boy who in himself reflects many men. In this he is similar to the precocious John Raskolnikov Gilson, but West's artistic texture is implied by the fact that Gilson is not only a satirical comment upon such artists as Rimbaud (who began to write at ten and abandoned poetry forever before the age of twenty), but also upon West's own precocity. Similarly West was probably mocking himself, as well as the self-consciousness of artists generally, when he had Beagle Darwin confess:

> You once said to me that I talk like a man in a book. I not only talk, but think and feel like one. I have spent my life in books; literature has deeply dyed my brain its own color. This literary color is a protective one—like the brown of the rabbit or the checks of the quail—making it impossible for me to tell where literature ends and I begin. (p. 47)

Obviously the artistic immaturity in West is more complex than in Fitzgerald's first book, for in *Balso* West satirizes his influences while he reflects them. In mocking books and their writers, *Balso* ridicules the fantasies of hosts of authors, among them Rimbaud, Baudelaire, Lautréamont, George Moore, Daudet, Huysmans, various Catholic mysties, Cabell, the Marquis de Sade, Dostoevsky, and Joyce.

Of importance to him were Cabell's *Jurgen* and Huysmans' *Là Bas* and *En Route*. From the former he may have gained aspects of his mannered tone and his questing plot. *Jurgen* is a narrative of a poet's journey into the past; it at one point dramatizes, as does *Balso*, the transformation of a beautiful maiden into a middle-aged woman; and it ends with the discovery that ultimate reality is sexual. From Huysmans, West probably gained his familiarity with such mystics as Saint Hildegarde, Suso, Labre, and Lydwine of Schiedam—all of whom Huysmans mentions in ways that invite parody. Huysmans' description in *En Route* of the torment of Suso (who bore a cross the nails of which pierced his flesh and wore gloves lined with nails) implies West's parody in the "agony" of Maloney the Aeropagite. And undoubtedly Huysmans' contention, in *Against the Grain*, that the sense of smell has a "grammar" and a "Syntax" of its own inspired West's conception of Samuel Perkins, whose nostrils were so acute that he "could smell a chord in D minor, or distinguish between the tone-smell of a violin and that of a viola" (p. 35).

Surrealism and the writings of James Joyce, two related sources, also illustrate how West reflects and yet satirizes his influences in *Balso*. The influence of the former is seen in the chaos of the dream life of Balso, for surrealism wished to capture man's disconnected dream life and preserve that mysterious world in art. However, to the surrealist's contention that the dream life may reveal an inner man who is higher than the purely animal creature, West directs his satiric attack. Even though a man may remove himself from everyday reality to the point of absurdity (as, for instance, when Balso reads a pair of letters within a dream within a dream), even then the simple truth is always the same: man is an animal. Both the orgasm of Balso's dream and the discovery of Darwin in Balso's dream within a dream reaffirm man's enslavement to the sheerly physical. To assert anything else, to conceive of the poet as the artist-priest, as the surrealists sometimes did, is absurd. Similarly, despite the fact that *Ulysses* deeply affected West, and his *Balso*, like *Ulysses*, is about a journey, West satirized what he felt was Joyce's artistic pretentiousness. This derision was once made clear in a reporter's interview with West; from the conversation, the interviewer concluded that West detested falsity, Joycean or otherwise, and therefore despised the phoniness of the inhabitants of the Trojan Horse: "Their conversation is *re-joycing*, but he [West] is not rejoiced."[14] The mockery is evident from the beginning of Balso's journey, for Balso begins his quest with a prayer satirizing Joycean rhetoric and agony. Joyce, or Stephen Dedalus, at the end of *Portrait of the Artist,* went "to encounter for the millionth time the reality of experience and to forge in the smithy of my soul the uncreated conscience of my race. . . . Old father, old artificer, stand me now and ever in good stead." Balso's invocation before he enters the Trojan Horse is less pretentious, but he, too, prepares to search for reality: "O Beer! O Meyerbeer! O Bach! O Offenbach. Stand me now as ever in good stead" (p. 4). What Balso finds in his search for reality is similar to what Joyce proclaims at the end of *Ulysses*. There, Joyce's "Yes" to the procreative principle is uttered in Molly Bloom's soliloquy, and West mocks that "Yes" in the series of affirmations with which he ends *Balso:*

> Moooompitcher yaaaah. Oh I never hoped to know
> the passion, the sensuality hidden within you—yes,
> yes. Drag me down into the mire, drag. Yes! And
> with your hair the lust from my eyes brush. Yes . . .
> yes . . . Ooh! Ah! (p. 61)

Most of all West satirizes the chaos and remarkable transformations of Joyce's famous *Walpurgisnacht* in *Ulysses*. In his satiric re-creation West fills *Balso* with every possible kind of chaos, and throughout the novel he has recurrent transformations, as, for example, when Balso, seeking the answer to the question, What is beauty?, is lured to embrace a nude young girl, only to find that in his embrace she slowly becomes a "middle-aged woman dressed in a mannish suit and wearing horn-rimmed glasses" (p. 32).

Obviously, West is satirizing Joyce, but even more obviously West reflects the influence of that great artist. The form of *Ulysses*, a journey through chaos, makes the form of *Balso* what it is. Even more, the dominant ideas of *Ulysses*, the quest for truth (or the father) and the rejection of false gods, are the central concepts of *Balso;* and West accepts the idea, if not the prose, of Joyce's "yes" to the body.

Two additional influences upon *Balso* remain to be mentioned. One is Fyodor Dostoevsky, whom West apparently intended to satirize in the tale of J. Raskolnikov Gilson. The trouble is that Dostoevsky overpowers West's satire, and before long West is deadly serious. The story of his Raskolnikov parallels that of the Russian Raskolnikov. The hero of *Crime and Punishment* commits murder because of his Superman theory, which divides man into the inferior mass and the superior few. The latter are destined to rule and are beyond the common laws of conduct. What Raskolnikov has to learn, and does learn in the horrible dream he has in the Siberian prison hospital, is that his concept of the higher morality, which allows the more spiritual person a freedom beyond law, is like a plague contaminating the world. Similarly West's Raskolnikov murders out of a spiritual, Superman drive, the desire to destroy the animal man. Because the total "unreasonableness" of the murder violates logical causation, the action fulfills the Superman dream of perfect freedom. However, like the Russian's Raskolnikov, West's hero must also learn his lesson. Though obscure in

Nathanael West:

the wit and weirdness of its statement, the lesson is that the root of all spirituality is the flesh, and any attempt to ignore or transcend the flesh will fail. The dualism of so many of Dostoevsky's characters, who struggle internally between good and evil, doubt and faith, spirit and flesh, suggests that the Russian author would have appreciated the lesson of West's Raskolnikov.

One other influence upon *Balso*, and in some ways it might be considered the most profound of all, is Dadaism. The movement, as has been noted, was much involved in disgust. This emotion was directed in part against the past and its works, but its primary attack was against the intellect. Contempt for the art of the past was shown by the Dadaistic painter Francis Picabia, who bought a toy monkey, glued it to a frame, titled it "Portrait of Cézanne," and exhibited it in a gallery which was entered through a public lavatory. The contempt for the mind was dramatized by the artistic productions of the Dadaists; most of the verbal art by its very unintelligibility scornfully mocked the intellect. Tristan Tzara's angry poem "Roar," which consisted of the title repeated 147 times, implied that artistic communication could be achieved only when the thought was extremely simple and naggingly reiterated. "Drink, don't think," was a refrain that ran through the entire movement, much as it dominates the O'Neill play *The Hairy Ape;* and such Hemingway characters as Lieutenant Henry and Jake Barnes are not only sad young men but Dadaists in their fear of thought.

For the Dadaists, such anti-intellectualism was merely the inevitable consequence of what they considered was the essential unreason of the world, an unreason so great that communication itself was almost impossible. To prove their point, five or six Dadaist poets once solemnly proclaimed a public reading, then read their works simultaneously while bells clanged in the background. Since true communication was, in the Dadaist's opinion, beyond man's capabilities, only egoistic and frustrated children would be tempted by the foolishness and the vanity of creative aspirations. When the Dadaists tried to explain the essential impulse that led to artistic creation, they tended to agree with Hans Arp, who, in his unpunctuated, Dadaist style, notes: "only the physically unfit among men compose poems pluck the lyre or swing the paintbrush."[15] *Balso* often echoes this attitude; for instance, John Gilson's pamphlet about the death of his mistress, Saniette, notes that Gilson's physical unattractiveness makes him "substitute strange conceits, wise and witty sayings, peculiar conduct, Art, for the muscles, teeth, hair of my rivals" (p. 26).

The obvious corollary to Dadaist anti-intellectualism is the worship of the natural man and the natural life. Arp comments on the need to leave the rational universe and accept the purely physical:

> dada wanted to destroy the rational swindle for man
> and incorporate him again humbly in nature. . . .
> dada is a moral revolution. dada is for nonsense. which
> does not mean bunk. dada is as senseless as nature and
> life. dada is for nature and against art.[16]

Disgust, anti-intellectualism, and glorification of the physical man are important aspects of Dada, and all are central to *Balso Snell*. The central scatological conceit of the novel is that art is an excrement, more closely aligned to bull-shit (note the initials of Balso's name) than to the "sublime excrement" romanticized by such writers as George Moore. The immediate source of this excrement is the mind, which rationalizes physical demands into supernal abstractions. Thus the mind is the cause of man's misery, for here dreams are born. The misery and frustration come when man finds, as he must, that the dreams are lies; this realization leads to that desire to destroy which is found in so many of West's creatures.

West's later novels contain only partial echoes of this first Dadaistic cry. Where *Balso* blasts at the intellect, the foundation of man's misery, the other novels dramatize the horrors that stem from specific dreams, the products of the mind. *Miss Lonelyhearts* presents the results of an attempt to live by the Christ dream. *A Cool Million* depicts the deluded life of a boy who takes the American, Horatio Alger dream seriously. *The Day of the Locust* portrays the horror of Hollywood, the lesser dream factory (for, of course, the mind is always the major dream manufacturer).

In the three novels that follow *Balso*, the end is destruction. Miss Lonelyhearts is shot as he runs toward the cripple who represents man and whom Miss Lonelyhearts would succor with love. Lemuel Pitkin, still believing in the American Dream despite the fact that he has been duped time and again, is shot at the end of *A Cool Million*. Tod Hackett, shrieking at the violent spectacle of a Hollywood premiere, is temporarily insane at the end of *The Day of the Locust*.

In truth West is thoroughly involved in destruction: certainly in that respect Dadaism dominated his work. *Balso*, however, does offer a trifle more. The novel ends with physical, sexual orgasm. In that alone, Balso finds the answer to the mysteries of the universe: "The miracle was made manifest. The two became one. The one that is all things and yet no one of them . . ." (p. 61). Thus in his search for the meaning of existence, for some central unity, Balso is successful. In copulation the multiplicity of two becomes the unity of one. However, this answer to Balso's search is unsatisfying, for it has no element of the spiritual about it: the unity is only transitory, and the rhythm of the sex act reflects the mechanics of the body's physical decay. The answer is bitter most of all because it implies that submission to the purely physical animal leads to happiness as high as man can expect on earth, and only in death will man's perfect peace arrive. To ask for more is to ask for dreams—and misery.

Finally, even the obscurantism of *Balso* suggests the Dada feeling that art is a private matter, best done when least understood. The Dada manifesto makes this point clearly: "Art is a private matter; the artist produces it for himself; an intelligible work is the product of a journalist."[17] The Dada hold on West is apparent in his declaration that *Balso* was written "as a protest against writing books."[18]

Still, despite his agreement with the Dadaist contempt of art, West was a writer, and, like many other artists, he preferred laughing defensively at himself to being laughed at by others. Yet he was a writer, and so when an interviewer asked him what he had done when he finished *The Dream Life*, West could only answer, with some astonishment, that he had begun another book. The new book was to be quite unlike *Balso*, in fact "of quite a different make, wholesome, clean, holy, slightly mystic and inane."[19] The new book was *Miss Lonelyhearts*.

3 The Christ Dream

WEST, EARLY IN 1927, returned to America. He had spent some three months in Paris. As he grew older, however, his stay lengthened in his own mind. In 1933, on the dust jacket of *Miss Lonelyhearts*, he claimed that he had lived there from 1926 to 1928. Still later he told his Hollywood secretary, Jo Conway, that he had spent six years in Paris.

On his return home, he told John Sanford:

I left Paris just before the New Year . . . and on New Year's Eve, I sent this gal a wireless message from the middle of the Atlantic: "Ring out wild balls." Shortly after getting home, I had a letter from her, saying, "Thanks for your kind holiday thought: 'Ring out, wild bells.'" What do you think happened this morning, though? I had another letter from her, and she told me she'd gotten an apology from the wireless company: "Message reading 'Ring out, wild bells' should have read 'Ring out, wild balls.'"[1]

West was bringing back to America what he considered the new sophistication. Jeremiah Mahoney recalls that in their first meeting after West's return from Paris, "He was dressed like a conservative dandy, with yellow gloves and the usual homburg. He seemed older, more poised, and evidently satisfied that he had attained some measure of cosmopolitan culture."[2] In reviewing his Paris impressions with Mahoney, West talked of Sylvia Beach's bookstore and of Ernest Hemingway. Wherever West went he passed vast amounts of time in bookstores, and it is no wonder that Miss Beach's fame as the publisher of *Ulysses* attracted him. Hemingway, whom West met briefly in Paris, impressed him as something of a poseur who talked at length, like a character from *The Sun Also Rises*, about Spain and the fishing and the bulls.

By the summer of 1927 West had resumed his friendship with Saul Jarcho and John Sanford. To Jarcho he gave a copy of the Paris edition of *Ulysses*, as well as a humorous volume by Stephen Leacock, *My Discovery of England*. Once he jokingly remarked that the New York police wished to arrest Petronius Arbiter for obscenity but were having trouble locating his hideaway. Jarcho and West occasionally took long walks together, and sometimes they stopped to visit a Greenwich Village speakeasy. Jarcho remarks:

. . . I entered medical school . . . [and] I used to see Pep. . . . Our conversations were long and serious

... We talked mostly about English literature, the
problems of literary composition, the problems of
authors and scholars in the materialistic American
environment. . . . We often talked of the worthless
comments on English literature tossed forth by
unqualified critics and dilettantes. Among Ned's
[West's] interests were Doughty and other travellers
to Arabia, also Norman Douglas. . . .

Once Ned asked me to describe an autopsy. He
wanted to see one. . . . He had some fantastic and
poetic conception—not serious—about the colors of
various viscera. He showed a tendency toward bizarre
images.[3]

With Sanford, also, West roamed New York. In their walks
West revealed how

He hated loud talk, ostentation, sharpie clothes, clichés,
public display of emotion, three-name women writers
(Thyra Samter Winslow, Viola Brothers Shore),
Bronx intellectuals (meaning Jews), Jewish girls
(bagels, he called them), sentimentality, and perhaps
above all himself.[4]

Sanford recalls that he and West often talked of writing
and painting.

These are some of the names I heard for the first time:
T. S. Eliot, Ezra Pound (Ezra Pfundt, West called
him), Walter Pater, a young guy named Hemingway,
Max Beerbohm, Aubrey Beardsley, Picasso, Modi-
gliani, Sherwood Anderson, Joyce, Kafka, William
Carlos Williams. Painters, writers of all kinds, but
never a composer. . . .

He had a library of four or five hundred books,
some of them pretty costly, but none too good to be
taken away. On the contrary, he offered them for loan,
and here are some of the items he started my reading
with: *Marius the Epicurean,* poems by Richard

Aldington, everything by Max Beerbohm, Coleridge's
Biographia Literaria, a novel about Theodore Gumbril
and his pneumatic pants (West thought Huxley made
stunning jokes).[5]

Sanford remembers that for a while after his return from
Paris, West worked with his father as a building contractor
and had "pocketfuls of money."[6] Possibly West seemed
well-off to Sanford, but in reality West's father was having
increasing financial problems and the Wallenstein and Weinstein families had their backs to the wall. Partially because
of this, and through the aid of his uncle Morris Jarcho,
West took a job in 1927 as assistant manager of the modest
Kenmore Hall hotel on East 23rd Street. The hotel became
a gathering place for a number of West's friends, notably
Quentin Reynolds, Isaak Orliansky, I. J. Kapstein, and S. J.
Perelman. Reynolds comments:

> I think it was during that year or so at the Kenmore
> that Pep became a writer by reading. Fate . . .
> picked out the perfect job for an embryonic writer;
> the Kenmore was a quiet place and Pep had nothing
> to do after midnight but be there. So he read. I
> suppose he read eight or nine hours a night. Not only
> Dostoevsky (always his favorite) and Stendhal and
> the emerging Hemingway and Sinclair Lewis and a
> man named Joyce . . . but anything else he could lay
> his hands on including *Black Mask,* a pulp magazine
> which specialized in detective stories. We both read
> that avidly, chiefly because Dashiell Hammett was a
> village friend of ours and he was the first man either
> of us knew who actually sold his stories. Dash was a
> free-wheeling spender who was always writing against
> the rent and one night I met him in Nick's and as usual
> he was in trouble with the "shorts." To make matters
> worse he was halfway through a serial for *Black
> Mask* but they wouldn't give him a dime until he had

finished it and he was about to be tossed out of his room.

"You've got a room at Kenmore Hall until you finish your serial," I told him grandiloquently heading for the phone booth. I told Pep about the problem Hammett faced and of my brilliant solution.

"Register him under a phony name," I said. "When he finishes his serial he can run like a deer and you can say that he was some skip artist who just blew the joint."

There was silence at the other end of the line.

"What is it, Pep?" I asked anxiously.

"I was just trying to think of a good name to register him under" Pep said mildly. "How do you like 'T. Victrola Blueberry'?"

"I'll be right up with Mr. Blueberry." We got a bottle of gin on credit from Nick's and that night the three of us stayed up late in the finest suite in the hotel talking of the kind of things we talked about in the 1920's.

"You got a title for the serial?" Pep asked.

"I think I'll call it *The Maltese Falcon*" Dash said.[7]

During these years in New York, West spent a considerable time exploring the Bohemian, the literary, and the radical veins of Greenwich Village. He and his closest friend, S. J. Perelman, who was contributing to *Judge, College Humor,* and *The New Yorker,* often dined at such Village restaurants as Siegal's and The Aurora, and at times West's sister Laura came down from Pembroke College to join the two men in their jaunts. Perelman and Laura were almost immediately attracted to each other, and on July 4, 1929, they were married and took an apartment near Washington Square. West was a frequent visitor, and, at their apartment and at other Village habitats, he listened (for he seldom spoke) to such Village luminaries as Philip Wylie,

Maxwell Bodenheim, Mike Gold, John Dos Passos, e.e. cummings, and Edmund Wilson, as they vividly enunciated their favorite iconoclastic, sensual, communistic, or anarchic theories. On one occasion Perelman introduced West to a columnist for the *Brooklyn Eagle,* and the columnist, who wrote under the pseudonym of "Susan Chester," told West and Perelman of the kinds of letters she received as a columnist for the lovelorn. The letters amused her, and she suggested that they might serve as material for Perelman. When West and Perelman read the letters, full of suffering and signed by such names as "Broad Shoulders," Perelman saw that they were inappropriate to his kind of verbal joking. West, however, responded to the unintended humor, the pathos, and the tragedy of the letters; and his receptivity was eventually sharpened and dramatized in the cries for help of such creatures as "Desperate," who writes to Miss Lonelyhearts:

> I am sixteen years old now and I dont know what to do and would appreciate it if you could tell me what to do. When I was a little girl it was not so bad because I got used to the kids on the block makeing fun of me, but now I would like to have boy friends like the other girls and go out on Saturday nites but no boy will take me because I was born without a nose— although I am a good dancer and have a nice shape and my father buys me pretty clothes. (p. 67)

With another part of his personality, West was attracted by a second circle of friends. These were young Jewish intellectuals, a number of whom had studied with Morris R. Cohen at City College, and all of whom had been influenced by the ideas of Spengler. More serious in their preoccupations than were his Greenwich Village acquaintances, this latter group often met at the home of George Brounoff, on Central Park West, and there, as they drank tea in the

Russian mode, they discussed art, music, philosophy, and literature. Generally the group was inspired by nineteenth-century Russian literature, most especially by the writings of Dostoevsky and Tolstoy, and Brounoff himself propounded the ideals of secular sainthood so persuasively, in the mode of Dostoevsky's Prince Myshkin, that he himself was often referred to as Prince Myshkin. In addition to this literary orientation, however, the group discussed Marxist ideas (especially those promulgated in such magazines as *International Literature* and *Inprecorps* and preached by such organizations as the John Reed clubs), visited *avant garde* exhibitions of modern art, and attended concerts of both *avant garde* and classical music. The tone of the group is implied by the fact that West, when he read a draft of *Balso Snell* to the members, was condemned for lacking seriousness in his writing.

During these years of the early thirties, West also became involved in two love affairs of some significance to him. The first was with Beatrice Mathieu, a writer specializing in Paris fashions for *The New Yorker*. A friend of the Perelmans, Miss Mathieu spent much of the winter of 1929–30 in New York, and by the time she returned to Paris in February, West was so emotionally involved that he was planning to visit her in June and beyond that was even dreaming of a future as an expatriate writer in Paris. These fantasies were strong enough for him to encourage Miss Mathieu to search for an apartment for him. His dreams were possibly induced by his hopes for an advance on *Miss Lonelyhearts*—of which he had finished four chapters by April of 1930—but Simon and Schuster (Clifton Fadiman read the manuscript) was not enthusiastic about the commercial prospects of the work, and not only did the firm fail to offer him an advance but it made no offer of a contract. Such harsh realities frightened West, and after a period of vacillation (during which he reapplied for a passport) he finally wrote to Miss Mathieu that he had abandoned, at least for the moment, his illusions of being a great artist or even of hacking out a living as a writer. Maybe, he wrote, he was a coward, a phony, but he had canceled his passage to Paris and was remaining in his hotel job.

An even stronger emotional commitment followed soon after. In the fall of 1930, West met Alice Shepard, the A. S. to whom *Balso* is dedicated. A college friend of Laura, West's sister, Miss Shepard was a Christian, of New England background. A truly beautiful woman, she was the chief model for the elegant and exclusive showrooms of Elizabeth Hawes, and she was also a gracious, sensitive, and intelligent human being. West was soon deeply in love with her, and she with him. Though both agreed that financial exigencies made marriage impractical at the moment, West got an application for a wedding license and carried it in his wallet as a promise for the future. Though he was to carry the application with him until 1939, the promise was to remain unfulfilled.

In the latter part of 1930, West, again with the assistance of Morris Jarcho, became manager of the Sutton Club Hotel on East 56th Street. It was a far more select hotel than the Kenmore, but a quaint depression pastime soon caused West to refer to its sun deck as Suicide Leap.

In his managerial capacity, West was especially kind to writers during the depression. Sometimes the kindness had a practical, depression-born basis: for instance, when West gave Erskine Caldwell a room at a reduced rent, he asked that Caldwell be sure to keep a light burning every evening. More often there was simply compassion. James T. Farrell remembers that West gave rooms to him and his wife Dorothy "when we had no money and no place to go; he did it simply and unobtrusively as though it were a matter of course. When I next saw him in '34–'35, he did not even mention it. He did us this favor without expecting any return, or any particular thanks."[8]

At the Sutton, West read and wrote and felt himself slowly suffocated in trivial business chores. While there he reworked *The Dream Life of Balso Snell* (which until 1930 he was calling *The Journal of Balso Snell*), but his efforts to interest a publisher were initially unsuccessful. Robert McAlmon's Contact Editions, before Moss and Kamin took over the Editions, refused the novel on the grounds that it was too much in the vein of Anatole France, and Brewer, Warren and Putnam, a small publisher, rejected it for being both obscene and blasphemous. Occasionally he amused himself by steaming open the mail of hotel residents (once abetted by his friend Lillian Hellman), and the lost hopes of which he read made him see the guests as grotesques and the hotel as a microcosm where men veiled their spiritual poverty by a thousand gilded disguises. At other times he agonized over the short stories with which he was experimenting. In one unpublished story, "The Adventurer," he dramatized (under the strong influence of Eliot's *The Waste Land*) the daydreams and recollections of former daydreams of a grocery clerk, Joe Rucker, so that the dreams become his sole reality. That truth West then extends to collective mankind, so that Joe sees "cripples" everywhere. Especially they lurk in libraries and congregate on park benches. Pale specters, without purpose, they exist only through their fantasies. Though Joe can dream of the myth of the wasteland, with its hope that the sexually wounded Fisher King may regain his manhood and the desert bloom again, there is in reality no Chapel Perilous, Joe is no savior, and there will be no regeneration for this world.

During this period West and Edmund Wilson shared occasional moments of amusement. West exhibited his cher-

ished Max Ernst illustrations, and both men enjoyed dis-
cussing hunting. West was proud of his gun and did most
of the talking about hunting. In his talk he exhibited "a quick
Jewish humor, and the quality of his imagination was, I
think, both Russian and Jewish."[9] Wilson, however, felt that
West's "hunting was largely a following of the Hemingway
fashion. He told me once about shooting a bear in the Adirondacks, but . . . the effect of the story was to make me
feel sorry for the bear."[10]

Once, letting memories of Paris break in on everyday affairs, West went into a crowded, steaming cafeteria in
downtown New York and commented, "If this were Paris,
we'd think it fun."[11] Always, though, the hotel was waiting,
and West had "an aura of sadness, as if he and his family
were constantly in trouble—there was a good deal of sickness and he did not have the money to get married."[12] Saul
Jarcho notes that, during this period, West "spoke quietly
but freely and often a little sadly and whimsically. He gave
the impression of being a slightly detached and somewhat
depressed observer of life."[13] Some additions to the picture
are made by John Sanford:

> . . . his [West's] pet phrase, "to coin a phrase"; his
> habit of speaking clichés in italics; his fat-lady joke,
> which he must've told you a dozen times; his being
> fresh out of matches everywhere and always; his odd
> stunt of buying a pack of butts, offering you one,
> taking one himself, and then giving you the pack
> as if he'd gotten it from you; his other nickname,
> Tweedy Boy; . . . his Brooks valise, five feet long
> and two feet wide; . . . his agony in the presence of
> sentiment, his physical agony; his good imitations of
> the Schnozzola. . . .[14]

In May of 1931 West proposed to Sanford that they spend
a summer in the mountains, and briefly West escaped the

city and the hotel. They rented a shack in the southern Adirondacks near Warrensburg, New York. The rent for the furnished house was twenty dollars a month, and with it "went 1200 acres of forest and a fifty acre pond in the middle."[15] With neither shirking the distasteful everyday chores, the men soon established a regular routine and got along very well together. In the morning they worked on their writing, West on *Miss Lonelyhearts* and Sanford on his first novel, *The Water Wheel.*

> A peculiarity of West's method of work that few know about was his habit of reading his stuff back to himself aloud. The walls of the cabin were plasterboard, and I could hear him as though he were in the same room. I squawked time and again, and time and again he'd quit and apologize, but always after a while he'd start again, and finally I realized that he was so rapt that he actually didn't know what he was doing. . . . In addition . . . West from time to time would ask me to listen to various passages. . . . Occasionally I did put in a comment, but it was generally limited to a matter of form, and once in a very great while West would accept the suggestion. . . . I noted, however, that he never asked me to try my own stuff out on him in return, and of course I never offered to read him a line. He did read that first book of mine, though, . . . One comment only comes back to mind —that I go over the manuscript very carefully and conceal the identity of a girl he happened to recognize. "But for Christ's sake, Scotty!" I can still hear him say. "You just can't write about real people that intimately. It isn't done!"[16]

The afternoons Sanford and West spent fishing and hunting. Since the rowboat they had bought was impractical for fishing, West suggested that they build a raft and anchor it in one of the deeper parts of Viele Pond. Using old oil drums for floats, they succeeded in constructing a fine raft. It served its purpose beautifully, except for the occasional dunkings that came when both men tried simultaneously to climb aboard. Once in a while, the men explored the fishing farther away: the Hudson for small-mouth bass, Brant Lake for pickerel. "What we caught we always took back to the cabin and cooked for supper, and we ate like swine."[17] Besides the fishing, there was the hunting. The two spent vast amounts of time shooting at paper targets, and one old tree near the cabin they almost cut in two with lead. Often the men tramped the woods in search of small game. With some irritation still, Sanford remembers:

> I have to say that there was no more dangerous man to be in the woods with than Pep West. It wasn't that he didn't know guns were meant for killing. It was simply that he was too bloody fumble-fingered to put the knowledge to use. He was not only capable of handing you a piece with the hammer cocked; he was also capable of nudging you with the barrel. He did that to me once with a loaded shotgun. . . . That was bad enough, but not till we'd changed pieces did I discover that the safe was off and the shotgun ready for firing. . . . I remember cursing West coldly for five minutes long. And I remember that he was astonished.[18]

Soon after this vacation West's first novel, finished long before, came out in a small edition. Ignored almost completely by critics and public, the novel bore the author's name as Nathanael West, not Nathan Weinstein. His adopted name did not immediately become a household word, but it did arouse some curiosity among his acquaintances. When asked how he had chosen his new name, West answered, "Horace Greeley said, 'Go West, young man.'

So I did."[19] Considering West's care in choosing the names for the characters of his novels,* the answer is provocative —especially in the implication that a pioneer, a quester, is leaving the old country, the ethnic homeland, behind and setting out on a journey toward a new land of hope and promise.

At this time also, West got an urge, as many young writers before and after him, to publish a "little magazine." He mentioned the idea to his friend William Carlos Williams, who agreed that they co-edit a new version of Williams' earlier little magazine, *Contact*. Because the editors felt that there were already enough outlets for commercial and scholarly writing, they agreed that *Contact* would publish in neither of these areas. The general purpose of the magazine would be to preserve true values and advance the *avant garde* in literature. In 1932 three issues of *Contact* appeared. Among the contributors were such people as West, Williams, Robert McAlmon, e. e. cummings, Parker Tyler, Yvor Winters, Erskine Caldwell, James T. Farrell, Nathan Asch, Eugene Joffe, and S. J. Perelman. Because the editors were unable to pay for contributions, the magazine soon declined

* The most thorough treatment of West's use of names in his novels occurs in C. Carroll Hollis' excellent articles "Nathanael West and Surrealist Violence," *Fresco* (Spring–Summer, 1957), and "Nathanael West: Diagnostician of the Lonely Crowd," *Fresco* (Fall, 1957). A single passage from the latter article indicates the close study Professor Hollis has made of West's use of names: "As in all of his novels, here too [in *The Day of the Locust*] West's names for his characters are carefully chosen to suggest the roles allotted to them. *Tod Hunter* is the God Hunter who can get no direction in his search from the friend who is crippled by success, the 'lame' Claude. But 'the leader of the chosen people,' the dwarf *Abe*, brings him to *Faye* (both 'faith' and 'fay') Greener. As her name suggests, she is the only faith Tod can find, and his desire grows as she rejects him. Her father Harry, 'the leader,' is an ineffectual failure. She herself has faith only in physical love and money but serves as the adored fay of *Homer Simpson*, the representative simple man, who sublimates his inherent evil as long as his blind love endures" (pp. 18–19).

in quality, and so, a little sorrowfully, West and Williams abandoned the venture. Though the creative writing in its pages was of no great literary importance, *Contact* published one of the first bibliographies of the little magazines. Compiled by David Moss, the bibliography was West's idea, and West insisted that it must include a full listing, no matter what the length, of the issues of Margaret Anderson's magazine, *The Little Review,* and Eugene Jolas' publication, *Transition.*[20] West's interest in these is probably explainable by their great importance in the history of the little magazine, but his insistence probably also came from the fact that his close reading of these particular magazines made them personally important to him. That he should have placed a high value on them is understandable when one notes a few of their contributions to American literary history: *The Little Review* had published goodly portions of *Ulysses; Transition* had published sections from Joyce's "Work in Progress" (eventually titled *Finnegans Wake*); and both magazines welcomed surrealistic and other experimental writing.

While West was working at the Sutton, he met Josephine Herbst, who was to be one of his closest friends. The meeting, which Miss Herbst remembers vividly, was arranged by Dr. Williams. It took place shortly after the publication of *Balso Snell* had finally been realized, and while West was doing the sixth revision of *Miss Lonelyhearts.* Miss Herbst recalls the spaciousness, even luxury, of the Sutton apartment where West was living. Nevertheless, he complained in his soft voice that it was a cage where he could do no work because of the continual interruptions. A dark, awkward, slender, and sinewy man, with brown hair, large firm hands, and a proud air and step, West had deep, large, brown eyes that, to Miss Herbst, suggested mystery, depths within depths, emotions beyond explanation. Like the dark brown eyes of West's sister Laura, West's eyes also suggested to Miss Herbst those of some long-lost child, searching and never finding, being hurt and never telling, caring and never showing.

To Miss Herbst and her husband, John Herrmann, West complained bitterly about his entrapment in the world of commerce. Typical of his own vision of people, West's description of the inhabitants at the hotel contained a paradoxical mixture of fascination and repulsion: "He had a certain enjoyment in the very details he deplored. I remember one occasion after he had been in Hollywood when he spent an entire evening relating the more sordid aspects of life in Hollywood with both revulsion and pleasure."[21] Similarly, the gusto with which West described the sordidness and suffering of the people in the hotel, the fascination which he found in portraying the hotel guests as inhuman clowns and grotesques, the way in which he reveled in the very details he deplored—all these, perhaps, formed some private masochistic alchemy by which West tried to erase the vision of suffering humanity he saw around him. To Miss Herbst it was a private, surrealistically Westian vision which distorted the harmless, innocent guests of the hotel.*

The death of West's father of bronchiectasis in June of 1932 left West heartsick—part of the despair of *Miss Lonelyhearts* stems from this source —and he considered leaving the hotel. His mother was opposed to such a plan and re-

---

* In a letter to Cyril Schneider, April 15, 1952, Allan Seager remembers that West, while in Hollywood, was still fascinated by the clientele of the Hotel Sutton. West "called the place 'Suicide's Leap' because there had been about half a dozen suicides in the place, one of them quite spectacular, which made all the papers. . . . It was not a place for the successful, and while West was aware that it was hardly a desirable hotel property, it fascinated him. Why did so many people jump from the sun deck? . . . I had the impression of a man who had a coherent view of 'our culture' but it was not a reasoned one. It was emotional, consistent, and gloomy."

peated over and over the dangers of the move, the need of a man to eat, and the foolishness of living on dreams. West listened and mused and listened some more. Finally, taking his small savings, he fled.

West drove to Erwinna, Pennsylvania, with the Herrmanns. A short while later, he read the completed portion of *Miss Lonelyhearts* to his sympathetic listeners. The Herrmanns' insistence that the manuscript be completed as soon as possible encouraged West to take a room at Warford House, a small hotel in Frenchtown, New Jersey. Here, working at the rate of about seven hundred words a week,[22] West completed the novel.

Nathan Asch, who was visiting the Herrmanns on one of the evenings when West crossed the river to make a social call, remembers the novelist as a sophisticated, ironic personality. He "looked as I suppose Michael Arlen would have liked to look," and he talked "as if he didn't actually believe that what was happening around him was really happening and he didn't much like it anyway."[23] Such a detached observer of the ironies in the human struggle hardly seemed to fit in with the class-conscious writers whom West apparently admired and with whom he was certainly friendly. The contradiction puzzled Asch. Not until he read *Miss Lonelyhearts* did he sense that behind the ironic, sophisticated front there was "a mentality that was tender and an eye that saw true."[24]

On the day that West completed *Miss Lonelyhearts*, he celebrated by going hunting. With a spray of buckshot, he brought down a pheasant. To end the day of celebration, West and the Herrmanns planned a pheasant dinner, but the eating was difficult since the buckshot had largely replaced the meat on the bird.

Another party shortly afterward caused the end of West's informal engagement to Alice Shepard. The reason for the broken engagement—which left West full of guilt—was not, however, that given by such friends as John Sanford:

> She [Alice Shepard] was . . . tall and good looking, conventionally so, as are five million American girls of any generation. She was Christian, and Pep, of course, was Jewish, and as I gathered it from him, that was the all-important difference. I believe it caused the ultimate break between them.[25]

The reason, instead, was far more fundamental: after a party West slept with another woman and Miss Shepard suspected it. When she confronted him, he confessed and pleaded for a reconciliation. She refused. Though he later invented causes for the rift, he never disclosed the truth.

About this time *Miss Lonelyhearts* was published by Liveright and met with a fine critical reception. Then came one of the publishing ironies that seemed to meet West throughout his career. Liveright did not advertise the book (the meager advertising for any of West's books is remarkable), and then, shortly after the novel's publication, Liveright went bankrupt. The printer, after delivering a few hundred copies of the book to bookstores, refused to deliver the remaining fourteen hundred copies of the edition. West frantically tried to get a release from Liveright so that the novel might come out under another publisher's imprint. His friend Sidney Jarcho, a lawyer, helped him in the involved legal proceedings. Together, they finally managed to place the book with Harcourt Brace. A new edition was soon published, but by then the name of *Miss Lonelyhearts* had faded from the public eye, and there was little chance the book would prove a popular success. A few hundred copies of the new edition were sold to a few readers who remembered the earlier reviews; then the novel went to the remainders tables.

Miss Lonelyhearts, like all of West's novels, is episodic. The narrative pattern is similar to that of *Balso Snell*. Though the tone of cynical mockery in *Balso* changes to fevered religiosity in *Miss Lonelyhearts*, both novels tell of a search. The search is for some spiritual reality to believe in and live by, and in both novels the search ends in tragic disillusionment.

Miss Lonelyhearts tells the story of a young man who writes a sob-sister column for the newspapers. Miss Lonelyhearts (in the original manuscript West had named his hero Thomas Matlock) gives advice in his column to desperate and helpless people who have no other place to turn. Miss Lonelyhearts has taken the job as a joke, and he hopes it will lead to his writing a gossip column. After a while the pathetic letters addressed to him make him feel that the joke has turned upon him. Here the novel really begins, and the action treats Miss Lonelyhearts' attempts to come to terms with his own helplessness. This he can do in no easy way. Instead he must go through what might be called a program for the attainment of salvation. This program, or pilgrimage, eventually leads to a mystical experience, but by the time it has reached this culmination Miss Lonelyhearts has become completely alienated from those around him; in the eyes of the world, he has become "sick." Though tragically ironic, it is only fitting that he should be killed by one of those desperate creatures who have led him to his ordeal and his mystical experience. The novel, as West claimed, is the "portrait of a priest of our time who has had a religious experience."[26] The portrait is painted in a succinct, imagistic style, and it attempts to fulfill West's claim that

> Lyric novels can be written according to Poe's definition of a lyric poem. The short novel is a distinct form especially suited to use in this country. France, Spain, Italy have a literature as well as the Scandinavian

writers. For a hasty people we are far too patient with
the Bucks, Dreisers, and Lewises. Thank God we are
not all Scandinavians.

Forget the epic, the master work. In America
fortunes do not accumulate, the soil does not grow,
families have no history. Leave slow growth to the
book reviewers, you only have time to explode.[27]

From the point of view of Miss Lonelyhearts, this priest
of twentieth-century America, the American scene is a deso-
late one. Its basic components are decay and violence and
pain. In this American wasteland, the decay is extreme.
Though the action takes place in the spring, the air seems
waxy and artificial, while the dirt of the city appears without possibility of generation. Even in the country, the vision is of death and rot. For Miss Lonelyhearts, the entire
world is dead, and only through hysteria, brought on by the
name of Christ, can the "dead world take on a semblance of
life" (p. 39).

In this decayed world, violence exists everywhere. Partly
its source is the Darwinistic struggle for survival; partly it
stems from the unsatisfied spiritual needs of man. Through
violence, modern man comes alive; it is the salt by which he
savors an existence without the Saviour. Before attaining
grace, Miss Lonelyhearts thinks that "only violence could
make him supple" (p. 49); or, comparing himself to a dead
man, he feels that "only friction could make him warm or
violence make him mobile" (p. 79).

Man is caught in a viselike trap: in a sterile world he
would still be alive, but only through violence can he feel
himself potent. The world of *Miss Lonelyhearts* is, therefore, filled with violence. Its everyday presence is suggested
by innumerable actions and images and by casual understatement. "Violent images are used to illustrate commonplace events. Violent acts are left almost bald."[28]

Man's desire for life leads to his seemingly instinctive preoccupation with sexual violence, the type most intimately associated with life. The letters to Miss Lonelyhearts are permeated with sexual suffering, from the nightmarish epistle of Broad Shoulders to the pathos of Sick-of-it-all, who writes that she is expecting her eighth child in twelve years "and I don't think I can stand it. . . . I cry all the time it hurts so much and I don't know what to do" (pp. 13–14). Miss Lonelyhearts' newspaper associates gain vicarious life from the violence of the sexual gang-shag tales they love to tell. Even Miss Lonelyhearts at one time tugs sadistically at a woman's nipples, at another time tears at an unwilling woman's clothes.

This emphasis on violence was in every novel West wrote. Even before the publication of *Miss Lonelyhearts*, West stated his defense:

> In America violence is idiomatic. . . . What is melodramatic in European writing is not necessarily so in American writing. For a European writer to make violence real, he has to do a great deal of careful sociology and psychology. He often needs three hundred pages to motivate one little murder. But not so the American writer. His audience has been prepared and is neither surprised nor shocked if he omits artistic excuses for familiar events.[29]

In this world of decay and violence man is able to exist only through dreams. The search for a dream to believe in is right—and in this contention *Miss Lonelyhearts* and *Balso* agree—for it is only through dreams that men can fight their misery. However, the commercialization and stereotyping of man's dreams have led to a weakening of their power, a puerility in their content. This is the worst betrayal of modern man.

Typically betrayed is Mary Shrike, the wife of Miss

Lonelyhearts' chief tormentor. In her early childhood she has been familiar with violence and suffering, but she romantically transforms her past when she speaks of it. Her alterations of reality make Miss Lonelyhearts realize that "People like Mary were unable to do without such tales. They told them because they wanted to talk about . . . something poetic" (p. 90). This desire for the beautiful attracts Mary to El Gaucho, and it is her poetic longing which explains the medallion she wears between her breasts. Both suggest romance, but both are obvious fakes. El Gaucho, with its romantic atmosphere, is only a commercialized dream, just as the medallion has no religious significance but is an award for a childhood racing contest. These small dreams are betrayals of man's true spiritual needs, but despite their limitations Mary must cling to them. Through such fantasies she attempts to satisfy her psychological need for mystery and romance. Her need unites her with the unfortunate correspondents who seek help from Miss Lonelyhearts.

Perhaps even more than the letter writers, Mrs. Shrike needs the help of Christ, the Miss Lonelyhearts of Miss Lonelyhearts. Not really able to believe in her tiny dreams, she, nevertheless, needs something on which to dream. The split personality which results can be seen in her inner conflict. On the one hand, she is pulled by the head's knowledge and fears; on the other, she instinctively reacts according to the body's desires. When Miss Lonelyhearts kisses Mary, she reacts with sexual grunts and scents; but never will her mind allow her to submit wholly to the sexual act. Because of the body-mind conflict, with the fears of the mind in eventual control, she will not sleep with Miss Lonelyhearts and cannot respond sexually to her husband. Being divided, Mary can submit totally to no one, and paradoxically one must give oneself to gain oneself. Mary becomes the eternal virgin; and the head, or reason, is the villain that makes her so. Rationalism dooms Mary, and much of modern man, to dream the small dreams rather than the big Christ dream; but the small dreams are psychologically inadequate to the spiritual needs of man.

A more powerful dream might have saved Mary by giving her a mystery and romance worthy of belief. But in this commercialized world the needs of the spirit have been betrayed. The modern dream merchants do not offer love as the dream by which man can conquer suffering. They do not even justify human suffering by stating that it is Christ's gift to man and that by suffering man comes to know Christ. Instead they offer the easy Technicolor evasions (from Art to the South Seas) that man so much wants to believe in. Unfortunately none of these escapes is powerful enough to salve for long the pain of existence.

In this world of decay and violence and pain, man can react in only a limited number of ways. He can, like Mary Shrike, who wavers between acceptance and non-acceptance of a lesser dream than Christ, become a split personality. By distortion and simplification, he can so blind himself to the suffering of man that he is capable of accepting a lesser dream. He can reject all dreams. He can accept the Christ dream of faith and universal love.

Miss Lonelyhearts' girl friend, Betty, follows the second of these paths. By her excessive simplification of the world, she is able to bring order out of chaos. When Miss Lonelyhearts first thinks of her, he muses "that when she straightened his tie, she straightened much more" (p. 49). Later on, when Betty visits Miss Lonelyhearts while he is ill, she puts the jumbled confusion of his room in order. This same ability to put her universe in order leads Betty to an inner peace that is reflected even in her physical smoothness. Because of Miss Lonelyhearts' own unsuccessful attempts to attain this harmony, he feels Betty is a Buddha, lacking only the potbelly.

For Miss Lonelyhearts, Betty's order is a false one. It excludes not only suffering but also the spiritual needs of man. It degrades man to a mere body and assumes that all his ailments can be cured by such drugs as aspirin. Still, while basically false, Betty's ability to limit experience allows her to retain her innocent, natural speech, and laugh. Such naturalness is more related to the primal simplicities of nature than to the elaborate artificiality, both physical and psychological, of the city. Inevitably Betty combats Miss Lonelyhearts' spiritual sickness by taking him to the zoo and talking of the country's sounds and smells. Then she takes him to the country. Though the visit does not cure Miss Lonelyhearts, Betty becomes an "excited child, greeting the trees and grass with delight" (p. 135).

Betty's vision of the way of the world is one of childlike order and harmony. It is akin to one of the childhood memories of Miss Lonelyhearts:

> One winter evening . . . he had . . . gone to the piano and had begun a piece by Mozart. His sister left her picture book to dance to his music. She had never danced before. She danced gravely and carefully, a simple dance yet formal. . . . As Miss Lonelyhearts stood at the bar, swaying slightly to the remembered music, he thought of children dancing. Square replacing oblong and being replaced by circle. Every child everywhere; in the whole world there was not one child who was not gravely, sweetly dancing. (pp. 64–65)

Such a world of simple patterns, however, is the world of childhood only; that it is based on children's limited, and therefore false, experience is suggested by what immediately follows: an unjustified punch in the mouth from a stranger loosens one of Miss Lonelyhearts' teeth. Violence and suffering exist in the real universe, and any harmony which eliminates these elements is false.

Though Betty's world is one of Buddhistic blindness, it can, through its limitations, become a universal of personal love, of "his job and her gingham apron, his slippers beside the fireplace and her ability to cook" (p. 52). This simplification makes Betty oblivious both to the world of suffering humanity and to the things of the spirit. The possibility of such a limited outlook continuing throughout life is slim.

Because the dreams sold by the modern dream merchants offer no adequate solution for conquering or justifying suffering in a world of rot and violence, some cynical sophisticates react toward dreams in still a third way. They reject all dreams. Shrike, Miss Lonelyhearts' chief tormentor, has made such a rejection. So have most of the newspapermen with whom Shrike associates. Once these men had felt that their devotion to Beauty and self-expression justified their existence, but under the commercialized mold of the news story they have lost all faith in Beauty. Shrike, as feature editor, has especially seen culture and Beauty and self-expression corrupted by commercialism. The loss of faith in Beauty deafens these men, whom Shrike epitomizes, to the call of any faith. Mechanically and cynically, they make jokes of man's dreams about the soil, the South Seas, Hedonism, and Art. The biggest joke, however, is the Christ dream, and Shrike reserves his most brutal attacks for man's aspirations toward Christ. Shrike sends a parodied prayer of the "*Anima Christi*" to Miss Lonelyhearts:

> "Soul of Miss L, glorify me
> Body of Miss L, nourish me
> Blood of Miss L, intoxicate me. . . ." (p. 11)

Or Shrike makes vulgar jokes about Christianity: "I am a great saint. I can walk on my own water" (p. 31). Or Shrike reads and shows others a news story concerning a condemned robber and murderer for whom a goat-and-adding-machine service, a religious ceremony, is to be held. Shrike proclaims that such a service embodies the true American religion. This assertion shows that Shrike has become dominated by the lust of the goat and the mechanicalness of the adding machine. To Shrike man is a thing of chemistry alone.

Except about the sexual reluctance of his wife, Shrike is as emotionless as a machine. His lack of emotion dominates the chapter entitled "Miss Lonelyhearts and the Dead Pan." The dead pan refers to Shrike's lack of facial expression, but the word *pan* also suggests the dead nature-god of flocks and pastures. In Shrike, *Pan* is dead, and Shrike is identified with the new mechanical world based on the emotionless physical sciences. These sciences, in their purest form, exist in the "triangles" of mathematics, and these triangles are symbolized in the novel by the triangular, hatchet-like face of Shrike. These triangles, representing the physical sciences with their tendency to destroy the world of spirit, perpetually bury themselves, as Shrike does, in the neck of mankind.

Shrike's lack of emotion determines his action throughout the book. He laughs at humanity by laughing at the pathos of Doyle. He invents a game which has laughter at the letters of the helpless as its purpose, and that game indicts him as the inhuman joke-machine he is. This lack of love and pity justifies the name Shrike, suggestive as it is of the bird that impales its prey upon a cross of thorns. Shrike has become the anti-Christ, crucifying those who strive for faith.

The final alternative to the inadequacy of modern dreams

is to attempt the Christ dream, which was once capable of alleviating man's suffering. Miss Lonelyhearts attempts this dream. Puritanical in appearance, he has a "bony chin . . . shaped and cleft like a hoof" (p. 18). The boniness connotes the man of spirit rather than flesh. The cleft chin indicates the split between the spirit and the flesh, between the devil and the saint. This opposition creates barriers to the Christ dream, and they crop up at every milestone of the spiritual journey.

One of the basic obstacles is materialism. Early in the novel Miss Lonelyhearts, like Shrike, accepts the idea of a materialistic and indifferent universe. He feels that if there were some spiritual manifestation, he could show his contempt by casting a stone. But in the indifferent sky there are "no angels, flaming-crosses, olive-bearing doves, wheels within wheels" (p. 25). Wanting to escape from a world dominated by decay and pain, a creation without spiritual manifestation, Miss Lonelyhearts, in true Shrike fashion, starts for a speakeasy.

Two other similarities between Shrike and Miss Lonelyhearts stem from materialism. Like Shrike, Miss Lonelyhearts attempts to become a worshiper of the flesh. Though without great enthusiasm, Miss Lonelyhearts pursues Betty and Mrs. Shrike. Later, he experiences a sexual act with Mrs. Doyle, who embodies primal, carnal, sealike sexuality, and when it is over, he knows that for him flesh-worship is no escape. A more important similarity between Shrike and Miss Lonelyhearts is that for a while Miss Lonelyhearts too attempts to become a joke-machine by laughing at his own sympathetic heart. For Miss Lonelyhearts the laugh is at first bitter and then dies in his throat. It is no wonder that West changed an early draft of the manuscript, in which he had Miss Lonelyhearts express the indictment of escapes found in "Miss Lonelyhearts in the Dismal Swamp," and placed the indictment where it really belonged: in the mouth of Shrike.

Materialism, with its corollaries of carnal love and cynicism, is no solution to Miss Lonelyhearts' need for an answer to the letters. Because of the failure of materialism, Betty, with her faith in personal love and a benevolent, therapeutic nature, finally succeeds in persuading Miss Lonelyhearts to go with her to the country. Momentarily he is able to accept Betty's limited world, but only momentarily. Violence quietly insists upon its existence, for in the country Miss Lonelyhearts sees in stark relief the ever-present animal struggle for survival. The ignorance and viciousness of man also persist; they are personified in the bigotry of a garage attendant who proclaims that it is not hunters but "yids" who have driven the deer from the countryside. Once back in the city, Miss Lonelyhearts realizes that "Betty had failed to cure him . . . he had been right when he said he could never forget the letters" (p. 145).

The ultimate barrier to the realization of the Christ dream is neither Shrike's materialism nor Betty's simplified world. That barrier is pride, and it resides in Miss Lonelyhearts as in all men. Its simplest manifestation is in man's revulsion from his fellow man, his unwillingness to lick lepers, as the saints of old had licked them, out of sheer humility and love. Though Miss Lonelyhearts "wants to lick lepers" (p. 62), he finds it difficult to attain sufficient humility. Rather than uniting himself to the unfortunate, he pities them. The first time he achieves identification is with the cripple, Doyle. The embodiment of broken humanity, Doyle has a primitive pathos that is totally repellent. When Miss Lonelyhearts, striving for complete humility, touches Doyle's hand, he instinctively "jerked away, but then drove his hand back and forced it to clasp the cripple's . . . he did not let go, but pressed it firmly with all the love he could manage" (p.

171). With this handclasp Miss Lonelyhearts symbolically licks his first leper.

This humility leads from the acceptance of Doyle, who represents suffering humanity, to the faith that some order, some pattern, does exist in the universe. There follows an interior calm so perfect that it seems either that of the dead man or of the religious fanatic who, in the perfectness of his faith, is in full accord with his universe. Miss Lonelyhearts' monastic retreat from the world further likens him to the ascetic religious. His asceticism, however, is clearly of the modern world: he not only drinks water and eats crackers but also smokes cigarettes. Still, his is a sainted calm, resting on the "rock" of Christ-like love and faith. Miss Lonelyhearts has achieved a life-in-death serenity, where "what goes on in the sea is of no interest to the rock" (p. 194).

Christ-like love and faith become the rock which leads to Miss Lonelyhearts' alienation from the sea of life. No longer is Miss Lonelyhearts bothered by intellectual problems such as the existence of pain and violence in a world created by a benevolent God, or the lack of order in a universe which, were it created by a purposeful God, should have order and harmony. The philosophic drama of the novel grows primarily from the first problem, but the lack of visible order has also affected Miss Lonelyhearts. He develops a need for order that he himself sees borders on insanity. He recognizes the sad truth that "Man has a tropism for order. . . . The physical world has a tropism for disorder" (p. 115). Man's intellect is constantly frustrated. Its human limitations make the mind unable to see the infinite order, yet its desires toward God demand that it seek a significant pattern. Philosophically Miss Lonelyhearts justifies his futile search: "All order is doomed, yet the battle is worth while" (p. 116).

Though the battle of the intellect is worthwhile in its direction toward the infinite, it is only by faith, by the abdication of the intellect, that the infinite order is perceived by man. Through humility Miss Lonelyhearts attains this simplified outlook. Now nothing remains of Miss Lonelyhearts save love and faith. Through humility he has united himself to suffering humanity, has accepted a universe whose order he cannot comprehend, and consents to marry Betty. The loss of all things save love and faith leaves "his mind free and clear. The things that had muddled it had precipitated out into the rock" (p. 204). After Betty tells him she is pregnant, he shows no emotional response and asks no questions about the future. In his faith, his loss of intellectual questioning, he can become the kind of person that Betty wishes him to be and can accept a future life circumscribed by her innocent but limited dreams: personal love, children, a farm in Connecticut.

Through his humility Miss Lonelyhearts has become dead to this world. Following Christ's injunction that whosoever would find his life must first lose it, Miss Lonelyhearts can now attain a mystical union with God. Transcending the fevered sickness of his body through a transforming grace of light and perfumed cleanliness, he becomes "conscious of two rhythms that were slowly becoming one. When they became one, his identification with God was complete. His heart was the one heart, the heart of God. And his brain was likewise God's" (pp. 210–11).

In this moment of hallucinatory ecstasy the cripple, Doyle, rings Miss Lonelyhearts' doorbell. Miss Lonelyhearts, wishing to succor with love all the desperate of the universe and expecting to perform a miracle by which the cripple will be cured, runs rapturously toward Doyle. But there is no miracle. Instead Miss Lonelyhearts is shot by Doyle, destroyed, like Christ, by the panic and ignorance of those whom he would save. Doyle, and in him suffering man, shatters the only solution to the intolerableness of man's pain, destroys the Christ-like man who perceives that love and faith are the only answers to man's pain in a universe he cannot understand.

True belief in the Christian answers, however, rests upon the dissolution of the self and the subsequent mystical experience of God's love and grace. Until such experiences (the price of which is alienation from this world), the very name of Christ, as Miss Lonelyhearts had felt before his "sickness," is a vanity on the lips of man. After God's love and grace, the personal ecstasy they bring is a "reality," but it is founded upon an insane delusion and even then the "reality" is incommunicable. Thus Miss Lonelyhearts runs toward Doyle with love in his heart, while the cripple, filled with hatred, makes his way up the stairs. In the ironic lack of communication, Doyle's gun, the symbol of a mechanical, loveless world, goes off, and the two men roll down the stairs together.

Although Doyle is the actual murderer of Miss Lonelyhearts, Betty is also indirectly responsible. She comes in while Miss Lonelyhearts and Doyle are grappling, and Doyle feels she is cutting off his escape. He tries to get rid of his gun, but in his panic at seeing Betty he causes the gun to explode. This involvement of Betty is meaningful, for Betty's fragmentary view of the universe would leave out pain and violence. With her belief that man's needs are always bodily ones and his ills are easily cured by aspirin, Betty would destroy the spiritual in man. Her approach to life would negate the need for Christ. It would kill the Christ dream, for without pain and violence there is no need for the relief of Christ-like love, no need for faith to reconcile unjustified suffering with the existence of a good God.

Betty's fragmentary view is false and cannot endure. Witnessing the murder of her unborn child's father, she will need an even greater blindness than she has shown before if she is to disregard the existence of violence. The pain of childbirth, which West emphasizes in the novel, will impress upon her the fact of suffering. Then she, like so many others, will have to reconcile pain and violence with a godly universe. Though there are answers that bring no peace, the love and faith of Christ could make for a better world, one founded on Dostoevsky's Christianity. Truly man needs Christ—witness the cry for "help" on which the novel begins—but Christ in our time has been dwarfed to a lovelorn columnist, his message has become a cliché, and his "agony" is a parody of the Christian myth. Even more ironically and horribly, the only "solution" for man's pain is Christian faith, yet that "solution" does not ease the pain of the letter writers, and it leads Miss Lonelyhearts to hallucinations, insanity, and death. That is the absurdity which illumines contemporary man's pilgrimate and quest.

In its fusion of form and content, *Miss Lonelyhearts* is the best novel West was ever to write. To the novel nothing should be added and nothing could be taken away. Its stark simplicity of language and sentence structure, a bareness achieved by continual pruning and sharpening through six revisions of the novel, creates a peculiarly nightmarish etching of shadows and decay unlike the art of any other American novelist. In addition the book has a warmth, a compassion, which exceeds that of West's other novels. The warmth is especially apparent in the increased depth with which West treats the dilemma of humankind in its need for a dream. Earlier, in *Balso Snell*, West had implied that the wisest thing man can do is to accept himself as an animal and to avoid dreams completely, for in dreams there is only misery. Such an attitude was naïve: an oversimplified solution of a very young man. In *Miss Lonelyhearts*, West probes deeper. The horror of a life lived without any dream is illustrated by the joke-machine called Shrike. Terrible as it is, even a bad dream is better than no dream at all, and this idea, from *Miss Lonelyhearts* on, is constant in West. Faye Greener, in West's last novel, *The Day of the Locust*, puts the insight most bluntly: "She said that any dream was better than no dream and beggars couldn't be choosers" (p. 60). Undoubtedly it would be better for mass man if he wanted a worthy dream instead of the nonsense offered to him by Hollywood or love story magazines, just as it would be better for him to like great art rather than the trash he prefers. His tragedy is that he doesn't make intelligent choices, and he doesn't because of what he is. The pathos of his need to dream, while forced by his nature to choose dreams that will not soothe his pain, is explored with both horror and compassion in *Miss Lonelyhearts*, and in *Miss Lonelyhearts*, unlike *The Day*, the pity is greater than the horror.

While *Miss Lonelyhearts* is wholly unique, one cannot leave it without being aware of how much West is indebted to other writers. Two of the more obvious are T. S. Eliot and William James. Like Eliot, West sees the world as a wasteland, though he is less optimistic than Eliot that a knight, a new Christ, may transform the land and its hollow men into human beings with purpose and direction. Like Eliot, West emphasizes the loss of love in this world, but West intensifies the pain of sex until it becomes a frightening, devouring nightmare—a vision that may be related less to Eliot than to the fact that West himself, while being treated for gonorrhea, sustained a slight injury to his prostate gland and thereafter suffered recurrent pain from the wound. Like Eliot's poem, West's novel takes the form of a Quest, and quite possibly West drew upon Eliot's chief source, Jessie L. Weston's *From Ritual to Romance*, for some of the details of Miss Lonelyhearts' trials; but unlike the "shantih, shantih, shantih" on which *The Waste Land* ends, West's novel ends in a total lack of communication between the "inspired" savior, Miss Lonelyhearts, and the earthbound man, Mr. Doyle. The final effect of the novel is less one of peace than of a confused universe in which the end of the Quest is meaningless, absurd death.

Just as obvious a source is James's *The Varieties of Religious Experience*. In that work James noted the classic states that precede religious conversion—from a feeling of deadness and disorder to despair and eventual submission to God —and that diagnosis accurately describes the psychological movement of Miss Lonelyhearts' mentality. For James the ultimate core of the problem of religion is the cry for "Help! Help!" that the victims of life call out, and that cry is the one that leads Miss Lonelyhearts to his agony. For James, men can be categorized into those who are healthy-minded (and see good as the essential quality of life) and those who are morbid-minded (and see evil as fundamental), and in the way in which she excludes evil, Betty is undoubtedly healthy-minded (and philosophically shallow), while Miss Lonelyhearts, who cannot limit his vision, is morbid-minded (and, for James as well as West, religiously profound).

More important than these influences are those of Dostoevsky, the French symbolists, and the French surrealists. None of these influences is surprising. West himself would have quickly admitted the influence of Dostoevsky, a fact brought out by John Sanford's comment that West had a constant "little brag that he could rewrite Dostoevsky with a pair of shears."[30] Josephine Herbst also remembers the numerous conversations she and West held upon Dostoevsky: how West commented on the power of *The Possessed*, with its grotesqueness and its violence, and how Stavrogin's rape of a young child tormented West.

In *Miss Lonelyhearts*, the Dostoevskyan influence is apparent in the character of Miss Lonelyhearts: he reads and ponders Dostoevsky; he wears the same hair shirt of guilt that tortures so many of Dostoevsky's heroes; he wears the hair shirt because he, like Dostoevsky's heroes, feels his inability to aid the helpless of the universe. Another Dostoevskyan concept is the dualism of good and evil which tugs at the heart of Miss Lonelyhearts and which fills him with the dream of attaining the love and humility of Christ and at the same time permits him sadistically to twist the arm of the clean old man.

Dostoevsky's influence on West is also shown in a letter West once wrote. In it he stated his conviction that the survival of humanity depended upon its acceptance of the Christian ideals of Dostoevsky.[31] This Christianity is probably best defined by Dostoevsky himself when he says: "If we do not follow Christ we shall err in everything. The way to the salvation of mankind leads through his teachings alone."[32] This is to say that whatever reservations he might have about whether God created man or man created God, Dostoevsky had no reservations about the perfect love and humility which Christ preached and lived. West understood Christ and his teachings in just the same way.

Whether West believed in the probability of man's free survival, however, is open to doubt. Always in West's writing, and above all in his last novel, there is the fear that there may be truth in Dostoevsky's "Legend of the Grand Inquisitor" in *The Brothers Karamazov*. In Dostoevsky's masterpiece, the Grand Inquisitor charges that God has given man not happiness but freedom. This freedom only the few can bear; for the many it leads only to untold suffering. The Grand Inquisitor, by enslaving man, has taken the burden of freedom from his shoulders; he has given man the semblance of earthly happiness even though at the cost of eternal joy.

In *Miss Lonelyhearts* and the novels which followed, this same freedom causes the suffering of West's characters. They strive for something to worship completely, yet never find anything which will wholly enslave them. There is no Grand Inquisitor in West's world to give the mass of men earthly happiness by giving them total enslavement. Most men are thoroughly contemptible creatures, doomed to misery, without a nature capable of choosing a dream worthy of dreaming. In their misery West's creatures turn to mere parodies of something to worship. In the world of the Grand Inquisitor, Christ at least exists as an attainable ideal for the few who can worship Christ by their own free choice. In West's world there is no such possibility. For the modern world, the big dream, the Christ dream, is just an ironic joke. Few men can even conceive of such a dream. He who dares to dream it dies clutching with Christ-like love the cripple, who is man, in his arms; but the darer dies in the most meaningless of ways, killed accidentally by a mechanical thing in the hands of the cripple he would save.

The French symbolist influence upon *Miss Lonelyhearts* manifests itself generally in the bareness and concentration of the action and the writing, as well as in the epigrammatic style and satiric manner. In addition certain of West's ideas are more common perhaps to French symbolism than to any other literature: for instance the flesh-spirit opposition, or the concept that the world is a hospital or a madhouse from which man cannot escape save by death. Villiers de l'Isle Adam, one of the symbolists whom West discussed with Saul Jarcho, uses both concepts in *Axël:* though Axël and Sara, at the end of the play, may have dominion over every earthly desire, they prefer to escape by suicide from this world of flesh and pettiness. Joris-Karl Huysmans, to whom West refers in *Balso*, dramatizes both ideas in *Là Bas*. Huysman's major character, the writer Durtal, wants to escape the humdrum, to get *out of the world*,[33] and Huysmans' villains, Marshall Gilles de Rais and Mme. Chantelouve, are satanists whose evil stems from the same out-of-the-world desire.[34] (The latter phrase is repeated often in the novel.) Durtal, however, learns, through a sexual rendezvous with Mme. Chantelouve, "that the flesh domineers the soul and refuses to admit any schism."[35] Therefore, the out-of-the-world dream is but a fantasy for either the religious or the satanist. At the end of the novel the hero of the people, the demagogue Boulanger, wins political victory. A little group listens to the fleshly beast, the people; they hurrah for their champion, and one of the group comments that such hurrahs would not greet those that might really help the agony of the people—a sage, an artist, or a saint. Listening, Durtal sees "whirlwinds of ordure . . . on the horizon!"

"No," said Carhaix [a simple, religious man], "don't say that. On earth all is dead and decomposed. But in heaven! Ah, I admit that the Paraclete is keeping us waiting. But the texts announcing his coming are inspired. The future is certain. There will be light. . . ."

Des Hermies [a doctor interested in satanism] rose and paced the room. "All that is very well," he groaned, "but this century laughs the glorified Christ to scorn. It contaminates the supernatural and vomits on the Beyond. Well, how can we hope that in the future the offspring of the fetid tradesmen of today will be decent? Brought up as they are, what will they do in Life?"

"They will do," replied Durtal, "as their fathers and mothers do now. They will stuff their guts and crowd out their souls through their alimentary canals."[36]

The symbolist whom West's writing most reflects is Charles Baudelaire. The influence of Baudelaire's prose poem "Anywhere Out of this World" is clearly seen in *Miss Lone-*

lyhearts.[37] West's reference to the poem in *Balso Snell* indicates that West knew the poem well. Its influence in *Miss Lonelyhearts* is especially apparent in the chapter "Miss Lonelyhearts in the Dismal Swamp." Baudelaire's poem compares life to a hospital in which all the patients long to change their beds. In the poem Baudelaire and his soul discuss the question of moving elsewhere. To his soul, Baudelaire suggests various possibilities of escape: Lisbon for its warmth, Holland for its tranquillity, Batavia for its tropical beauty, Tornéo, the Baltic, the Pole. To all of these escapes the soul is silent until at the end of the poem it explodes: "N'importe où! pourvu que ce soit hors de ce monde!" In almost exactly the same way Shrike offers escapes to Miss Lonelyhearts: the South Seas, Art, Hedonism, Suicide, Art, and Drugs. At the very last, Shrike mockingly offers the escape of Christ. It is after Shrike's mockery that Miss Lonelyhearts most desperately strives for the love and humility and faith of Christ. His growing involvement with the Christian dream leads to his alienation from the rest of the world, his mystical experience, and eventually his death. Ironically, the big dream will not work in this loveless world, and so can only lead *out of the world.*

Most important to the eventual impact of *Miss Lonelyhearts* are the images that West creates. These images owe a good deal stylistically to the surrealists—probably more than West himself realized. The nihilistic side of surrealism wished to destroy the world of rationalism, to replace it with the surrealistic world of individual perceptions. This world at its most truthful was the product of dreams and visions. The rational relationship of objects was replaced by the subconscious and truer vision, where Dali clocks hung without suspension in varicolored skies, where an umbrella and a sewing machine copulate on an operating table, where the symbol of the surrealistic is the *sur réalité* of the objects in a drugstore: douche bags piled against aspirin bottles and both outlined against a toothpaste ad. In this kind of surrealistic perception, suggestive of the cosmic chaos, the surrealists felt that there was a shocking humor, the humor of the Jacobean writer of conceits. It is this kind of humor, destroying the stereotyped perceptions, laughing at the normal human relationships, that the surrealists strove for in their work. This humor of conceits is shown in Picabia's painting of "A Young American Girl in a State of Nudity," in which the girl is portrayed as a clean, dry spark plug. It was even better illustrated by Dali, who painted a pair of scales to fulfill a teacher's assignment to paint a Gothic virgin. When the teacher expressed astonishment, Dali replied by saying that although others might have seen a virgin, he saw a pair of scales. This same desire for conceits led to the search for new images in literature, for the revolution of the word that Eugene Jolas preached so often in *Transition*. The revolution was to be accomplished by new arrangements of words, and the search for the new sometimes led to strange literary amusements: for instance, some writers plucked by chance, out of a paper bag or a newspaper, two or more words and then yoked them together to create a shocking effect. The chance combinations eventually bore fruit in such weirdly titled, surrealistic poetic texts as "L'Homme Approximatif," "Mouchoir de Nuages," and "Les Vases Communicants," such a startlingly titled painting as Dali's "Debris of an Automobile Giving Birth to a Blind Horse Eating a Telephone."

This metaphysical humor of conceits is at the root of West's macabre wit in *Miss Lonelyhearts*. Even the basic concept suggests the metaphysical in its yoking of Christ to an advice-to-the-lovelorn columnist. The progress of Miss Lonelyhearts toward his "sickness" leads to distorted, unique perceptions: a man's tongue is seen as a fat thumb, and a man's cheeks as rolls of toilet paper; a woman's buttocks are seen as enormous grindstones and a woman's nipples as little red hats; a woman is seen as a tent, veined and covered with hair, and a man as a skeleton in a closet; the stone shaft of a war memorial becomes a penis, sexually dilated and ready to spout seeds of violence.

As a writer, West took great pride in his image-making ability. His pictorial eye was active as far back as college, where he spent a good deal of time drawing. His interest in painting lasted throughout his life, and shortly after college he began his collection of Max Ernst's surrealistic prints. That West was proud of the images he created is evident in his statement that *Miss Lonelyhearts* is indebted for its psychology to William James's *Varieties of Religious Experience*, but "The immagery[*sic*] is mine."[38] This pride in his imagery is again evident in his statement that he had originally intended to subtitle *Miss Lonelyhearts*

> "A novel in the form of a comic strip." The chapters to be squares on which many things happen through one action. . . . I abandoned this idea, but retained some of the comic strip technique: Each chapter instead of going forward in time, also goes backward, forward, up and down in space like a picture.[39]

In these imagistic terms the characters subordinate to Miss Lonelyhearts become merely simplified states of mind. Juxtaposed pictorially against the growing alienation of Miss Lonelyhearts from the world of reality, the minor characters serve primarily as contrast and chiaroscuro. This static, pictorial quality is also true of the actions, which seem like candid snapshots of people caught in mid-air against a background of dull sky and decaying earth. Each action becomes a symbol of an abstract state of mind and heart, and leaves one remembering a series of almost independent pictures rather than with a memory of the developing actions: Miss Lonelyhearts bringing the knife down upon the lamb; Miss

Lonelyhearts twisting the arm of the clean old man; Miss Lonelyhearts entwined about Doyle while Betty watches the two roll down the stairs. The pictures are, in reality, sensory portrayals of the inner heart and mind of Miss Lonelyhearts. They portray in archetypal imagery Miss Lonelyhearts' guilty mind (the murder of the lamb); his self-torturing, flagellating heart (the beating of the clean old man); his deluded, mystical vision (the entwined pair). In West's hands the case histories of James and Starbuck and Freud become merely the necessary folklore tradition, the Bullfinch, that instigates him not to psychologize but to pictorialize. This pictorialization, West felt, was the writer's fulfillment:

> Psychology has nothing to do with reality nor should it be used as motivation. The novelist is no longer a psychologist. Psychology can become much more important. The great body of case histories can be used in the way the ancient writers use their myths. Freud is your Bullfinch; you can not learn from him.[40]

This use of Freud as the inspirer of images revealing states of heart and mind is continually apparent in the novel. A simple illustration is the deliberately sinning mind of Miss Lonelyhearts which envisions sex as a way of escape from the letters and then involuntarily pictorializes the sex act in the tent-and-skeleton image of Mrs. Doyle. In a more extended way, this imagistic style is shown in the description of Miss Lonelyhearts' feeling that in sex is the core of pain: a mental state objectified in Miss Lonelyhearts' image of himself

> in the window of a pawnshop full of fur coats, diamond rings, watches, shotguns, fishing tackle, mandolins. All these things were the paraphernalia of suffering. A tortured high light twisted on the blade of a gift knife, a battered horn grunted with pain. (p. 115)

Later on this imagistic, surrealistic style is evident in the externalization of Miss Lonelyheart's feeling of himself as a rock unaffected by the sea of life. Miss Lonelyhearts visualized that

> a train rolled into a station where he was a reclining statue holding a stopped clock, a coach rumbled into the yard of an inn where he was sitting over a guitar, cap in hand, shedding the rain with his hump. (p. 188)

Or again this use of Freud as Bullfinch is suggested in Miss Lonelyhearts' inner sensation of himself as a dead man, in a world of dead things, being reborn through grace. The feeling is pictorialized in the vision of

> the Christ that hung on the wall opposite his bed. As he stared at it, it became a bright fly, spinning with quick grace on a background of blood velvet sprinkled with tiny nerve stars.
>   Everything else in the room was dead—chairs, tables, pencils, clothes, books. He thought of this black world of things as a fish. And he was right, for it suddenly rose to the bright bait on the wall. It rose with a splash of music and he saw its shining silver belly. (pp. 209–10)

These images make the abstract concrete. They pictorialize the inner feelings. They partially explain the peculiar power of West's writing, with its nightmarish involvement in a world of hallucinations and shadows. In this approach to writing, West owes a good deal to surrealism. In the success with which he makes his distorted world of half-light come alive, perhaps more alive than the world of everyday toast and tea, he is indebted only to the intensity and power of his own imagination.

The critical reception given *Miss Lonelyhearts* heartened West (any comment would have been encouraging after the almost total chill with which *Balso* had been received) even while he was worrying himself almost sick over the publishing problems of the novel. Though he couldn't buy fine shoes or suits with critical notices, the encouragement helped him believe in himself, helped a state of mind which must have been similar to that once described by a friend of West:

> To be a young man with literary aspirations is not to be particularly happy. . . . One moment the young writer is energetic and hopeful. The next he is catapulted into a fit of despair, his faith in himself infirm, his self-confidence shattered and broken, his view of the future one in which he sees futile self-sacrifices, ending only in failure.[41]

Such a despairing mood was undoubtedly altered somewhat by the reception given *Miss Lonelyhearts*. True, there were some bad reviews. The *Boston Transcript* sneeringly noted that the book was smartly phrased, with not much more to commend it, and then added that the novel was essentially phony, the kind that might, perhaps, last as dinner table conversation for three months or so.[42] *The Nation*, though conceding that the book was unique, sardonically commented that the universe presented was "all very sad, bitter, and hopeless." The reviewer then went on to condemn the book because it confounded the actual and the fanciful too often; in so doing he showed a total inability to comprehend what West had done artistically.[43] *Harrison's Reports*, a reviewing service directed at movie interests, noted:

> Never have I read anything to compare in vileness and vulgarity with . . . *Miss Lonelyhearts*. It is so obscene that I am surprised that its publication should have been permitted, particularly because of its implications of degeneracy. It cannot be defended on the grounds of art; it has none: it is just low and vulgar, put out undoubtedly to appeal to moronic natures.[44]

Such totally derogatory reviews disheartened and wounded West to so great an extent that in the case of the *Reports* he seriously considered the feasibility of a lawsuit. For the most part, though, the reviews gave West confidence. The *Saturday Review* said that West's novel was "a solid work as well as a brilliant one," and then compared West's satire favorably to the tragedy that Dreiser might have made of the same material.[45] The *New York Times* felt the bitterness of West's despair was equal to that of Swift and saw "a philosophical undercurrent . . . similar to that in Dostoevsky." The reviewer concluded with the opinion that "*Miss Lonelyhearts* stands to be one of the hits of the year, to win both popular and critical acclaim."[46] Even more heartening than any of these single reviews, however, was the news that *Contempo,* one of the more prominent little magazines of the period, was to devote most of its July 25th issue to a number of reviews of *Miss Lonelyhearts.* There, Angel Flores, wonderfully perceptive, noted the progenitors of West as Dostoevsky and Cocteau. To Dostoevsky, West was indebted for the bloody hairshirts and mystical quavers of his characters; to Cocteau, West was indebted for "that peculiar nightmarish quality, that pervasive uncanniness which hovers over the canvasses of Giorgio de Chirico and Salvador Dali." Flores concluded:

> Nathanael West's most remarkable performance has
> been to bring Fyodor's dark angels into the Haunted
> Castle. He did not recur to the drab realism which is
> so responsible for the stagnation in the works of the
> younger American writers—a realism which generally
> produces accurate reporting, easy-to-handle bulletins
> and time-tables, and ALSO bad literature. Mr.
> West has given us anguish and terror and fantasy
> (Dostoevsky-Ribemont-Dessaignes?) at the very
> crucial moment when the current vanguard taste insists

on directing literature towards the casehistory, gravy-mashpotato tradition.[47]

Bob Brown wrote a rather foolish review of the novel as pro-letarian literature, which it certainly was not, but Josephine Herbst made up for this with one of the most perceptive re-views West received in his lifetime:

> Miss Lonelyhearts reads like a detective story. Its realism is not concerned with actuality but with the comprehension of a reality beyond reality. The furniture of the speakeasy, the upside-down quality of New York night and day life provide a background that only a fine movie camera could actually inter-pret. . . .
>
> Miss Lonelyhearts floundering among the problems of humanity, stuck in the Slough of Despond of bankrupt emotionalism to the accompaniment of high-powered motors, jazz music, weeping drunks and men out-of-work reflects much more than his own minute destiny. The entire jumble of modern society, bankrupt not only in cash but more tragically in emotion, is depicted here like a life-sized engraving narrowed down to the head of a pin. Miss Lonely-hearts stricken with the suffering of the underdog, seeks an answer. . . . The pathological intensity of this seeking leads him to the desire to embrace hu-manity and that embrace pitches him to death. The ecstatic moment, realistically furnished, in which this occurs approaches the miracle of the old Mystery Plays.
>
> It is significant that although all the scenes are not night scenes, in retrospect they appear to take place in semi-darkness, in that sort of twilight that occurs in dreams. The characters too are those of the dream, faces out of line, some distortion. Miss Lonelyhearts himself, in his dilemma, seeking a way out, is without distinct features. As he goes down, he seems to be

someone wearing the huge nose of a clown who has
been tightrope walking and has suddenly been discovered to have broken legs. He falls into the pit and
even as he sinks the clown nose tortures us with a
desire to laugh, the same kind of laughter that hysterically crops up in a tragic moment. If the characters
are not sharpened in an individualistic way, it is
because they much more nearly serve their purpose in
this book as types. . . . Doomed by the society that
roars around them to live ignominiously and alone in
rabbit hutches, poking their heads out to wail to
their father confessor, who, like them, is lost, they
are not puppets so much as they are representatives of
a great Distress.[48]

Finally, William Carlos Williams answered a critic's charge
that *Miss Lonelyhearts* was sordid by commenting that the
critic had mistaken the writer's use of his materials for the
writer's intent; if Miss Lonelyhearts was sordid, so also were
Macbeth and *Crime and Punishment.*[49]

All of these comments gave West confidence. By December of 1932 he felt enough faith in himself and his writing to
buy, in cooperation with the Perelmans, a comfortable farm-
house in the vicinity of Erwinna, Pennsylvania. Soon he was
writing to Josephine Herbst of his future plans. In his next
book, he commented, he planned to satirize the American,
Horatio Alger dream.[50]

4 *The American Dream*

Shortly after the republication of *Miss Lonelyhearts* by Harcourt, Brace, Max Lieber, West's agent, sold the novel. The purchaser was Darryl F. Zanuck, who had recently founded Twentieth Century-Fox, and the price was, for West, as astronomical $4,000 (or over $3,000 more than he had previously earned from his writing). Such money was highly tempting, and when Columbia Pictures offered West the opportunity to write an original film script he seized the chance. Early in July of 1933 he joined the Perelmans in their rambling, adobe-style home, and on July 7 he began work, as a junior writer, on a week-to-week contract with a salary of around three hundred and fifty dollars a week (a pleasant rate compared to his hotel salary of fifty dollars a week). His hours, or so he claimed to his Eastern friends, were from ten to six; he was expected to work a full day on Saturday; he, like the other junior writers, worked in a "cell" in a row of cells; his typewriter was expected to be continuously clacking; he was expected to judge the artistic merit of screen writers by the size of their salaries; and all in all he saw little difference between the commercialism of movies and that of hotels.

On this Hollywood sojourn, West worked on two studio projects. One was a "treatment" and then a first-draft script of a story idea for a movie to be called *Beauty Parlor*. About a beautiful manicurist in a swanky beauty parlor, the script is full of the adolescent dreams of the thirties (manicurists dating rich men who pose as chauffeurs) and contrasts the luxuries of sin to the simplicities of virtue. In doing so, the script implies that virtue is a better way of life than sin, but on the way to this message, to contribute to the dreams of the audience, the script dramatizes a considerable amount of gaiety, temptation, and extravagance. Even more strongly directed toward the archetypal, mass dreams of man was West's script *Return to the Soil* (the title recalls Shrike's indictment of Betty's favorite dream of escape in "Miss Lonelyhearts in the Dismal Swamp"). In large part, through the dramatization of the trials of "Father" Anderson and his son, West writes a paean to the soil, which ennobles men, and an indictment of cities and machines, which enslave and corrupt men. When Father Anderson's son fails in the city, he returns to the soil to cry, as his father had earlier done, that all things, all life, come from the soil, and human rejuvenation and redemption can only be accomplished by a return to its truth.

In late August West finished the third draft of *Return to the Soil,* but Columbia decided not to renew his contract. For a while West remained in Hollywood, and watched with some bitterness as his novel, in the movie version, was slowly twisted and tormented out of shape. The Hollywood version of the novel, a comedy melodrama which was credited to Leonard Praskins, bore no relationship to West's narrative, and the movie came to the screen as a murder thriller titled *Advice to the Lovelorn* and starring Lee Tracy. Soon after the movie appeared, West was released by Twentieth Century, and in July, 1933, he returned East. Confiding his impression of Hollywood to Saul Jarcho, West noted especially

> the contrast between the ignorant and wealthy
> Philistine and the impecunious scholar and writer.
> This subject recurred after his first visit to Hollywood,
> which disgusted him. He said that a trip to Hollywood
> was like a ride in the glassbottomed boat in the waters
> near Bermuda, where you could see garish improbable
> fauna swimming about.[1]

This attitude West expressed in a story called "Business Deal," which he published in *Americana* in the latter part of 1933. The story opens with the West Coast head of Gargantua Pictures, Eugene Klingspiel, working ceaselessly.

> First he read *The Hollywood Reporter, Variety,* and
> *The Film Daily.* Then he measured out two spoonfuls
> of bicarbonate and lay down on the couch to make
> decisions. Before long Mr. Klingspiel had fallen into
> what he called a gentle reverie. He saw Gargantua
> Pictures swallowing its competitors like a boa
> constrictor, engulfing whole amusement chains.[2]

Onto this pleasant scene comes Charlie Baer, a writer for Gargantua. Soon Klingspiel and Baer are wrangling over

Baer's new writing contract. Klingspiel, in an attempt to induce Baer to work for less than five hundred dollars a month, emotionally recalls the story of Adolf Rubens, a "poor little furrier" with a dream:

> "Everybody laughs at him and calls it Rubens' Folly, but he doesn't care. Why? Because in his brain he sees a picture of a mighty amusement ennaprise bringing entertainment and education to millions. . . . This ain't a business, Charlie; it's a monument created by the public to Adolph Rubens' ideals, and we're building all the time."
> "Five hundred dollars or I stop building," said Charlie in the same metallic tone.[3]

Eventually Baer gets his five hundred dollars, and the story of Hollywood's falsity and tasteless greed ends. Unimportant in itself, the story has interest in its foreshadowing of West's last novel, *The Day of the Locust,* for the concentration on Hollywood phoniness and tastelessness and the dominant animal imagery of "Business Deal" will appear again in *The Day.* In "Business Deal" the conflict between Bear and Klingspiel is described as one between a mongoose and a cobra, and occasionally Baer speaks "bovinely" and Klingspiel quivers "like a stag." The whole story reveals West's contempt for what he calls the "pants pressers" among Hollywood's Jewish overlords, and the tone illuminates the disgusted fascination with which West always observed Hollywood's "improbable fauna."

West's brief Hollywood experience impressed him once again with the knowledge of the lie inherent both in Hollywood and in life itself. This notion West used in the still-unpublished short stories, "Mr. Potts of Pottstown" and "The Sun, the Lady, and the Gas Station." These stories end with the revelation that the universe is rotten, but man, in his foolishness, attempts to disguise the decay, to cover up the fake, the falsity, that is life. In "Mr. Potts of Pottstown," Mr. Potts is the leader of a hunting club in a part of Tennessee which has no game and where hunting is but a masquerade and not a serious concern. The club is disrupted by the interference of a number of practical wives of the members. When a new mountaineering club is formed, Mr. Potts is not asked to join. Hurt, he goes to Switzerland to climb some real mountains, and there he meets a boy from home who states a Westian fact: everything is a fake everywhere. In Europe, then, Mr. Potts learns that his hunting club was no more foolish in its masquerading than is the general falsity of life everywhere. A better story is "The Sun, The Lady, and the Gas Station," which opens with the description of how all things look rotten under the pitiless truth of the sun's glare. Ironically, this decay is even noticeable at the 1933 Century of Progress, where the narrator stops for a few days on his way to the ultimate in rottenness and fraud: Hollywood. Finally, the decadence and deceit of modern existence is symbolized in a story which the narrator hears after he arrives in Hollywood. It tells of an old actress who wishes an affair with a gas station attendant. To attract the young man, the old woman gets her face lifted with paraffin. She then attempts to lure her prey, but the merciless sun betrays her. In the heat the paraffin melts, and the age and decay (the realities of existence) become plain. The attendant roars with laughter. With him West seems to be laughing at the gigantic deception that Hollywood and most of mankind like to live by. Perhaps most of all, however, West is laughing at a Western culture, or a capitalistic system, which in the depression year of 1933 was in its decadence, or seemed to be, but despite this still liked to paint, to pretend to be a thing of beauty.

After his Hollywood release, West returned to Bucks County. In the high, stiff, white house in Erwinna, set in a small hollow a hundred yards or so off the dirt side road that ran upward past it, West began to live and to write. The living was attended with numerous chores. With the help of S. J. Perelman, West attempted to install power and plumbing, and it was not long before West was referring to the house as "eight ball."[4]

Having a place in the country allowed West to keep a dog. He had always been a dog lover, though he had never had a prize hunter. Now, in his new "eight-ball" house he had plenty of room, and he succeeded in acquiring a special raccoon-hunting dog which he imported from the South. At the same time he bought an ornate hunting outfit which made him look like Sherlock Holmes. The fine hunting dog, however, turned out to be a fraud. It shivered miserably (and a little comically) through one abortive hunt, and then West gave it away in disgust. This love for, and poor luck with, dogs seemed constant in West. Malcolm Cowley remembers that West

always pictured himself in roles, and Nimrod was one of them. He had a big pointer named Danny to whom he ascribed extraordinary virtues, although I'm sorry to say that Danny was a biscuit eater. Or rather a raw liver eater—he got pounds of liver per day, and often when taken out into the field he'd show no interest in birds. Men die by what they live—Pep was killed on his return from a shooting trip. Danny was given to the Coateses, who couldn't work up the same affection for him that Pep had shown—nobody could have shown that affection, nobody but a mythomaniac loving one of the other characters in the drama he lived from day to day.[5]

A little later West bought a new car which he habitually drove at high speeds over back country roads, where its springs shrieked in protest. A close friend recalls that

> Pep's poor driving was Pep . . . it was something he could no more have unlearned than he could have unlearned his way of walking, which was a sort of shamble, awkward and out of sync, or his way of putting on a coat, which made you think he was always trying to climb down the arm hole. . . . He was always tripping, always fumbling, always ill-related to still objects. . . .[6]

In many ways West, in the country atmosphere of Bucks County, took on the appearance of a country squire. Gun in hand, he sauntered around his property. Here and there he planted trees. He watched workmen as they built a dam which he envisaged as the first step to an idyllic retreat flocked with wild birds—a dream never to become reality.

The country squire was not the only side of West that showed in Bucks County, or if it was, it was a decidedly democratic aristocrat. He loved wandering the countryside and hunting and talking with the local farmers. Miss Herbst remembers that he was fond of lecturing on the primitive equalities that ruled, unsophisticatedly, under the open sky, where the ability to notice the animal smells and the riffle of the grass were the simple tests of adequacy, where man's sophistication had not led to his misery.

Soon West's mother joined him in his new home. The lavish meals she prepared for him forced West to take longer and longer walks to avoid getting fat. Perhaps the walks were also an attempt to avoid the pragmatism of his mother's mind and the constant suggestions that he return to the hotel, to security and a steady future, to the assurance of three meals a day and a place to sleep at night. Already he had spent too much time at this writing foolishness. The last two books hadn't sold at all; what made him think a new one would be different? Yes, she knew what some of those critics had said about *Miss Lonelyhearts*. But you couldn't eat those fine words, could you?

Truly, West's mother had little interest in his writing. His father had been more sympathetic, for there was true attachment, emotional rather than intellectual, between father and son. John Sanford recalls this bond vividly.

> Except in one case, it was impossible for Pep to parade affection. The exception was his father—Max, he always called him. A shy man, Max was, and a very simple and homely man, but gentle to the limit of the word's meaning, and quiet, and warm. . . . Pep was plain wild about him.[7]

But West's mother, pale, with a large, round face and a thick body, had little regard by now for West's nonsensical writing dreams. West almost feared his mother, a woman who, apparently, wallowed in suffering and who gained much pleasure from nagging. Her needs were constantly in the back of West's mind. If he stopped in for an evening visit with the Herrmanns, who lived hardly a hundred yards away, he always remembered to call "Mamma" if he stayed a little late. If he dropped in for an afternoon, he always remembered when dinner time came, and no matter how stimulating the occasion, he left for dinner at home "because Mamma has fussed over it so." Once, because of a tardy train, the Herrmanns were late for a dinner date with West and his mother. The sorrowful complaints of Mrs. Weinstein were vivid and lengthy.

Once West asked Miss Herbst to explain to his mother something of art and the needs of the artist. Mrs. Weinstein sat placidly in her chair, calmly rocking, her hands folded quietly in her lap. In all the literary clichés, Miss Herbst talked of the artist's duty to himself and society, of how such a talent as that of West should not be allowed to die, of West's misery in the commercial world of the hotel, and of how a hotel job such as West had held would rot away the inner artist. Mrs. Weistein's chair never missed a beat in its steady rocking, and at the end of the trite but high-minded plea she only asked calmly and placidly, "How's he going to eat?" Another close friend of the time comments that West was

> a deeply disturbed person, aware of the repressed violence in himself and others, fascinated by the macabre and offbeat. He was monopolized by a possessive mother and quite unable, at the time, to free himself from this thralldom. Certainly he was a lonely man and quite often full of despair. What saved him was that he was immensely alive, full of curiosity about everything. His strong sense of the droll and the ironical colored all his thinking.[8]

In Erwinna, West ate the heavy, spicy food that his mother loved to prepare, took long walks, polished his hunting gun incessantly, talked to the country folk, and dreamed of the completion of his idyllic bird retreat. At the same time that West was acting his role as country squire, he was also, somewhat contradictorily, deeply aware of the world of economic reality.

By 1932 the American depression had tightened its hold on the country. Immediately following the debacle of 1929, a common chant had been that "everything would be all right in the long run," but that optimistic invocation was soon replaced by the knowledge that people don't eat only in the long run. By 1932 millions of Americans were still wondering where their next meal was coming from. Out of their plight came long lines waiting to be served from public soup kitchens, and out of it, too, came the long trek of in-numerable dispossessed farmers, contemptuously called Okies, to the promised land of California. By 1933, there were twelve million workers, better than one out of five, according to William Green's estimate, out of jobs. Between 1929 and 1933 farmers saw their annual gross income shrink 57 per cent. All of this was reflected in a national income which fell, between 1929 and 1933, from its majestic height of eighty-five billion dollars to a shrunken forty billion.[9] In New York City, where Central Park's "Hoover Valley" be-came a symbol of a system's failure, twenty-nine people died of starvation in 1933, and the admissions for malnutrition to the New York Health Center rose from 18 per cent of total admissions in 1928 to 60 percent in 1931.[10] To his disciples, Father Divine's assertion that "the real God is the God that feeds us"[11] seemed only common sense. It is understatement to say that there was growing dissatisfaction with an eco-nomic system that seemed to be unable to avert periodic depressions and unable to do anything about them when they arrived.

This discontent was not only apparent in such scenes as that of the "bonus army" routed on Hoover's lawn, but it was also reflected in the minds of douce citizens living com-fortable lives in American suburbia. The concern of these people was evinced by Daniel Willard, the president of the Baltimore and Ohio railroad. Envisioning himself as a work-ing man with no job and no prospect of one, seeing his family starving, Willard announced in a proclamation that must have shocked the staid guardians of respectability: "While I do not like to say so, I would be less than candid if I did not say that in such circumstances I would steal before I would starve."[12] The academician Nicholas Murray Butler rejected the conventional depression solution of waiting for prosperity to appear just around the corner:

If we wait too long somebody will come forward with
a solution that we may not like. Let me call your
attention to the fact that the characteristic feature
of the experiment in Russia . . . is not that it is
communist, but that it is being carried on with a plan
in the face of a planless opposition.[13]

A special commission of the Federal Council of the Churches
of Christ drew a pitiable picture of men in want, and finally
declared the moral obligation of the churches

to demand fundamental changes in present economic
conditions; to protest against the selfish desire for
wealth as the principal motive of industry; to insist
upon the creation of an industrial society which shall
have as its purpose economic security and freedom for
the masses of mankind.[14]

The noted theologian Reinhold Niebuhr predicted that

It is not at all out of the realm of probabilities that
the middle-class paradise which we built on this
continent, and which reached its zenith no later than
1929, will be in decay before the half-century mark is
rounded.[15]

In an America of want and discontent, prophets and false
prophets arose. Howard Scott's pseudoscientific Technoc-
racy briefly lured American dreamers in the winter of 1932–
33. With his slogan "Every Man a King" and his tactics of
threat and denunciation, Huey Long strode to the virtual
dictatorship of Louisiana. Though Long's most bitter oppo-
nents could hardly maintain that his desire to "Share our
Wealth" did not bring considerable benefit to the Louisiana
poor, not even Long's best friends could deny that in violence of language and promise of impossible gifts Long bore
two basic marks of the demagogue. By the same tests Father
Coughlin (and his Christian Front) and Dr. Francis Town-

send (with his plea for an Old Age Revolving Pension) played upon the prejudices of the foolish and the dreams of the old. Even worse demagogues scurried hither and yon across the continent: George Deatherage, with his Knights of the White Camellia; Fritz Kuhn, "Der Fuehrer," with his German-American Bund; William Dudley Pelley, with his Silver Shirts and his call for white supremacy; and Gerald L. K. Smith, with his frank and fervid anti-Semitism and his admiration of German "efficiency." A *Fortune* poll in April, 1939, acknowledged the growth of anti-Semitism during the thirties in the big cities of America. In addition the poll found that many American citizens had unconscious anti-Semitic attitudes which often parroted Nazi talk at its worst, and often flippantly and irresponsibly classified Jewish citizens as Communists or "international bankers." The wave of the future couldn't rise here—of that most Americans were sure—but to some American prophets, hatred and bigotry seemed to be lapping at the shore.

Abroad, Il Duce noted "we have buried the putrid corpse of liberty,"[16] and to prove it Italian soldiers marched against helpless Ethiopia. In 1931 Japanese troops marched into Manchuria, and in 1937 Japan began its full-scale offensive against China. The agony of civil war began in Spain in 1936, and the Loyalist cause won such writers as Hemingway and Dos Passos, as well as a number of young American idealists and radicals. In Germany, Hitler proclaimed the doctrine of Aryan supremacy, began the systematic humiliation and decimation of German Jews, and roared, "Only force rules . . . force is the first law."[17]

At home, in 1933, Americans sang the theme song of *Three Little Pigs:* "Who's Afraid of the Big Bad Wolf?" Shirley Temple, by 1934, had replaced Mae West and Jean Harlow as Hollywood's top personality and box-office attraction, and saccharin rather than sex seemed to many Hol-

lywood producers to be the way to wealth. By 1931 Charlie
Chaplin, in *City Lights*, had treated briefly the serio-comic
elements of the stock-market crash, as well as the tragedy of
unemployment; but in 1934 most of the overlords of Hollywood were still hoping that if the depression were just ignored, it would go away.

It did not go away. In an America filled with want and
despair, West would have been less than human if he had
not reacted with sympathy for the oppressed, but *Miss
Lonelyhearts* had shown the exact opposite of this. Miss
Lonelyhearts' desire to identify himself with suffering humanity (as well as Miss Lonelyhearts' repulsion from the sufferers and the guilt that followed) was quite possibly also an
emotion of the creator of *Miss Lonelyhearts*. At any rate
West reacted to the depression with pity for the sufferers,
as well as concern that he himself should not be caught in
the same desperate situation. Compassion caused him to
clutch at possible economic solutions. Like many thinking
people of the time, he debated with himself and others the
possibilities of communism as a solution to economic problems. He wrote a "Christmass [*sic*] Poem" celebrating the
death of Christianity and the birth of Marxism:

> The spread hand is a star with points
> The fist a torch
> Workers of the World
> Ignite
> Burn Jerusalem
> Make of the City of Birth a star
> Shaped like a daisy in color a rose
> And bring
> Not three but one king
> The Hammer King to the Babe King
> Where nailed to his six-branched tree

Upon the sideboard of a Jew
Marx
Performs the miracle of loaves and fishes

The spread hand is a star with points
The fist a torch
Workers of the World
Unite
Burn Jerusalem[18]

Often during this period West and James T. Farrell breakfasted together and talked about the Communist movement. The two disliked the Communist credo that art was to be harnessed and used for the good of the state rather than as the individual expression of the author. The restrictiveness of such a concept, like other rigidities in the Communist literary line, was hard for the serious and honest artist to accept. Even harder to accept were certain Stalinist methods. West and Farrell agreed that Stalin's use of bad means for good ends was hard to justify; it was doubtful if a better world could ever be created by such methods.

Nevertheless, around 1935, West's sympathy with the workers involved him in a strike. West and a number of other prominent people picketed Ohrbach's in an attempt to gain publicity for the strike. Eventually many of the group, including West, were arrested for obstructing traffic. In the cell, West was "quiet and sullen while the rest of us were enjoying ourselves." After being released from jail, West "kept coming back to how much he had hated being locked up even for those few hours." Later he and his friendly jail companion "got to embroidering on our memories of our life in prison and it got sillier and sillier and we worked up a kind of comic routine . . ."[19] Another friend adds that West was really pressured into this strike; he didn't want to get involved because he had to start work soon in California.

When West was arrested, he didn't wait for trial, but instead "went to California . . . and . . . received a suspended sentence *in absentia* for disturbing the peace."[20]

Probably West was sympathetic to communism and saw hope in the Russian system of a planned economy. However, West's tendency to pity the human affliction while at the same time standing a trifle above it must have militated against his joining the Communist party and accepting its discipline. West's aloofness is borne out not only by the comic routine that he evolved from his prison "martyrdom," but also by Farrell's comment that "We used to talk at breakfast and in the Brevoort, a little bit sardonically of the foibles of our friends and the CP line. . . ."[21] Certainly West was always, above all, the artist. Never did he propagandize for propaganda alone. Once he tried. In *Miss Lonelyhearts* he attempted a chapter called "Miss Lonelyhearts and the Communists." Because the chapter was artificial, he was unable to finish it.[22]

Even more, this tendency to stand aloof is suggested by West's association with the magazine *Americana*, of which he became an associate editor in August, 1933. The detachment of *Americana* had been suggested in a front-page editorial of the opening issue in November, 1932. That editorial first noted that the editors were neither Republicans nor Democrats nor Socialists, and then went on to add:

> We are not COMMUNISTS because the American Communist party delegates its emissaries to bite the rear ends of policemen's horses and finds its chief glory in spitting at the doormen of foreign legations. We are also unconditionally opposed to Comrade Stalin and his feudal bureaucracy at Moscow.[23]

What, then, was the position of *Americana?* The editorial concluded on a Dadaistic note of disgust:

We are Americans who believe that our civilization
exudes a miasmic stench and that we had better prepare
to give it a decent but rapid burial. We are the laughing
morticians of the present.[24]

The editors' disgust was apparent in the cartoon by
George Grosz in the opening issue. Titled *Genesis*, the picture showed, in the foreground, two foul, hard-faced creatures, a man and a woman, neither of whom in their insensi-
tivity could have a thought for anything but self. In the
background a young girl with prominent hips and buttocks
is walking a dog. The ironic caption for the cartoon was
taken from Genesis: " 'So God created man in his own image . . . and God said . . . have dominion . . . over
every living thing that moveth upon the earth.' AND THE
REST IS HISTORY." In the same issue, the cynicism is
emphasized by the article "Viva Capone." It laments the un-
warranted persecution of American gangsters and concludes
with the opinion that Capone "can be bought, but at least
he would stay bought—as good a definition of an honest
man as we have ever encountered." After *The Nation* called
this first issue of *Americana* "unpleasantly sadistic," Gilbert
Seldes, one of *Americana*'s editors, answered:

> I will suggest to the editors of *Americana* that they
> reform. No more sadism. Only pretty pictures of sweet
> communists welcoming Trotsky back from exile;
> sweet capitalists washing the feet of the ten million
> unemployed; and sweet editors of liberal magazines
> smiling broadly at love triumphant.[25]

These attitudes had not changed at all by the time West
became an editor of *Americana*. The August, 1933, issue ran
a Grosz cartoon in the series called *Proven Proverbs*. The
cartoon simply pictured an old tramp rummaging in a gar-
bage pail. Underneath was the caption: "Mother was right,

the first million is always the hardest." If there was any change in editorial policy, it was in the tendency to run more and more photographs. Sometimes these photographs consisted of different pictures joined together incongruously, often almost libelously, into a composite picture; the favorite subjects for insult in these creations were Hoover, Hitler, and Roosevelt. Occasionally numerous photographs were shown in a collage on a single magazine page, and the ironic juxtapositions often created a surrealistic effect. The collage "Chicago Welcomes You" was run in the August, 1933, issue, and it depicted such scenes as two white-masked hold-up men robbing an office worker; a bum sitting on white steps; a dead dog lying in a road; an alley spotted with liquor (or blood) and three bums lying or sitting in contorted positions; a woman, apparently dead, lying on the ground with an open purse nearby; and a workman looking down musingly on black waters.

The magazine obviously saw the tragedy of the times, but it offered no solutions, unless bitter laughter could be called one. West himself sympathized with the magazine's position as spectator, impartially deriding Hoover and Hitler, Stalin and Roosevelt, and the Dadaistic and surrealistic tendencies of *Americana* were close to his own art. Yet, as a human being with—whether he liked it or not—a sympathetic heart, West could hardly be content with mere laughter. Too obviously the capitalistic system seemed to be creaking at its very foundations. Looking abroad, he could only shudder at the German solution to its economic and psychological problems; the German need for a scapegoat and a father image might be a universal desire. It might be used in America by some potential Hitler.

Certainly there were no easy answers to the problems created by the depression. Quite possibly West felt he could offer no solution. Yet he could not be satisfied with the attempts that were being made. As he turned back to his writing, he must have felt, as he was later to write Jack Conroy about another novel: "I believe there is a place for the fellow who yells fire and indicates where some of the smoke is coming from without actually dragging the hose to the spot."[26] *A Cool Million* was a strong and fearful cry of fire: the first to indicate that fascism could happen here.

A Cool Million was published in June, 1934, well before American fascism had reached full cry. Subtitled "The Dismantling of Lemuel Pitkin," the novel tells of the adventures of a young country bumpkin and his girl, Betty Prail, in their progress through life. According to the American dream—one sedulously mythologized by the American educational system, one fervently preached not only by Horatio Alger but also by Franklin and Jefferson and Whitman, one symbolized by Lincoln and his progress from log cabin to White House—according to this dream, by honesty and industry the road to fame and fortune is magically opened. But the progress of Lemuel is quite the contrary: his is a slapstick mockery of the Alger theme of *Bound to Rise, Onward and Upward*, and *Paddle Your Own Canoe*. *A Cool Million* shows not how Lemuel wins his way, but how he gradually sinks rather than swims, how, on his pilgrimage through life, he loses such physical accoutrements as his teeth, an eye, a leg, a thumb, and his scalp. The progress of Betty Prail is a feminine counterpart of Lemuel's, and it is made, for the most part, while she is flat on her back. The novel shifts back and forth between the adventures of Lemuel and Betty. In true Algerian style, the shifts usually occur when an especially fearful action is approaching its climax. The whole is treated in a broad, lewd prose, more appropriate to the washroom than to the drawing room. For his use of incongruities in action, West is slightly indebted to certain mannerisms of S. J. Perelman, to whom the novel is dedicated, but the plodding prose, some of it lifted almost intact from Alger novels, lacks the wit and grace of Perelman.

Full of coincidences, the action of the novel is largely slapstick; the characters are broad stereotypes; the style, save for a brief surrealistic section treating the "inanimate" exhibit of the "Chamber of American Horrors," is one extended cliché. As a whole, the book reflects the extensive reading in Alger that West did preparatory to writing the novel. Above all, West dramatizes the lie that, for him, the American success dream had become.

At the opening of the novel, Lawyer Slemp comes to tell the Widow Pitkin that the mortgage on her home will soon be foreclosed. With no hope for money, the widow and her son Lemuel search for a way to "keep the roof over their heads" (p. 146). In desperation Lemuel goes to see the president of the Rat River National Bank, Nathan "Shagpoke" Whipple, about a loan. To Lemuel's plea, Whipple answers that he would not help even if he possibly could. He advises that it would be far better for Lemuel to "go out into the world and win your way" (p. 149). To aid Lemuel, Whipple advances thirty dollars and takes a lien on the family cow as security. After Whipple deducts 12 per cent interest in advance, Lem is off to make his fortune.

But not quite off. First, Lem must prove his mettle, and this he does on the way home from the Rat River Bank. As he wends his way homeward, he sees the slight figure of his boyhood love, Betty Prail, pursued by a fearful dog, obviously mad. A red-blooded American youth, Lem goes to Betty's defense. Soon he leaves the dog dying, with the mad foam still upon its mouth. The action is in the heroic pattern of the American Boy, and, like the true American Girl, Betty admires Lem's fearlessness. The two of them, however, have forgotten the town bully, Tom Baxter. Soon he is upon the scene. He confronts Lem and demands five dollars in payment for the death of his dog. Lemuel asserts the dog's madness, but Tom coarsely refuses to listen.

The two boys begin to fight. Lemuel does quite well for a while, even though he's smaller and lighter than Tom. Lem peppers his opponent's nose and eyes until Tom sheepishly admits he's bested and offers his hand. Instead of the Algerian pattern of friendship that should follow, Tom jerks Lemuel "into his embrace and squeezed him insensible" (p. 154). In emulation of the frail Victorian female, Betty screams and faints. The chapter ends with Tom surveying the charms of Betty, while "His little pig-like eyes shone with bestiality" (p. 154). This animality is apparently satiated in the following chapter even though the author, in his adopted Algerian pruriency, feels he "cannot with propriety continue my narrative beyond the point at which the bully undressed that unfortunate lady" (p. 155).

Obviously the race is not to the industrious and honest, the fair-minded and pure. It is Tom and all the Toms like him for whom the world is an oyster. And the Lemuels? They get it, eternally get it, in the neck. The Bettys? In an even more vulnerable spot.

The point is made at length, and then it is repeated again and again. Often it is made, especially when Betty is the subject, with an adolescent smirk, a crude, bathroom-wall humor. After Tom Baxter has had his will with Betty, she is captured by white slavers—Italian, of course—who bring her to New York. Then, after being forced by the Italians to "serve a severe apprenticeship to the profession they planned for her to follow" (p. 167), Betty is sold to a brothel keeper—Chinese, of course—who, beneath a laundry façade, runs a prosperous whorehouse based upon the principles of the House of All Nations. Betty is ensconced in the colonial room of this brothel, dressed in colonial costume and served by a Negro in livery. Everything is in perfect harmony, for Wu Fong, the brothel owner, is an artist in his trade. The author, in Algerian fashion, moralizes in a parenthesis:

> (Wu Fong was a great stickler for detail, and, like many another man, if he had expended as much energy and thought honestly, he would have made even more money without having to carry the stigma of being a brothel keeper. Alas!) (p. 160)

Soon Betty is waiting for her first customer, a pock-marked Armenian. She is assured of a busy future, for, as all true, Protestant, white, patriotic, red-blooded Americans know, "it is lamentable but a fact, nevertheless, that the inferior races greatly desire the women of their superiors. That is why the negroes rape so many white women in our southern states" (p. 169).

Later on, West treats the effect of the depression upon Wu Fong's brothel. Just like so many other merchants, Wu Fong decides he is overstocked and must cater to the new fashion of "Buy American" popularized by Hearst.

> He decided to get rid of all the foreigners in his employ and turn his establishment into an hundred percentum American place.
>
> Although in 1928 it would have been exceedingly difficult for him to have obtained the necessary girls, by 1934 things were different. Many respectable families of genuine native stock had been reduced to extreme poverty and had thrown their female children on the open market. (p. 202)

West goes on to describe with relish the new decorative patterns of the girls' rooms, from Pennsylvania Dutch to Modern Girl interiors. He describes the costumes of the girls, from that of Princess Roan Fawn, who "did business on the floor" (p. 204), to that of the Modern Girl, Cobina Wiggs, who "had broad shoulders, no hips, and very long legs. Her costume was an aviator's jumper. . . . It was made of silver cloth and fitted very tightly" (p. 204). Even the food and drink are appropriate to the various girls and their customers: groundhog and rye is served to Lena Haubengraber's clientele and "tomato and lettuce sandwiches and gin" (p. 205) to that of Cobina Wiggs.

Such smirking is, of course, not great writing, and it is doubtful if it is even good writing. Yet *A Cool Million* is more than a mock-melodramatic burlesque of the American success dream. It is a fearful cry against the dangers inherent in that dream. Used by opportunists, even those who believe the clichés they mouth, the American dream could by the stepping stone to a dictator. As the first significant novel satirizing the incipient fascism West saw in America, *A Cool Million* is worthy of study.

In terms of this fascism, the most interesting character of the novel becomes Nathan "Shagpoke" Whipple. Molded in the image of Calvin Coolidge, Shagpoke is thrifty to the point of miserliness. He has been President for four years, and then has "beaten his silk hat . . . into a plowshare . . . to . . . become a simple citizen again" (p. 146). It is Whipple, who, as Lem's mentor, preaches the American success dream; but it is he also who mouths a flag-waving America-firstism, a narrow, cracker-barrel insularism, a suspicion of all sophistication, all things European, all that is not good, white, Protestant culture. This Americanism communes with its own simplified vision of Abe Lincoln and Henry Ford. It sees them as embodiments of the success dream, and from their example preaches a simple rugged individualism. In his favorite clichés, Whipple utters his sermon:

America . . . is the land of opportunity. She takes care of the honest and industrious and never fails them

as long as they are both. This is not a matter of
opinion, it is one of faith. . . .
       . . . . The story of Rockefeller and Ford is the
story of every great American. . . . Like them, by
honesty and industry, you cannot fail to succeed.
(p. 150)

Americans who can believe in the bromides preached by
Whipple are just the ones who can also accept blindly any
number of other simple-minded, black and white ideas.
They accept such bogeymen as that in which the Negro becomes an animal lusting for white flesh. They find no difficulty in believing in the bogeymen of international conspiracies. For them, danger lurks in all things strange.

In the hands of an opportunist, these simple-minded people can be used, as Shagpoke uses them, for a ladder to
dictatorship. Shagpoke forms the American Fascist party
(called the National Revolutionary Party in the novel) on
the dreams and fears of the simple-minded. With uniforms
of leather shirts and coonskin caps, he hands the party members the mass identity, and individual suicide, they so desperately wish. He bases the intellectual appeal of the party,
ironically enough, upon the cliché of rugged individualism.
Its mass appeal he ensures in the fears and hatreds of the
simple and the unemployed. In his addresses, Shagpoke
arouses his followers through their fear of Capital (under
the specter of the International Jewish Bankers) and Radicalism (under the nightmare of the Bolsheviki):

There was enough work to go around in 1927, why
isn't there now? I'll tell you; because of the Jewish
international bankers and the Bolshevik labor unions,
that's why. (p. 187)

As a corollary to the suspicion of the vaguely foreign
and fearful unknown, the National Revolutionary Party

(N.R.P.) also evinces a heightened praise of "American-ism," a flag idolatry, and a hatred of all "foreigners" and foreign countries. Every true, red-blooded American must, as Shagpoke expresses it, "be made to realize that the only struggle worthy of Americans is the idealistic one of their country against its enemies, England, Japan, Russia, Rome, and Jerusalem" (p. 243). Or, more frankly, Americans must continually be on their guard against the foreign ruses of Jews and Catholics, Communists and Orientals, as well as those sophisticated Englishmen in white tie and tails. Above all "we must purge our country of all the alien elements and ideas that now infest her" (p. 188).

Dreams, fears, and hatreds form the appeal of Shagpoke's party of Leather Shirts and Storm Battalions. Soon Shag-poke is marching from the stronghold of his "Americanism," the white, Protestant South, upon the "foreign" city of New York. In New York, Commander Lemuel Pitkin has been acting as a stooge in a comedy routine. By now he has been deceived, deluded, and dismantled over most of Amer-ica. He has had his teeth pulled in a jail where the warden believes that all criminals are really sick and that the cause of their sickness usually lies in faulty teeth. He has lost an eye while rescuing a rich man and his daughter from stam-peding horses. (This is, of course, an Algerian situation. But the rich man here offers Lem neither employment nor the hand of his fair daughter. Instead he mistakes Lem for an irresponsible groom and scolds him for letting his horses get out of control.) He has lost a leg in a bear trap and has been scalped by Indians. Now, in New York, he has grate-fully accepted a stage role in which he is physically bela-bored until "His toupee flew off, his eye and teeth popped out, and his wooden leg was knocked into the audience" (p. 250). The audience is convulsed by Lemuel's agony.

Unlike another Lemuel, Pitkin learns nothing and remains

gullible to the end. Never does he lose faith in the clichés preached by Shagpoke. When he is asked to give an N.R.P. speech before the audience where he is performing, he knows his duty. While making the speech, he is shot and becomes a martyr to the N.R.P. cause.

The epilogue, below a row of bravely waving American flags, tells of a parade on Pitkin's birthday, a national holiday in memory of the All American boy. Marching for Pitkin, thousands of American Fascists sing the Pitkin song of martyrdom. The leader of American fascism, the great man Shagpoke Whipple, deifies Pitkin:

> Of what is it that he speaks? Of the right of every American boy to go into the world and there receive fair play and a chance to make his fortune by industry and probity without being laughed at or conspired against by sophisticated aliens. . . . But he did not live or die in vain. Through his martyrdom the National Revolutionary Party triumphed, and by that triumph this country was delivered from sophistication, Marxism and International Capitalism. (p. 255)

In the triumph of Shagpoke the reader sees the danger. The Pitkins, eternal simpletons with dauntless faith in the American dream, go forth to make their way in the world. They do so believing that if a man is only honest and industrious, he is sure to reap the just rewards of fame, fortune, and *the* girl. Instead of these, the American Boy receives jail, poverty, violence, and death.

On the way to the last reward, the All American Boys become bewildered. In the perplexity of these bumpkins is bred the danger. They need a dream, and, under the irresponsible leadership of men such as Whipple, can easily accept a new fantasy. This new bromide condemns all sophisticated thought as foreign and un-American. In stark simplicity, the cliché proclaims that the rewards of Lemuel's honesty and industriousness are being kept from him by the twin bogeymen of the International Jewish Bankers (I.J.B.) and the Bolsheviki. According to the bogeyman fantasy, the I.J.B. and the Bolsheviki are allies in their fight against The American Way. As allies, they have in their employ a mysterious spy and terrorist (he is operative 6348XM when he reports to the I.J.B.; comrade Z when he reports to the Bolsheviki). In addition they have a joint cultural representative, the poet-impresario, S. Snodgrasse, who conducts the subversive "Chamber of American Horrors" because he "blamed his literary failure on the American public instead of his own lack of talent, and his desire for revolution was really a desire for revenge" (p. 238). The I.J.B. and the Bolsheviki are constantly conspiring—so comes the whisper from Whipple, and then the speech—to keep the bumpkin from the fame and fortune and girl which are his due rights. Lemuel believes, and he follows. In Whipple's bogeyman lies and Lemuel's foolish fears, says West, American fascism is being born. What he has to say is an object lesson for an America continually beset by the fearful fantasies of its Bilbos and Longs and Rankins, its McCarthys and Maddoxes and Wallaces. The fantasies have a purpose, and West shows clearly what it is.

A Cool Million is a sad commentary upon the confident faith of the founding fathers: a sad decline from the lyric of Hail Columbia! happy land! or the concept of America, the land of the free and the home of the brave. But in the face of the American depression, it would have been surprising if West had not written such a book. What West does is to restate his constant theme in a contemporary context. The quest for something to believe in continues, and it again ends in despair. Where *Balso* indicts the folly of the quest of art, where *Miss Lonelyhearts* mocks man's dreams of Christ, *A Cool Million* attacks the American success dream. West had hoped to make *A Cool Million* an American *Candide,* but though it is not that, it does present an essential Candidean truth: the progress of the industrious and honest man is from shirtsleeves to shirtsleeves.

Like the previous novels, *A Cool Million* offers no real solutions. It mocks the American way, derides the "conspiracies" of the Bolsheviki and the International Jewish Bankers, and attacks bitterly the American Fascist movement. If the novel suggests anything affirmatively, it is that life was better in an earlier time. Then the complexities of existence had not led to such falsities as those exhibited in the inanimate section of the "Chamber of American Horrors," where stood

> a Venus de Milo with a clock in her abdomen, a copy of Power's "Greek Slave" with elastic bandages on all her joints, a Hercules wearing a small, compact truss.
> In the center of the principal salon was a gigantic hemorrhoid that was lit from within by electric lights. To give the effect of throbbing pain, these lights went on and off.
> All was not medical, however, . . . Paper had been made to look like wood, wood like rubber, rubber like steel, steel like cheese, cheese like glass, and, finally, glass like paper.
> . . . . The visitor saw flower pots that were really victrolas, revolvers that held candy, candy that held collar buttons, and so forth. (p. 239)

This is the progress of man, and for West such glorifications as Chicago's "Century of Progress" exhibition could not disguise the irony of man's advance. No wonder that in *A Cool Million* the Indian Chief Satinpenny looks backward longingly to a simpler time when America was "a fair, sweet land" uncontaminated by the "white man's civilization, syphilis and the radio, tuberculosis and the cinema" (p. 232).

No wonder Chief Satinpenny, too sophisticated to believe in the possibility of a return to the past, advocates, in a Dadaistic disgust with which West seems to sympathize, a war against the white man and the future under the war cry: "Smash that clock" (p. 233). As Spengler and Valéry had suggested (and West had read their criticisms), man's "progress" is leading to the end of Western civilization. West agreed with such viewpoints, though perhaps more emotionally than intellectually. Along with other friends of West, Robert M. Coates has noted: "I think the key to his character was his immense, sorrowful, sympathetic but all pervasive pessimism. He was about the most thoroughly pessimistic person I have ever known."[27]

A Cool Million had been written, more than any other book West wrote, to make money. West hurried the writing in hopes of profiting by the good notices of *Miss Lonelyhearts*. But *A Cool Million* fell sadly short of its objective. When it died quickly on the bookstands, the doubts of West's mother tormented him more strongly than ever. Though he could rationalize the failure of the book by asserting that it was too premature an examination of native American fascism, still self-doubt nagged. He hated to think of money, but with the practical reminders of his mother, he found himself hardly able to think of anything else. This excessive concern for money is implied in Edward Newhouse's memory that West, shortly after the publication of *Miss Lonelyhearts*, commented that "he was going back into the hotel business and make large batches of money and do nothing but write for the rest of his life."[28] Miss Herbst remembers that, as West's money grew less and less, he sometimes would make ludicrous plans for getting rich quickly. At one time he schemed, half jokingly, half seriously, to grow rubber in Brazil; at another, he dreamed of buying an old junk and trading in the China seas.

A Cool Million made little money for West, and certainly not enough to justify the purchase of the expensive suits and sixty-dollar shoes that West occasionally longed for. Nor were the reviews of the novel favorable enough to bolster West's confidence as an artist, even if he was one whose books did not sell. One reviewer sneered that he had struggled "through another of Mr. West's books. I can only report that I can't see it. I don't think good writing is laid on with a trowel."[29] Herschel Brickell's comment was hardly better: "Seemed to me a dull book while I was reading it and seems even duller as I look back on it."[30] Even the good reviews were patronizing. The critic of the *New York Times* compared the book to *Candide,* and then added:

> *A Cool Million* is not so brilliant and original a
> performance as . . . *Miss Lonelyhearts.* . . . But as
> parody it is almost perfect. And as satire it is a keen,
> lively and biting little volume. . . . It is funny, but
> there's a method in its absurdity.[31]

In the same vein, T. S. Matthews reported in the *New Republic:* "*A Cool Million* is not so successful a caricature as his earlier *Miss Lonelyhearts,* and it can be taken at a glance, but the glance is worth it."[32]

If there was neither money nor critical recognition in writing, what was there? It was a hard question to answer, and one that his mother seldom let West forget. Perhaps he should return to the hotel. There he had security at least. In an America where, seemingly, as many people were unemployed as employed, where those people that had jobs were on strike, where bread lines were a common sight, where brother-can-you-spare-a-dime was more than a line from a sentimental song—in such an America, security was not to be sneered at. True, West sympathized with the unfortunate, but he did not want to be trapped himself. Nor did he like the picture of the great artist, unrecognized and starving in some secluded garret. Such visions were for fools and children. Pathetic creatures, they were also laughable, and he would not be laughed at by anyone but himself (as he, the artist, had suggested in *Balso*). If he went to the arty Greenwich Village hangouts, it was "only to get laughs out of them."[33] If the true writer was really an outcast, he liked the role no better than that of the Pagliacci clown. Perhaps the hotel would be better.

It was a despairing prospect that lay before him. At times he longed to be a "boyscout" or a "Western Union Boy"—his skeptical terms for reformers—but he was unable to give himself wholly to fantasy, even of the communistic variety preached by such friends as Mike Gold, and he revealed his larger vision in such a story as the unpublished "Tibetan Night." There he dramatized not the evil of wealthy capitalists and the nobility of exploited proletarians, but instead emphasized the links that bind the classes: their inward emptiness and their compulsion to dream. Thus he begins his story with the concept that the proletarian revolution has been successful and the capitalists who remain alive have retreated to Kaskaz, Tibet. In that isolated world, they live in their private fantasies, and are kept alive by visions of regaining their wealth and returning to their genteel habits and Connecticut estates.

During the spring and summer of 1934 he toyed with a number of projects. Drawing upon his extensive knowledge of American folklore and legend, he outlined a revue, which he submitted to Leland Hayward's office, of a number of scenes, combining music and ballet, out of the American past; among the sequences he proposed were sketches of

Father Mapple's sermon in *Moby-Dick* (which would capture the magic and flavor of Nantucket whalers in their days of glory); of the Mississippi river boat, with its dandified gamblers and coarse river men (which would emphasize the music of whorehouse ballads of the mid-nineteenth century); and of a Harlem rent party (which was to capture the frenzy of jazz music of the 1920's). Two one-act interludes, possibly using works by Paul Green and Eugene O'Neill, were to supplement the folk-quality, and so was a master of ceremonies, who was to draw upon such writers as Mark Twain and Artemus Ward for the monologues with which he brought unity into the performance. The conception was ambitious but before its time, and West was unable to interest a producer.

Yet another abortive project of this summer was a play, *Even Stephen*, on which West collaborated with S. J. Perelman. Probably inspired by the furor aroused at Brown on the publication of Percy Marks's novel *The Plastic Age*, the play tells of how a female novelist, Diana Breed Latimer, visits a girls' college and pieces together wild tales, on inadequate evidence, about the sexual frustrations and frantic orgies of the girls and their professors. Lacking effective satirical focus, the play failed to interest a producer and deepened West's uncertainties about his future as a writer.

The most bitter blow of all, however, came yet later in the year. In the late summer or early fall of 1934 he applied for a Guggenheim fellowship. The project that he outlined on his application was an autobiographical novel, similar in form to Malcolm Cowley's narrative, *Exile's Return*, or James Joyce's *Portrait of the Artist as a Young Man*. Unlike Cowley, however, West did not plan to illuminate the search for identity that Cowley's adventurers in the arts attempted in the 1920's in Paris. Instead, after exploring his American education in the first three chapters, West planned in his fourth chapter to dramatize the difficulties, even the impossibility, of modern man's finding a real emotion. In his fifth chapter West planned to dramatize the influence of Spengler and Valéry upon his hero, so that he perceived the inevitability of contemporary violence and of the decline of the West, and in his last chapter West planned to have his hero discover the significance of economics (and possibly, though West did not say so, of Marxist theory). To lend support to his application, West requested letters from George S. Kaufman, Malcolm Cowley, F. Scott Fitzgerald, and Edmund Wilson, all of whom responded with generous praise. The Guggenheim Foundation, however, was left unimpressed; its awards went elsewhere.

In despair, West drifted aimlessly. When he was not dreaming of get-rich-quick schemes, or seeing romantic omens in dreams and commonplace events, or having a beer or an idle chat with one of the village farmers, he was reading Dostoevsky. For several months he pursued this life of dreaming and reading and waiting.

5   *Reprise*

IN HIS LIFE West was full of contradictions and ambiguities. Distrusting emotions, he nevertheless was intensely aware of the pathos of the lost and helpless of the universe. Without religious belief, he could still see the desperate needs of man for the Christian myth. Contemptuous of dreamers, he was, nevertheless, obsessed by the dreams of men. He might well have been describing himself when he depicted the hero of *The Day of the Locust* as "a very complicated young man with a whole set of personalities, one inside the other like a nest of Chinese boxes" (p. 260). Yet despite this complexity a pattern emerges. To note it is to oversimplify and to distort it, for the pattern is but a general design, and it leaves out the variety and the richness of the man and the work. Yet in the distortion there emerges a simple truth. John Sanford is aware of this "truth," which is neither The Truth nor the only "truth," when he comments:

> More than anyone I ever knew, Pep was dedicated to his writing; more than anyone I ever knew Pep writhed under the accidental curse of his religion. I'm Jewish myself, and I've had many a painful moment . . . but Pep stands at the head of the list when it comes to suffering under the load. So far as I know, he never denied that he was a Jew, and so far as I know he never changed his faith (it's a joke to call it that, because he had as much faith as an ear of corn). But he changed his name, he changed his clothes, he changed his manners (we all did), in short he did everything possible to create the impression in his own mind—remember that, in his own mind—that he was just like Al Vanderbilt. It never quite came off.[1]

Such a comment implies not only West's rejection of his racial heritage but also a deep-seated insecurity, and the obvious answer to that insecurity should be evident by now. The answer is perhaps even more apparent in West's unpublished short story, "Western Union Boy," than in his better known works. The central incident of the story concerns a recollection of a middle-aged man who feels that he has been unsuccessful in life; he then remembers one of his early boyhood failures. As a boy he had dropped an easy fly ball at a critical point in a baseball game, and as a result was chased from the field by a throng of angry spectators. Trembling, the boy had hidden in a nearby woods, where he spent the remainder of the day. Even after the episode was over, his fear remained.

This incident is autobiographical. In later life West told of the episode frequently, and seemed to enjoy each retelling. The image of the crowd in pursuit was important to West, and it served as the pivotal image in his last novel, when a mob, the cheated of life, chase a number of the Hollywood cheaters of mankind. The fictional locusts are intent on capturing and destroying the fleeing cheaters; and West's memory of the fearful flight of the boy is similar. Wells Root, a close friend who listened frequently to the baseball story after West came to Hollywood, remembers that West felt that "If they [the mob] had caught him they would have killed him."[2]

Whether West's feeling is based on reasonable appraisal is irrelevant. What is important is West's own evaluation and the insecurity it implies. Ultimately the reason for this haunting fear is unknown, but the image of the persecuted human fleeing from his tormentors is an archetype deep in the collective unconscious.[3] In the Hebraic collective unconscious, if such a thing does exist, the image dates back to a time long before the flight of the Jews out of Egypt. In West's own time the image was unusually pertinent because of Hitler's deliberate and horrible pursuit of scapegoats. Such an image implies the source of West's insecurity: he was a member of a minority group, a Jew.

The typical pattern of such groups in America has been treated at some length by the religious sociologist Will Herberg. It is seen in the Jew's reaction to the two societies between which he is torn. In the first-generation American Jew, the basic ties are with the fatherland, and there is a rejection of the new country. (While this reaction is typical of other first-generation groups, such as the Italians, Irish, and Poles, these groups tend to assimilate more quickly into the American cultural and religious pattern.) Most of the second generation reacts differently. Somewhat ashamed of the old folks, it tends to reject the language, religion, and culture of the family. Its members insist on being Americans, but the omnipresence of the first generation reminds them constantly of the ties with the old country. The individual of this generation, more than any other, becomes a marginal man, one "who lives in, or has ties of kinship with, two or more interacting societies. . . . He does not 'belong' or feel at home in either group."[4]

These second-generation Jews, of whom West was one, had the problem of finding their own identity. "To what do I belong?" they often asked, in order to find an answer to an even more important question: "Who am I?" Without answers, "the second generation found itself in an intolerable position, consumed with ambition, anxiety, and self hatred."[5] To change one's name, as many second-generation Jews eventually did, was often an affirmation of the Americanism which these Jews wished to display, but as an answer to their insecurity, such name changing was woefully inadequate. Often the change in name only led to contempt from other Jews, to suspicion on the part of most gentiles, to increased knowledge that one must forever dangle between two worlds and never really be a full member of either. If one were fairly insensitive, such a fate might be almost unnoticed. For a sensitive man, however, such dangling would be a constant torment, the kind of anguish, for instance, that we find in Miss Lonelyhearts, who, suspended in a world of disorder, finds himself

> . . . developing an almost insane sensitiveness to order. Everything had to form a pattern: the shoes under the bed, the ties in the holder, the pencils on the table. When he looked out of a window, he composed the skyline by balancing one building against another. If

a bird flew across this arrangement, he closed his eyes
angrily until it was gone. (p. 47)

Harry Haller, the steppenwolf (or outsider) of Herman
Hesse's novel *Steppenwolf* makes the point in these words:

> Human life is reduced to real suffering, to hell, only
> when two ages, two cultures and religions overlap.
> . . . Naturally every one does not feel this equally
> strongly. A nature such as Nietzsche's had to suffer our
> present ills more than a generation in advance. What
> he had to suffer through alone and misunderstood,
> thousands suffer today.[6]

Similar to Miss Lonelyhearts and the steppenwolf is the one
Jew whom West creates in any detail in his novels. This
Jew is Abe Kusich, the dwarf of *The Day of the Locust*.
He is both an outsider, suspended outside the normal pattern of existence and yet unwilling to accept his difference
from others, and the epitome of human suffering. Symbolic
of his status as an outsider are his constant and futile attempts to experience a satisfactory sexual experience with a
normal woman. As the epitome of suffering, the dwarf identifies himself with the pain of the dying cock in the grue-
some and bloody cock fight of *The Day;* and Abe's identity
as sufferer is made even clearer by Tod Hackett's comment
to Homer Simpson, himself a personification of the suffering of the simple man, that Homer could learn of agony
from Abe.

Now it is probably unwise to state dogmatically that
West's insecurity or the desire of the characters in his fiction for order and peace in a chaotic universe can be explained wholly by any theory. Man and his art are too complex for that, and West was more complex than most men.
Yet the theory does illuminate the character of West. Even

more it illuminates West's writing. This is true because if there is any constant pattern in the novels of West, it is the pilgrimage around which each novel centers. In each the hero is in search of something in which he can believe and to which he can belong. The search may be made skeptically as in *Balso,* or with religious fervor as in *Miss Lonely-hearts,* or ironically as in *A Cool Million* and *The Day;* but the result is always the same: tragic disillusionment. The quest is similar to the dominant motif of *Ulysses,* and it is undoubtedly this concept in Joyce's work, as well as the pathos of the Jewish outsider Bloom, which impressed West so tremendously and made him read *Ulysses* again and again. Not to bend the knee to either church or Mother, to reject and then to seek: it was a theme worthy not only of an Irish Catholic but of an American Jew.

It is more than likely, therefore, that the reason West's novels are involved in the Quest is his rejection of a heritage, both familial and racial, that burdened West just as Joyce's heritage weighed on that great nay sayer. West's consciousness of his theme is evident from the beginning epigraph of *Balso,* "After all, my dear fellow, life, Anaxagoras has said, is a journey" (p. 2); and it is as a journey, dominated by a quest which ends in disillusionment, that West's novels should be read.

But what is this promised land that is being sought in the novels of West? It is no land of milk and honey, nor is it one of perfume and spices. It is an interior land, and the search is for interior security and order, for the "beloved balance" that J. Raskolnikov Gilson seeks so desperately in *Balso.* The reason that such a search permeates the work may be the needs of West, the man, rejecter as well as seeker, and these needs are present not only in West's early life but in his later years as well. For instance, West's attraction to left-wing causes while in Hollywood brings to mind

Will Herberg's comment that the second-generation Jews, in their desire to belong wholly to something, often turned to internationalism or radicalism.

Though the idea can easily be carried to absurdity, the need for order that is present in West's fiction is also at the center of much modern fiction by "assimilated" Jews. Salinger's *The Catcher in the Rye* is dominated by Holden Caulfield's need for moral order in the universe; its absence is suggested by the omnipresent obscenity that Holden feels obliged to erase wherever he can. In his plays, Arthur Miller preaches, sometimes a little stridently, the need for a world of cooperative harmony and human dignity; but what Miller sees, and agonizes over, is a world of chaos, a zoo, in which the human animals struggle viciously to destroy one another. More obviously, the need for order is dramatized in the middlebrow novels of Herman Wouk; *The Caine Mutiny* and *Marjorie Morningstar* are basically indictments of those Bohemian men of air, those Noel Airmen, who would disrupt order by violating convention or questioning the rightness of some supreme naval commander. For those with higher brows, Saul Bellow's *Dangling Man* dramatizes an anti-hero who, in a time of war, seems suspended midway between existence and non-existence, war and peace; such an anti-hero, therefore, seems to dangle, forever waiting, in a world without focus or center or pattern. In another of Bellow's novels, *Henderson the Rain King*, the hero, though more dynamic, is at first lost in the maze of American civilization. In his heart there arises constantly the cry, "I want, I want," and to still this cry he goes to Africa on a "quest" (the word is Henderson's). In the simplicity of Africa he finds that what he wants is reality, which is the noble and the great, not the pig but the lion, in man. For Bellow, the search, the quest for order, ends in affirmation, and Henderson ends as a *be-er* and not a *be-*

comer. As a *be-er*, Henderson stands for stability; he has found a meaningful order:

> "Oh, you can't get away from rhythm, Romilayu,"
> I recall saying. . . . "You just can't get away from it.
> The left hand shakes with the right hand, the inhale
> follows the exhale, the systole talks back to the diastole,
> the hands play patty-cake, and the feet dance with
> each other. And the seasons. And the stars, and all of
> that. And the tides, and all that junk. You've got to
> live at peace with it, because if it's going to worry you,
> you'll lose."[7]

Though the rage for order is hardly a Jewish monopoly, it is certain that "assimilated' Jews in America have worked well with it. Doubtless their preoccupation with the theme, and West's, has some relationship to their bicultural status in America. Possibly that bicultural status explains, as well as it can be explained, the agony, so largely inexplicable in ordinary, logical terms, that lay deep in West's heart and that made him write the cries for "Help" which are implicit in all of his novels.

6　*The Dream Factory*

In the summer of 1934, Columbia Pictures purchased the film rights to *A Cool Million,* and though the studio soon lost interest in producing the work West was encouraged enough by the sale to consider anew the possibility of a movie assignment in Hollywood. By March of 1935 he had decided to seek work there, and in the summer of that year he took an apartment at The Pa-Va-Sed apartment hotel on N. Ivar Street. A shabby hotel, similar to that in which Tod Hackett lives in *The Day of the Locust,* The Pa-Va-Sed had a clientele of seedy Hollywood types—bit players, comics, stunt men, and full-time tarts and part-time prostitutes —and seemed especially to attract midgets, one of whom West observed as he picked himself up after being thrown bodily out of an unfriendly tart's apartment.

Despite his writing credentials, West found it difficult to get a writing assignment, and he gradually grew more and more impoverished and confused. In addition he contracted gonorrhea, the cure of which was complicated by a congested prostate gland; he was often in pain and he lost considerable weight. His clothes slowly grew more ragged and ill-fitting—at times he noted that he was beginning to talk and look like Gandhi—and his dependence on the Perelmans for financial help left him increasingly guilty and desperate. Lying on his pull-out, hotel bed in the summer heat, he listened to fire engines tracking down eternal fires in nearby canyons, and he may have thought of writing an apocalyptic work like that upon which Tod Hackett muses in *The Day:* "He was going to show the city burning at high noon, so that the flames would have to compete with the desert sun. . . . He wanted the city to have quite a gala air as it burned. . . ." (p. 334).

During this period West became friendly with a number of his fellow inmates at The Pa-Va-Sed, occasionally even loaning his car, for professional purposes, to some of the hotel girls, and with time he enlarged his acquaintance of the seamy side of Los Angeles. Through Stanley Rose, primarily known for his Hollywood Boulevard bookstore, West met not only a number of writers but also some of the derelicts and petty gangsters among Rose's varied acquaintance; with Rose and his friends West occasionally attended illegal cockfights at Pismo Beach. Through another screen writer, Sy Bartlett, West was introduced to a number of newspaper reporters and police officers, and West liked to go with them on police calls, sometimes involving homicide, to seamy, bizarre neighborhoods. Occasionally West visited the local Mexican community, and there he made a number of acquaintances familiar with the more sordid aspects of the lower depths of this world. On yet other occasions he attended Hollywood premieres at such movie temples as Grauman's Chinese Theatre, and watching the mob that gathered outside the theater (some members of which had been waiting since early morning for a sight of their favorite idols), he saw not worship of the stars, as did most people, but instead a vast hatred and a desire to tear the clothes and rend the flesh of the glamorous, beautiful people. At still other times West visited the temples of local religious cults, among them the gaudy $1,500,000 Angelus Temple of Sister Aimee McPherson, and his experiences there, barely distorted, were similar to those he ascribed to Tod Hackett in *The Day of the Locust*: "He visited the 'Church of Christ, Physical,' where holiness was attained through the constant use of weights and spring grips; . . . the 'Tabernacle of the Third Coming' where a woman in male clothing preached the 'Crusade Against Salt'; and the 'Temple Moderne' under whose glass and chromium roof Brain-Breathing, the secret of the Aztecs, was taught" (p. 365). Truly, West traveled much in Los Angeles, and he came to know the guises of a vast range of Angelenos. In addition he listened closely to the talk of the tarts, madams, racehorse addicts, and movie extras that he came to know so well (and whose dialects he captured in the speech of such characters in *The Day of the Locust* as Mary Dove, Faye Greener, and Abe Kusich), and at one time he even considered compiling a dictionary of the speech of prostitutes.

During 1935 West may have written a seventeen-page movie "original"—a treatment of the Seminole Indian Osceolo in which West revealed his awareness of the brutality, heroism, and pathos implicit in the fate of the American

Indian—but he could not sell the script, and he did little other writing during this year of frustration and despair. At times, in his darkest moments, he sent moody telegrams, signing himself "Melvin Apple," in which he parodied in a vein of black humor the religious agonies of such Dostoevsky characters as Alyosha of *The Brothers Karamazov.*

Finally, however, West managed in January of 1936 to secure a week-to-week writing contract with Republic Productions. There he shared an office with Lester Cole, but he often visited the office of his friend Sy Bartlett, where he would lie on the floor, his hands under his head, and thumb through a pack of dream-cards until he came across a suitable romantic cliché; undoubtedly he had this method in mind when he described Faye Greener's fantasies, and undoubtedly he would also have agreed with Faye's admission that "her method was too mechanical for the best results . . . it was better to slip into a dream naturally" (p. 317). Yet, for West the technique worked in writing screenplays.

After four months with Republic, at a salary of $200 a week, he had proved himself sufficiently to be offered a six-month contract with a raise of fifty dollars a week. Though Republic was the most commercial of the Hollywood dream factories, the contract offered a modicum of security as well as the possibility that West might be able to do some of his own writing. For that stability, such as it was, West was grateful; he was content for two years to conceive cheap dreams, manufactured on tight budgets, to satisfy the stereotyped fantasies of a mass audience. Not until January of 1938 would he leave Republic to seek a better contract at a more pretentious, or more artistic, studio.

Though at times West complained about Hollywood, he was, on the whole, happy to be at Republic, and then, later on, at such studios as RKO, Universal, and Columbia. One reason was his pessimistic conviction that good writing had little chance for popular success: mass man by his very nature preferred trash to art. Often West and his friend Robert M. Coates discussed this point. West constantly asserted that the writer, if he were to gain time and freedom to do good work, had to turn for a livelihood to hack drudgery. Since this had proved to be true in his case, it was obviously only intelligent to do the hack work where it was well paid—ideally, Hollywood.[1]

In Hollywood, as he had expected, West was a writer who was not a creator. Instead, he was an employee, and he produced his work for materialistic furriers and pants-pressers whom he despised. Usually he wrote in collaboration with others, so that individual artistic expression was further diluted. The difference that he felt existed between his novel-writing and his screen-writing was apparent in his work habits. Where he wrote and rewrote his novels on the typewriter, his screenplays he wrote "out in longhand. . . . When it came to a treatment, an adaptation or an outline, he could dictate it in a few hours."[2] Working in this way for Republic Studios, West collaborated in 1936 on *Ticket to Paradise, Follow Your Heart,* and *The President's Mystery.* For the same studio, he wrote an adaptation of *Rhythm in the Clouds* in 1937 and an original screenplay, *Born to be Wild,* in 1938. Around the same time, West worked for Universal on a Deanna Durbin picture which was never produced, and with Boris Ingster he wrote a screenplay for RKO which was not used but which eventually became the Hitchcock movie *Suspicion.*

Of these early movies, the most interesting to West, and the most successful critically, was *The President's Mystery.* The title was inspired by the fact that the movie was based on an idea of President Franklin D. Roosevelt. The President's idea was "whether it was possible for a man, weary of faithless friends and a wasted life, to convert a $5,000,000 estate into cash, disappear and start anew in some worthwhile activity."[3] Using this idea as a springboard, West and his collaborator told a story of a lobbyist, James Blake, who is the tool of big business. By wining and dining legislators, Blake defeats the Trades Reconstruction Bill, a piece of progressive legislation which would have helped the nation's smaller industries and cooperatives during the depression of the thirties. Spiritually and physically weary from his labors, Blake wanders to a town named Springdale, which would have benefited greatly by the passage of the Trades Reconstruction Bill. In Springdale, Blake attends a town meeting. The meeting moves him to remorse. He decides to disappear from his Washington haunts, to convert his securities into cash, and to back the town's cooperative experiment. Blake's disappearance from Washington and his wife's murder on the same night make for a thread of melodramatic plot, but the movie's basic concern is with the cooperative movement in America. Even before the movie was publicly shown in New York, the *New York Times* commented that a preview had "set the industry buzzing. The feeling is that the film should attract attention. It . . . may possibly bring about serious consideration of the screen as an editorial medium."[4] When the film was actually reviewed by the *New York Times*, the reviewer praised it lavishly and concluded:

> Although there is no disputing its propagandistic intent, the film . . . has not reduced its narrative to a moralizing bludgeon. . . . *The President's Mystery* is a well-constructed essay on one means of achieving a more abundant life, and it is an interesting picture as well.[5]

Meyer Levin in his *Esquire* column "The Candid Cameraman" went even further. He devoted most of his lengthy column to *The President's Mystery*, which he called "The first Hollywood film in which a liberal thesis is carried out to its logical conclusion."[6] Levin noted how big business, in the film, tries to destroy the cooperative movement in Springdale; using a variety of the filthiest tactics possible, big business seems finally on the verge of breaking the co-operative:

> Now this is where the picture might go screwey. By all that is Hollywood, we might have expected a compromise solution here, in which the corporation takes over the orders of the cooperative and fills them on schedule, proving that corporations have good hearts. But what happens? . . . The farmers hop onto their trucks, their hay wagons, their Model T flivvers, they swarm into the town, halt the riot, load the goods on their motley caravan and deliver it to the main line of the railroad, thus saving the cooperative and establishing, at least for movies, the idea that cooperatives can work in America.
> In other words: a Hollywood movie goes the whole hog. . . .
> Republic is to be violently congratulated for this picture. I hope it even lifts the studio from the independent to the major studio ranks.[7]

Undoubtedly West was gratified by the reception given *The President's Mystery*, but he had little real pride in his screenplays. Despite this, he gradually rose from low-budgeted C films to the commercially successful movies upon which he worked, alone or in collaboration, in 1939 and 1940: *Five Came Back* (RKO), *I Stole a Million* (Universal), and *Men Against the Sky* (RKO). The best of these artistically was *Five Came Back*, which starred Chester Morris and an unknown actress named Lucille Ball. The movie told a rather stereotyped tale: a plane with its varied group of twelve passengers (including an anarchist being escorted to his execution) crashes in a tropical wilderness and so sets off a series of adventures from which only five of the original twelve come back. The movie was commended by the *New York Times,* which noted it was "a rousing salute to melodrama, suspenseful as a slow-burning fuse, exciting as a pinwheel, spectacularly explosive as an aerial bomb."[8] Such praise largely left West unmoved. A close Hollywood friend, Wells Root, has commented upon West's detachment from his screen work:

> I think he figured in respect to producers and directors that movies were their business, not his. He was a sort of architectural assistant, working on plans for a house. . . . Whatever happened to him in pictures, good or bad, up to the time of his death, had affected in no way his real work, which was writing novels.[9]

Possibly, as Root points out, had West lived longer, he would have lost this artistic detachment, for he would "have progressed to A-bracket pictures, which are formidably budgeted, competently directed and acted. . . . Had this happened, his attitude toward films might have been less detached."[10]

That point never arrived for West, so he spent his time writing fluff, into which he occasionally tried to intrude social commentary. Typical of West's movie work is the screenplay *The Spirit of Culver,* which he wrote in 1939 in collaboration with Whitney Bolton. The movie starred Jackie Cooper (as Tom) and Freddie Bartholomew (as Bob), and it began in Indianapolis in 1932. Scenes of depression, "No Help Wanted" signs and people getting food from relief agencies, flashed onto the screen. These scenes dissolved into others of boys hopping freight cars. The camera then shifted to a news headline, "Youth Problem Acute," and from there it flashed to a food line in which young boys were waiting. After some quarreling among the boys, the scene shifted to two army officers in charge of the food line:

> Captain: "You're doing a great service to youth, Major."
> Major: "What frightens me is the terrible waste. The whole country will suffer if the strength and courage of these boys goes to pot. The government *has* to take over the problem."
> Captain: "Put them in the army."
> Major: "Not necessarily. Feed them—clothe them—house them. Give them something to do. Conservation—reforestation—maybe road building. There is still plenty of fight and decency left in those kids out there. But another two years in soup kitchens—and they'll be beaten and useless."[11]

From this social commentary, the movie turns into a tale full of sentiment and coincidence, with an impossible, but happy, ending. Essentially the movie is the familiar one about a poor and cynical boy, Tom, at a school of storied military tradition. Inevitably the poor boy has a chip on his shoulder; he antagonizes his classmates and is especially offensive to his roommate Bob, a wealthy English boy with a kind heart. By the end of the movie, however, the two boys are friends, and through the convolutions of the plot—including the rebirth of Tom's father, who everybody thought had died in World War I—the cynic Tom has learned what Bob has always known. Bob expresses this knowledge during a history lesson when he says, "Sometimes it is better to *die* on your feet than live on your knees." At the end of the movie, Tom expresses the same thing: "There will always be things worth fighting for, sir, even dying for." Because of the conquests of Hitler and the fact that America might soon become involved in some

European holocaust, the statements were more than mere clichés, and some fervid America firsters objected strongly to the expressions. Both statements were probably the work of West, for he did occasionally insert political overtones into non-political movies. According to his collaborator on the movie, West

> . . . insisted on inclusion of a scene in the picture which either took verbatim or paraphrased a fiery statement by La Pasionara, the then explosive Spanish woman in the troubles in Spain. I think it was: "It is better to die on your feet than live on your knees."[12]

From the writing of such fluff, even with its sometimes irrelevant social commentary, West gained security and some time to travel, to read, to hunt, and to write his own unique work. Occasionally he went East for vacations. Once he traveled to Mexico, and at another time he went to Key West. He liked neither of the latter places, primarily because he disliked intensely the inconvenience and the dirtiness of traveling. For the most part he remained in Hollywood, where he entertained well, though never garishly. He read voluminously and spent considerable time in the bookstores and at the homes of his friends Stanley Rose and Larry Edmunds. He liked to eat in Musso Frank's, a favorite dining spot for writers, and he spent considerable time in the art galleries of Los Angeles. For his own amusement he sometimes returned to his drawing, and Jo Conway, his secretary, served as the model for a number of sketches. With such friends as Root and Conway and Rose, West occasionally talked of the things that disturbed him. Frenzied hatred in West was rare, "he saved it for arrogant, unjust, and particularly for pretentious people,"[13] but West did despise "the conventional public villains such as Hitler and Franco and could work up quite a head of steam about ultraconservatives here at home such as Herbert Hoover.["14] A constant subject of conversation among West's liberal circle was the situation in Germany:

> Nat's attitude toward Nazism was rather like a doctor's attitude toward cancer. It was a plague, to be stamped out, cured, or controlled. In other words, his distaste —deep as it was—seemed objective rather than subjective.[15]

A subject that West himself often introduced was the Catholic Church. Toward it

> he had some special aversion. . . . He had read widely on the subject, from earliest church history to the present. Any historical hypocrisies or decadence were documented in his mind with relentless clarity. His characterization of the Church as big business, complete with facts and figures, amounted to an indictment. He could even tell you how much real estate it owned in New York, with formidable statistics on the taxes it did not pay because it was a religious institution.[16]

West's greatest pleasure came in hunting, which he did at every opportunity with such friends as Wells Root, Stuart and Darrell McGowan, and William Faulkner. Faulkner remembers that he and West took occasional trips to Santa Cruz island and the Tulare marshes. West, he says, was an excellent marksman and did his share, and more, in the chores of the hunt. Though both men were novelists and were employed as screen writers, they were friendly as hunters, not writers, and never talked of their own writing or the books of others.[17] Stuart McGowan remembers the fear of West's fellow hunters as West drove to or returned from the hunt:

He had a habit of becoming so interested in his conversation that he would forget to watch the road. . . . there were many times I would take the steering wheel and turn the car on the right side of the street to keep from meeting on-coming traffic—most of the time without interrupting Nat's discourse.[18]

Jo Conway recalls how West

followed the season from when it began in Oregon down through California and into Mexico each year. He had two dogs . . . Danny and Julie. . . . Pep would have trusted a person with his bank account, his life almost, before he would trust his dogs to you. He always had to have a house and servants just because of the dogs. . . . He would hunt every weekend he could, and never missed opening day. In fact, on Monday and Tuesday, I would get a rundown on the weekend's hunt; then we might work Wednesday and Thursday, but on Friday the preparation for the hunt began.[19]

Once Danny, West's favorite hunting dog, was hit by a car, and Jo Conway received a long letter from Oregon about the event. West told vividly of holding the mangled, bleeding dog in his arms while he searched endlessly for a trustworthy veterinarian. For Miss Conway the narrative was "literature."[20]

While in Hollywood, West learned the craft of screen writing, but he never lost the desire to do his own writing. Reading Liddell Hart's *The War in Outline: 1914–1918*, he was struck by the stupidity of the British generals, and in 1937, with this as his source, he and an M.G.M. writer, Joseph Schrank, began the play *Gentlemen, the War*, which, in 1938, ran for two performances on Broadway under the title *Good Hunting*. The play was a satire upon an older, more picnicky kind of war, a Gentleman's War, and it made its point through an old-fashioned British warrior, Brigadier General Hargreaves, who insisted that there be no gunnery activity in the early morning (one's sleep, you know) and demanded that there be no shop talk (bad taste, you know) before breakfast. The central satiric action dramatized the confusion of war and the accidental nature of victory: campaign orders were delivered to the wrong commander, and through the mistake an enemy position was taken.

Brooks Atkinson called the play "nitwit theatre," and then added, "If you hurry, you may find some reputable actors defying doom. . . . The jokes are faint and tedious; the direction is disastrous."[21] West and his friends attributed the play's failure to the fact that it opened during the war crisis of Munich week, when jokes about war not only sounded hollow but also seemed in the worst of taste.

The failure of the play hurt West, but the pain was softened by the fact that *Good Hunting* was sold for a substantial price to Hollywood. On his own return to Hollywood, West resumed what was, on the whole, a comfortable life. Yet at times, as an artist, he despaired. His position as employee, not creator, engendered the vague discontent that seems to be the lot of most serious writers in Hollywood who are forced to compromise with their historic roles as poet-priest, rebel, and oracle. Leo Rosten has analyzed this dissatisfaction among writers in his study of Hollywood:

> The writer who has tasted the joys of independent creation is thrown into abysmal discontent by Hollywood. He wants to write something in which he "believes." He wants to set down his honest conceptions—of people, emotions, events—without making compromises to costs, "business sense," "a fourteen-year old public," or other demons in the producer's cosmology. . . . He finds it hard to cope

with the sense of futility which overpowers him in
the middle of another story about the heiress and the
reporter, the duchess and the jewel thief. . . . He
cannot suppress the self-indicting feeling that he
ought to be writing "something significant."[22]

Possibly it was guilt of this kind, at least partially, that
led many Hollywood writers to become embroiled in leftist
political activity. One cannot really say, and certainly such
political involvement had no simple explanation. Deeper
emotional elements were often more basic, and, of course,
the time, with its human misery (and consequent human
guilt), made leftist activity fashionable. Whatever the reason, numerous Hollywood people, West among them,
tended toward leftist outlooks. Even before he came to
Hollywood, West had unmistakably shown his political
leanings when he, with numerous other well-known writers, signed his name to the manifesto of the 1935 American
Writers Congress. The call of the Congress read, in part, as
follows:

> The capitalist system crumbles so rapidly before our
> eyes that, whereas ten years ago scarcely more than
> a handful of writers were sufficiently far-sighted and
> courageous to take a stand for proletarian revolution,
> today hundreds of poets, novelists, dramatists, critics
> and short story writers recognize the necessity of
> personally helping to accelerate the destruction of
> capitalism and the establishment of a workers'
> government. . . .
> A new renaissance is upon the world; for each writer
> there is the opportunity to proclaim both the new way
> of life and the revolutionary way to attain it. Indeed,
> in the historical perspective, it will be seen that only
> these two things matter. The revolutionary spirit is
> penetrating the ranks of the creative writers. . . .[23]

Soon after he arrived in Hollywood West joined the embryo Screen Writers Guild (he was elected to its Executive Board in 1939), even though the Guild had been painted with a leftist reputation and the overlords of Hollywood frowned upon Guild membership. During the Spanish Civil War, West worked many hours and contributed a considerable amount of money to the Spanish Loyalist cause—a cause for which most intelligent people of the time worked and prayed. Similarly he worked numerous hours on a committee formed to aid the migratory workers of California, the kind of worker depicted in *Grapes of Wrath;* and he sympathized with and aided the Anti-Nazi League of California. Jo Conway, West's secretary from early 1937 until his death, remembers, "Pep was pretty far to the left in his political thinking. . . . His sympathies were easily aroused and he had so much heart that he was a sucker for any cause. . . . We used to have fabulous political arguments."[24] Stuart McGowan, with whom West often hunted, and Whitney Bolton, with whom West worked, also recall West's determined political position. When Tom Mooney, a leftist prisoner of international fame, was released from prison, West suggested that Bolton, who wrote a column for the *Morning Telegraph,* might do a feature story of Mooney. Because Bolton was interested, West invited him to visit one of his friends. Mooney also appeared at the friend's home, and "West made a great show of 'Tom' this and 'Tom' that, when speaking to Mooney, and, obviously, looked upon Mooney as some kind of a hero."[25] When James T. Farrell last saw West, in September, 1938, West was in New York for the opening of his play *Good Hunting;* they seemed to be conscious of their political differences.

> We didn't have much to say to one another, and we
> only talked for a few minutes. I do not know if politics

had too much to do with this or not. I might add that
at the time I was deep in the fight . . . against the
Moscow trials, and I had heard rumors that "Pep" had
come closer to the Party. I know that I felt that when I
met him. However, I cannot say whether this was true
or false. We parted friendly.[26]

Certainly West had come closer to the Communist party,
but he was not a member. He scorned the confusion and
hypocrisy of some Hollywood Communists and rejected the
ideological shifts that followed the Russian nonaggression
pact with Hitler in 1939. He implied his feelings in a letter
in which he noted that he spent considerable time on pro-
gressive movements, but could not use such material
in his fiction because it seemed a melodramatic falsification.
Despite trying, he could not believe in the "mother" of
Steinbeck's *Grapes;* and his own effort to describe a meeting of the Anti-Nazi League of California resulted in his
depicting a brothel and a pornographic film in *The Day*.[27]

To put it simply, West possessed a sympathetic heart,
but he tended to be too detached in his viewpoint on the
human dilemma to be able to propagandize in his novels—
the art he believed in—and it is likely that this detachment
kept him from membership in the Communist party. Because of this detachment he could never, as a good party
member was expected to, see things in simple black and
white terms. This inability is related to the kind of schizo-
phrenia one so often feels in his writing: his attitude toward his characters shows sympathy, yet, at the same time,
repulsion. Unlike his master, Dostoevsky, West seldom
seems able really to love the sordid people he depicts. Like
Miss Lonelyhearts, West appears to be repelled by the
primitive pathos he portrays, but unlike Miss Lonelyhearts,
West seems unable to overcome the repugnance he feels for
such sordid humanity. Sympathy, pity, he could give, but

identification was beyond him. He could want to love, to lick lepers, but do it, he could not. West's tendency to see things in terms of gray, not black and white, is suggested by the end of *The Day*. On one level, the end is given to the mob which has risen to pursue and possibly to overthrow and destroy its exploiters, the Hollywood cheaters. Yet the end is certainly no piece of communistic propaganda: the skepticism with which West views the upheaval is too great. The mob is no simple proletariat, bringing in an era of good will and brotherhood. Instead it is a ravaging locust, with death in its vitals, destroying meaninglessly and futilely, and West's view of it is one of horror and fear, not hope. Such skepticism and despair hardly fit the Communist mind.

Numerous friends and acquaintances remember this aloofness as a central trait of West. Whitney Bolton notes:

> He had an unusual detachment about Hollywood. . . .
> I think the only time he relaxed from impersonality
> was one morning when he had just received his
> weekly check as a screen writer, and, with a smile,
> exclaimed: "I like working out here. It makes me rich
> beyond the dreams of avarice."[28]

This detachment, however, did not keep West from being fascinated by the grotesqueries of the world in which he found himself. Miss Herbst remembers West's telling her a host of stories about Hollywood vulgarism. He told the stories with a typically ambivalent mixture of attraction and revulsion: he reveled, for example, in the story of the Hollywood titan who would neither wipe himself nor flush his own toilet, but instead always kept a lackey to do such menial chores. However, at the same time that West inwardly writhed at the Hollywood cast of mind habituated to such actions, he learned a great deal from his observations. Robert Coates feels that "the garishness, etc., of Hollywood . . . satisfied his pessimistic outlook on life."[29] James T. Farrell recalls, "He was fascinated by the grotesqueries of Hollywood. . . . Also, without being Puritan, there were things that he didn't like about the sexual behaviour. . . . I recall him once remarking about some Hollywood people who would hire two prostitutes and take them into a hotel room at the same time."[30] Allan Seager adds:

> A footnote on the wooden-headed cowpoke in *Locust:* The saddle shop with the hitching-racks in front where he hung out was just across from the old KNX radio station on Sunset. No horse was ever hitched to the racks but I have seen the movie cowpunchers sitting on them by the hour. I am sure West was put to no trouble in getting the character. All he would have to have done was walk by two or three times. Having known something of the Hollywood West saw at the time he was seeing it, I am of the opinion that *Locust* was not fantasy imagined, but fantasy seen. All he had to do was recognize it and know when to stop.[31]

In a long talk with Miss Herbst about the artist caged in Hollywood, West said that he felt he was relatively unharmed by the Hollywood atmosphere, but he agreed that the Hollywood world was not the right kind for a serious writer. For himself even, he was fearfully apprehensive: he considered writing as "a way of life, a time for reading and reverie," and felt strongly that the neurotic fearfulness of life in Hollywood was slowly destructive of the creative artist.[32] As time passed in Hollywood, this feeling possessed West even more. At times, with the knowledge that the youthful artistic impulse was gone, West even questioned whether it was worthwhile to write creatively at all. He wondered if it was not mere personal vanity that made one dream of doing something significant. His message, "Beware," was one that the world did not want to hear. His style, which he felt lacked both the warm chuckle and the hearty belly-laugh, found few admirers. As a matter of fact, he wrote to George Milburn that

> all my books fall between the different schools of writing. The radical press, although I consider myself on their side, doesn't like my particular kind of joking, and think it even Fascist sometimes, and the literature boys whom I detest, detest me in turn. The highbrow press finds that I avoid the big significant things and the lending library touts in the daily press think me shocking. . . . I've never had the same publisher twice—once bitten, etc.—because there is nothing to root for in my work and what is even worse, no rooters.[33]

Feeling that the reaction to his novels was occasionally highly enthusiastic but more often grossly vituperative,[34] West often, in his later Hollywood years, wondered exactly who his audience was. He conceived of himself as a comic, but not a humorous, writer, in a tradition older than Benchley or Frank Sullivan,[35] but with so slight a public that he often wondered whether the writing of unwanted novels was really worthwhile. His answer was always a tentative, doubting *yes.* Both the doubts and the answer are suggested by a letter he wrote to Edmund Wilson:

> I once tried to work seriously at my craft but was absolutely unable to make even the beginning of a living. At the end of three years and two books I had made a total of $780 gross. So it wasn't a matter of making a sacrifice, which I was willing enough to make and will still be willing, but just a clear cut impossibility. . . . I haven't given up, however, by a long shot, and although it may sound strange, am not even discouraged. I have a new book blocked out

and have managed to save a little money so that about Christmas time I think I may be able to knock off again and make another attempt. It is for this reason that I am grateful rather than angry at the nice deep mud-lined rut in which I find myself at the moment.[36]

For some three years, while continuing to write Hollywood fluff, West brooded over the Hollywood grotesqueries. Twice he got false starts on a novel. The first of these was inspired by a newspaper story about a boat. The boat was called the Wanderer, and it was involved in "a kind of round-the-world . . . yachting adventure . . . which wound up in scandal in a California harbor; a kind of high-seas, sleasy, cafe-society thing . . . which appealed to his pessimism."[37] The second false start stemmed from West's conception of a boardinghouse in Hollywood. He retained much of this material for his last major work.

> Thus, the father of the girl, the Eskimos and the other vaudeville characters in "Day of the Locust" were originally figures in a different novel he had vaguely planned. . . . (It was to be, as I recall it, laid entirely in a kind of old-vaudevillean's boarding house hangout in Hollywood, and the whole action was to be a sort of endless double-take, people clowning at funerals, pretending to be sad at weddings, etc.; in short, acting endlessly.)[38]

From these two false starts a new form gradually evolved, and in the spring of 1938, working five hours a day, West slowly, painstakingly completed *The Day*. Even after the proofs of the novel began coming in, West continued to polish and sharpen the writing. In his search for exactness he was constantly making changes and additions, for which he was willing to pay if necessary.[39] More than ever the message of his work was "Beware," and he wanted no one to miss it.

The Day of the Locust, like West's earlier novels
a desperate need for something worth believing
searching for. In *The Day,* however, the narrative is
complex than in the other novels. The viewpoint c
novel shifts back and forth between Tod Hackett and
Homer Simpson. Homer Simpson is one of the searchers of
the universe who, seeking after Paradise, has found in Hollywood only a place to die, and Tod Hackett is one of
those who attempt to satisfy the emotional needs of the
searchers of the world. Dominating the novel are the twin
elements of the search and its frustration. Always the searchers are cheated, not only by Hollywood but by life itself,
which promises so much and delivers so little. The cheating
is suggested by repeated images of falsity, in which nothing is what it seems, all things are in essence lies. The need
for order and security makes the search go on, and if some
super-Hitler, some Dr. Pierce-All Know-All can promise
such security, the cheated of mankind will destroy and
burn because of their need to achieve it. Always, though
obliquely and episodically, with a kind of Grecian inevitability, the action of the novel is moving toward increasing
violence, toward the mass destructive orgy in which the
novel hysterically ends.

The characters that West uses in this nightmarish novel
are grotesques, and they are similar in the cause of their
grotesqueness: the need for an emotional life. Both comic in
the tastelessness of its results and tragic in its yearning, this
emotional need leads to architectural monstrosities built
formlessly of plaster and paper; it leads to brothels and
cockfights and pornographic movies and endless attendance
at funerals, to vicarious lust and violence furnished by movies and newspapers, to violence even in the Hollywood
premieres. For both rich and poor, however, there is an ever
lessening sensibility to such shocks, and as the sensibility de-

creases there comes the emotional death which leaves each person with the vague feeling that he has been betrayed. West expresses the ennui of the living-dead when he says:

> The sun is a joke. Oranges can't titillate their jaded palates. Nothing can ever be violent enough to make taut their slack minds and bodies. They have been cheated and betrayed. They have slaved and saved for nothing. (p. 157)

Charles Baudelaire, who could not have been far from West's mind as he created the universe and the inhabitants of *The Day,* expressed the concept in "Au Lecteur" in this way:

> But in this den of jackals, monkeys, curs,
> Scorpions, buzzards, snakes . . . this paradise
> Of filthy beasts that screech, howl, grovel, grunt—
> In this menagerie of mankind's vice
>
> There's one supremely hideous and impure!
> Soft spoken, not the type to cause a scene,
> He'd willingly make rubble of the earth
> And swallow up creation in a yawn.
>
> I mean *Ennui!* who in his hookah-dreams
> Produces hangmen and real tears together.
> How well you know this fastidious monster, reader,
> —Hypocrite reader, you!—my double! my brother![40]

Both West and Baudelaire agree that the destruction of the universe may occur because of man's ennui. For some men, in the world of West, this boredom can never be alleviated, but their search for a way to realize some kind of emotional life effects actions that slowly lead toward the supreme shock of violence. In America, West felt, such destruction was waiting only for a forceful leader and his demagogic promises. Germany had already found such a leader; filled with hatred, the bitter and cheated of America awaited a new messiah of violence.

The world of *The Day* is a limited world which excludes the ordinary working man completely, but West knew he was painting a partial world, and, as he pointed out in a letter to the proletarian novelist, Jack Conroy,

> If I put into *The Day of the Locust* any of the sincere, honest people who work here and are making such a great progressive fight, these chapters couldn't be written satirically and the whole fabric of the peculiar half-world which I attempted to create would be badly torn by them.[41]

The half-world can be divided into spectators (the cheated whose emotional needs demand satisfaction) and performers (the cheaters who are attempting to satisfy the emotional needs of others). The roles, however, occasionally shift, for in the world of grotesquerie all men are both performers and spectators; for instance, Faye Greener serves as a performer in her screen roles, but off the screen she attempts to satisfy her emotional needs by thumbing through a pack of mental dream-cards until she finds one on which to dream.

The spectators are on the fringes of the novel, all except Homer Simpson who, in his eventual explosion, functions as the living symbol for all of them. Having no life in themselves—no inward vitality or beliefs or dreams—they must seek life elsewhere, and often their search leads to the Sargasso Sea of dreams: Hollywood. Symbolically these people, who exist everywhere, are suggested by the aged who have come to Hollywood to die physically the death they have already experienced emotionally. These embittered spectators fascinate Tod Hackett, and he draws numerous sketches of them for his picture "The Burning of

Los Angeles." Watching them as they frequent their religious temples, monstrosities which serve only to mock true religion, Tod appreciates their "awful anarchic power . . . aware that they had it in them to destroy civilization" (p. 110). Singly, these people are barely noticeable, "almost furtive," but when they join their own kind, as in the mob scene which ends *The Day,* they become "arrogant and pugnacious" (p. 156). Through mass violence they may for a brief while fulfill themselves, become performers in the drama called life, and it is the revolutionary transformation from spectators to performers that Tod Hackett envisions in his painting of "The Burning."

At the center of the novel are the performers. The most important of these, Abe Kusich and Faye and Harry Greener, Tod Hackett is painting in his series of lithographs called "The Dancers." Abe Kusich is a performer, partly because he is a race-track tout who sells lies and dreams to all who will buy. A dwarfish Jew, loud-talking and aggressive, Abe is painted with more compassion than any other character in *The Day,* and in his struggles and suffering he is comparable to the cock he handles in a horrible cockfight. Nature's grotesque, Abe parallels in his physical monstrousness the distorted mentalities of the other grotesques. Because of this physical monstrousness Abe belongs among the performers, for it is his physical grotesqueness that titillates the sensibilities of onlookers just as that of the bearded seven-foot lesbian might have done. Thus Abe's grotesqueness arouses Tod at times to a "sincere indignation," and at other times to an excitement which makes him feel "certain of his need to paint" (p. 5).

Another of the performers, Harry Greener, is a comic and a failure. In his role Harry purveys a burlesque act consisting of violent kicks in the belly and falls on the back of the neck. Like another performer, Lemuel Pitkin, Harry occasionally gratifies his insatiable audience by the extremity of his agony. One fictional critic feels the violence of Harry's routine approaches the purgative function of tragedy, so that "The pain that almost, not quite, thank God, crumples his stiff little figure would be unbearable if it were not so obviously make believe" (pp. 25–26). Even in the everyday world, Harry acts the comic. His role is mostly a matter of defense, for he has learned that people do not like to hurt a comedian, but he also seems to get a masochistic pleasure in comic routines given before bar audiences. So involved is he in the stage world that in his real illness, from which he dies, he groans "skillfully . . . a second act curtain groan, so phony that Tod had to hide a smile" (p. 80). Beyond death, even, Harry's acting seems continued: in his coffin, waiting for his final curtain, he is "newly shaved, his eyebrows shaped and plucked and his lips and cheeks rouged. He looked like the interlocutor in a minstrel show" (p. 88).

The most important of the performers is Faye Greener, a movie extra who speaks an occasional one-sentence role badly. Where her father, because his audience wishes it, has simplified the subtleties of humor into the violence of slapstick, she has simplified the complexities of love into the horror of lust. This she has learned from the screen, just as she has learned from it all the other falsities, all the other dreamplot lies, that dominate her existence: the artificial voice, the elaborate gestures, the lustful suggestiveness. The precipitant of lust and violence, she herself has an "egglike self sufficiency" (p. 63). Thus she can become a whore to gain money for her father's funeral and yet remain unaffected by the experience "because her beauty was structural like a tree's, not a quality of her mind and heart" (p. 89). Nothing can harm her, for, like Mary Shrike, she is the eternal virgin, capable of giving pain but incapable of giving herself.

She, therefore, cannot really gain herself, and so, like the celluloid clichés on which she dotes, she never really comes alive. In her falseness, she suggests the whole Hollywood lie, and her promise, like that of the Hollywood dream-products, leads not to satisfaction, only to increased frustration. What Faye becomes, and to a lesser extent her father and the dwarf, is the grotesqueness of the screen made into real flesh. In essence her lure is like that of the screen, where shadows talk to shadows against a background of shadows. It is the lure of self-destruction, but in the nightmare world of West the death wish lures men as meat attracts flies.

Especially lured by Faye, and thus by self-destruction, are Homer Simpson and Tod Hackett. As the name implies, Homer is representative of the timeless, suffering man. He is a simple creature, kindly, passive, humble, and resigned, but he is doomed to a life without hope. His is the misery of all those whose "anguish is basic and permanent" (p. 58).

Homer is a symbolic representation of the spectators of life, forever cheated. He has come to Hollywood from a small city near Des Moines. His life before Hollywood had been lived between deep sleep and a plantlike calm. For a time in Hollywood, Homer exists in the same way. Then Faye comes into his world. After Homer has met Faye, he feels thoroughly awake, more completely alive than ever before. The living which Homer has achieved, however, is painful, just as life for West is basically frustration and pain. Even more, Homer's new life is based on a lie, for Faye is no more a real woman than are the shadows on the screen. Still, Homer must grasp this chance at life, just as the movie-lovers grasp after life in their attendance at the movies, and must invite Faye to come and live with him. Faye comes, but their relationship is totally sexless, just as the love affair between screen lovers and movie audiences is a totally sexless one. Soon Faye persecutes Homer maliciously; she lures him toward the destruction which he had instinctively known he was inviting when he lusted after her. Then Faye sleeps with another man and leaves Homer with his misery. It can never be purged, can never come to a climax and be forgotten. It is the misery of the victims of life, and Homer evinces it in a sobbing "like an ax chopping pine . . . repeated rhythmically but without accent. . . . It would never reach a climax" (p. 143).

Without relief, the only thing for Homer to do is to attempt escape. This he seeks by the device he had earlier used: sleep. Watching the sleep into which Homer falls, Tod compares it to uterine flight, the perfection of escape:

> Better by far than Religion or Art or the South Sea Islands. It was so snug and warm there, and the feeding was automatic. . . . It was dark, yes, but what a warm, rich darkness. The grave wasn't in it. (pp. 148–49)

Homer, however, awakens. He wanders to the world premiere of a movie and sits down near the premiere mob. Adore Loomis, a child actor, is hiding behind a tree close by. Adore is playing a childhood game: he has tied a string to a purse, and he wishes to attract Homer's attention so that Adore can snatch the purse away. Homer totally ignores the purse. This irritates Adore, so that he first makes faces at Homer and then gestures insultingly. Nothing arouses Homer until Adore throws a stone full in his face. This action, added to the metaphorical stone he has taken from Faye, arouses Homer from his trance. He pursues Adore, and when the boy falls, Homer jumps on him repeatedly. The mob surges violently toward Homer, and the last sight of him shows him "shoved against the sky, his jaw hanging as though he wanted to scream but couldn't" (p. 161).

The incident with Adore is obviously symbolic, for Adore is another Hollywood-created grotesque. Deprived of a normal childhood and a true mother's love, Adore has become capable of singing a sexual song in a practiced blues voice and with extreme sexual gestures, and yet, horribly enough, he has not the slightest idea of what he's doing and suggesting. No wonder his mother notes that Adore believes he is the Frankenstein monster. As that horrible creation, he offers a cheat that is similar to that which Faye offers. Both his cheat and Faye's are merely symbols of the larger lie which is Hollywood, and Hollywood is merely suggestive of the greatest cheat of all: life itself.

West's first instinct was to call *The Day* by another name, *The Cheated,* and certainly the latter name is an accurate indication of the fate of Homer and those for whom he stands. Homer's saga is the potential tale of all of the innumerable cheated people who have come to die, and, further, of all people anywhere who are betrayed by life. Like them, Homer, in Hollywood, lives the same deathlike existence he had lived before he came to Hollywood. Like them, Homer tries to come "alive": Homer through Faye and they through the Hollywood screen. With this "living" comes frustration and pain. In addition the "living" is a lie, for it is based on deathlike shadows which have neither life in themselves nor the ability to bestow life—whether the shadow be that of Faye or the screen itself. Eventually the frustration and the pain and the cheat that are Faye and life itself torment Homer beyond endurance. He erupts into violence and attempts to destroy one of the cheaters. The host of the cheated everywhere, subconsciously aware of the lie offered them by Hollywood and life itself, are capable of the same kind of violence, and show it in the mob scene which ends the novel. In their fury they become for a moment something more than the cheated; they become ravaging locusts.

In this twilight world of West, Eros, the god of love, lies dead between the violence celebrated by newspapers and the escape of liquor bottles. In this world, men like Homer are trapped between a plantlike existence of suppressed emotion and a futile attempt to satisfy their emotional needs. The constant emphasis placed on Homer's hands shows this human dilemma. Like the hands of Sherwood Anderson's Wing Biddlebaum (in *Winesburg, Ohio*), Homer's hands have "a life and will of their own" (p. 39), and they dramatize Homer's suppressed, but only partially controlled, emotional needs. Thus the external Homer is revolted by sex, as is shown by his attitude toward a hen's copulation, but shortly after Homer has met Faye, his hands become intolerable in their itching and he has to hold them under water. Eventually the desires of the internal man become so strong that Homer's "fingers turned like a tangle of thighs in miniature. He snatched them apart and sat on them" (p. 56).

The underground man, however, is never satisfied, and Faye only arouses him to further frustration. The result for Homer, as for the other cheated, is an involuntary turn to some dwarfed escape: in Homer the hands "left his lap, where they had been playing 'Here's the church and here's the steeple,' and hid in his armpits. They remained there for a moment, then slid under his thighs" (p. 134). For the other cheated, always betrayed, there are the miraculous religions of all the Drs. Pierce-All Know-All. These religions preach easy ways of salvation: through vegetarianism, through physical fitness, through invocations of ghosts. Most often, however, the cheated turn to the dwarfed religion of the silver screen and its dreams. The movie temple is the place of worship for these particular cheated people, and they go to their church primarily to satisfy the spirit's need for a dream, but also to appease a basic sexual demand. Thus the mob at the end of the novel is compared to an ecstatic congregation with spasms passing continuously through it. Men tell sexual jokes, while hugging complacent, contented, and laughing women. Tod feels a sobbing young girl pressing against him. Her clothes are torn, and an old man "was hugging her. He had one of his hands inside her dress and was biting her neck" (p. 162). Tod manages to free the girl, but then another "spasm" passes through the mob, and "He saw another man catch the girl. . . . She screamed for help" (p. 163).

Tod Hackett, primarily a symbolic dramatization of the Hollywood cheaters, is the second of Faye's admirers. A sensitive and complicated young man, he is perceptive and often seems much like West himself. He lives for a while on Ivar Street, where West also lived temporarily; he is interested in military lore, and, like West, has childhood memories of perusing old volumes in search of military pictures; he has, perhaps, even the same artistic problem as West:

> During his last year in art school, he had begun to think that he might give up painting completely. . . .
> He had realized that he was going the way of all his classmates, toward illustration or mere handsomeness. When the Hollywood job had come along, he had grabbed it despite the arguments of his friends who were certain that he was selling out and would never paint again. (p. 3)

Despite his awareness of the entrapment of the cheated, Tod is still one of Faye's admirers. He himself is thereby entrapped, even though he realizes Faye is just as false as the sets and costumes he designs, even though he realizes that as a love object Faye suggests the grotesqueness and destruction of the screen. In this entrapment, Tod is associated with the cheated (or the spectators) so that he would throw himself upon Faye (and self-destruction) just as would Homer or the barber in Peoria who pursues the glamour and amour of the screen.

Primarily, however, Tod's association is with the performers (or the cheaters). He designs Hollywood sets as false as the scripts which Claude Estee, a writer, creates. Here is the artistic tragedy. As artists, Claude and Tod are doomed to an artistry that rises no higher than the wishes of the cheated. They could, the modern artist could, do better. Perhaps they could create such music as Bach had produced in his confidence that Christ, the earth's lover, would eventually come to his mate. But Bach is not for the cheated. They demand, even though it is their own betrayal, the grotesqueness of violence and slapstick and lust. This fact West once noted in a book review:

Maybe the men who make the pictures are not to blame. Perhaps we should blame the man for whom the pictures are made—"the barber in Peoria. . . ."
It is strange, but the movies are always trying to forget "the barber." Even Mack Sennett tried *once* to forget him. He lost several hundred thousand dollars, then took another look at the sign hanging on the wall of his scenario department. "Remember: the extent of the intelligence of the average public mind is eleven years. Movies should be made accordingly."[42]

Obviously artistic democracy, in which the wishes of the mass dictate the work of the creator, is artistic tragedy, but even more it is mankind's tragedy. The art and the religions of today, which should satisfy man's emotional needs, salve the pain of his existence, have been forced to forfeit their function. This betrayal is demanded by the cheated, but it is resented as well, and from this ambivalence arises their

181

desperate bitterness. The final result of the betrayal Tod envisions in his picture "The Burning of Los Angeles":

> Through the center . . . came the mob carrying baseball bats and torches. For the faces of its members, he was using the innumerable sketches he had made of the people who come to California to die . . . all those poor devils who can only be stirred by the promise of miracles and then only to violence. A super "Dr. Know-All Pierce-All" had made the necessary promise and they were marching behind his banner in a great united front of screwballs and screwboxes to purify the land. No longer bored, they sang and danced joyously in the red light of the flames. (p. 165)

Fleeing from the crusading mob are all the Hollywood cheaters—Faye, Harry, Claude, and Tod—as well as Homer, who seems to be falling out of the picture and thus not rightfully a part of it (as he, who is one of the cheated but is, ironically, destroyed by them, should not be). Fleeing, Tod stops to throw a small stone at the mob. *The Day* is such a stone, but West had few illusions about its potency as a weapon against the onrushing fascism that he feared.

Even a superficial examination of the novel reveals that the dominating effect is that of fear: fear of that great beast, the mob. Though surcharged with pity, this terror still dominates the novel as it dominated the novelist (though "insecurity" would be a more appropriate term in reference to the novelist). Explicitly this fear leads to the rejection of American mass culture and "art," but there is also an underlying fear (earlier suggested by *A Cool Million*) of democracy itself. This emotion is easily understandable in a member of a minority race. It is even more understandable when that minority is being persecuted by a majority, as, during the thirties, the Jews were being persecuted in Germany.

The image of that archetypal fear is that of the mob in full pursuit of those it would tear asunder, and it was shown earlier that such an image possessed West from childhood. This image, and the host of other images of violence in *The Day*, fulfills in West's terms the artist's duty: to use Freud as Bullfinch in presenting pictorially, symbolically, the mythology of our day. The particular mythology that West was concerned with in *The Day*—pertinent to West's own time but timeless in its implications—is a drama about man's emotional needs, the frustration of those needs, and the need for a scapegoat to vent one's rage upon. This is, of course, good Jung, and it is completely pictorialized in the vision of the cheated pursuing those they have forced to do the cheating.

In *The Day*, there is a rejection of the mob and its culture, as well as a dominant archetypal image. At the same time, however, that there is a total revulsion from the living dead who compose the mob and complete hysteria at the destructive potentialities of the rabble, there is also a close identification of Tod Hackett with the mob. As a Hollywood artist he is a performer who creates for it, but he also, in his feeling for Faye, identifies himself with the longings of the mob. These longings of both Tod and the mob are first of all wishes for that world of dreams which Faye and the movies represent. Just as important, Tod and the mob long for the destruction which Faye, and the movies, offer: "Her invitation wasn't to pleasure, but to struggle, hard and sharp, closer to murder than to love. If you threw yourself on her, it would be like throwing yourself from the parapet of a skyscraper" (p. 12). Psychologically this death wish of Tod (and its identification with similar desires in Homer and the mob) might be compared to the attempt at total assimilation by the Jew—where the Jew attempts to destroy the old, the unwished for Jewishness, in an attempt to unite himself with the new, the majority, the mob. The parallel with West's dilemma as the marginal man is obvious.

This simultaneous repulsion from and identification with the mob on the part of Tod indicates the psychological tension, in which a man hates the thing he loves and loves the thing he hates, which is at the center of every novel West wrote. In *Balso Snell* the repulsion-identification is associated narrowly with the adolescent artistic impulse and broadly with the entire Western cultural heritage. In *Miss Lonelyhearts* the repulsion-identification is associated with the modern Christ figure and also with the hordes that the modern, and futile, Christ would save through love. In *A Cool Million* the repulsion-identification is with the American dream and the mob of gullibles deluded by its falsities. In *The Day* the psychological tension is associated with the "art" and the political system of the great unwashed beast, the people. It is possible that West's own bicultural status, with its consequent repulsion from and identification with both the traditional Jewish heritage and the new American one, is responsible not only for the ever-present tension but also for a good deal of its power.

Finally, one should note a basic result of this psychological tension: the need to resolve it. Thus West's fiction dramatizes the quest for order, security, but always the search ends in failure. In *The Day* the lack of order is dramatically, and ironically, shown in Homer's destruction by the very mob for whom he stands as a living symbol. Perhaps the rabble may be forgiven, for they truly know not what they do. They cannot know, for in their world, West's world, whirl is king, and Dada is his prophet.

Part of the impact of *The Day* stems from the way in which West strives in prose for effects similar to those of certain painters. One of the artists whom Tod Hackett turned to when he grew discontented with the "fat red barns" (p. 3) of Homer and Ryder was the great Spanish master Francisco Goya. So, in painting the gloom, pain, potential violence, and terrifying blankness of the human starers (or cheated), West worked in Goyesque style, painting in the darkest colors and with the most frightening of distortions. In treating the mob, West did not satirize or paint with pity. Like Tod Hackett, West painted the mob with respect, for he knew "its awful anarchic power" (p. 109). This mass, chaotic power is most effectively suggested by images of "wild, disordered minds" at work (p. 109). One such image is of a man who

> had the same counter-sunk eyes, like the heads of burnished spikes, that a monk by Magnasco might have. . . . He was very angry. The message he had brought to the city was one that an illiterate anchorite might have given decadent Rome. It was a crazy jumble of dietary rules, economics and Biblical threats. He claimed to have seen the Tiger of Wrath stalking the walls of the citadel and the Jackal of Lust skulking in the shrubbery, and he connected these omens with "thirty dollars every Thursday" and meat eating. (p. 110)

The chaos of such minds, tortured by their confused ideas of betrayal and "religion," is constant in *The Day*, and the power, anarchy, and religious frenzy of the starers are fused perfectly in the last chapter of the novel. There, the mob is whipped into "ecstasy" by a radio announcer who is compared to a "revivalist preacher" (p. 155). Like an irrational animal, ultimately sexual in its motivations, the mob "roars" furiously when it is so directed, but the fury has no focus, and so the mob, like a "bull elephant," goes churning back and forth, each "spasm" undirected, but still powerful, irresistible.

The art of Goya is helpful in understanding the imagery of *The Day*, but just as important is the art of Daumier, another of the masters of Tod Hackett. The influence of Daumier's caricatures is most apparent in the depiction of the Hollywood performer-cheaters. Earle Shoop, for instance, speaks a language that caricatures the talk of movie cowboys, and he has a "two dimensional face that a talented child might have drawn with a ruler and a compass" (p. 66). Harry Greener has a mask for a face. It is described in the same terms as that of the face of the idiot in *Balso*, and, like the idiot, Harry is capable of only extreme grins and frowns, with no expression between. Harry talks in the language of the burlesque comedian, and by so doing he caricatures any real feeling or humanity. Faye Greener's every action is described in terms of its affectedness, and her inward dreams are caricatured simplifications of movie clichés. Claude Estee makes fun of, and at the same time participates in, this world of caricatures: at one time he poses against his Mississippi mansion (a Hollywood duplication of the real thing) as a Civil War colonel rubbing his belly (he has no belly), and yells orders to a "black rascal" (actually a Chinese) for a mint julep (which turns out to be a Scotch and soda). Obviously Claude is aware that he is living in a world of make-believe just as funny and just as false as that world of good guys and bad guys, cowboys and Indians, purveyed by the black and white two-dimensional screen. Knowledge is no salvation, however, nor does laughter destroy the world of caricature. It exists, and Claude, as creator-performer for this world, lives in it and by it, even while he laughs at it. In this, Claude is like West himself, and that West felt close to Claude is suggested by the fact that in an early draft West tried to tell a part of *The Day* in the first person and through the eyes of Claude.

The reason West draws the performers as caricatures is

made clear not so much by *The Day* as by *Balso Snell*. In *Balso*, West spoke of a "natural antipathy felt by the performer for his audience" (p. 44). West noted that a practical reason for the natural dislike came from the necessity of the performer to be constantly straining, through ever growing exaggerations, to please his audience. The inhuman demand on the performer is noted by the precocious John Gilson in *Balso:*

> My relations with Saniette were exactly those of the performer and audience.
>
> While living with me, Saniette accepted my most desperate feats in somewhat the manner one watches the marvelous stunts of acrobats. Her casualness excited me so that I became more and more desperate in my performance. (pp. 25–26)

In *The Day*, West makes the same point in Tod Hackett's set of lithographs, "The Dancers," which portray Hackett's division of the world into the starers and the performers, a world in which the starers

> stood staring at the performers in just the way that they stared at the masqueraders on Vine Street. It was their stare that drove Abe and the others to spin crazily and leap into the air with twisted backs like hooked trout. (p. 5)

This constant straining to please, never with success, makes the performers, or artists, caricatures both in appearance and thought. In addition the inability of the artist-performer to satisfy his audience induces a feeling of inadequacy that is easily transformed into hysteria. The opera basso in *Balso* and the Greeners in *The Day* are similar in their laughter, a kind that West notes in *Balso:*

> People say that it is terrible to hear a man cry. I think it even worse to hear a man laugh. (Yet the

187

ancients considered hysteria a woman's disease. . . .)
    One night at the movies, I heard a basso from the
Chicago Opera Company sing the devil's serenade
from Faust. . . . When the singer came to the laugh
he was unable to get started. He struggled with the
laugh, but it refused to come. At last he managed to
start laughing. Once started, he was unable to stop.
    (pp. 18–19)

In *Balso*, however, West did not really dramatize the antagonism of performer and audience; nor did he carry the
hostility to the lengths he does in *The Day*. In the latter
novel the hostility becomes a social condition, and the end
of the novel implies a kind of revolutionary overthrow: for
a while the hostile starers unite, become a group entity—
what Steinbeck would call a "group man"—with a personality of its own, and violently turn upon the performers. This
kind of social division and this kind of revolutionary overthrow could easily be equated with the Marxist divisions of
mankind and the eventual hope of Marxist victory by the
proletariat over their exploiters. There is one drawback to
such a simple reading. Just as Beagle Darwin in *Balso* had
seen the audience as essentially "sweating, laughing, grimac-
ing, jeering animals" (p. 51), so in *The Day* the starers are
irrational and embittered animals. To look toward them, toward the typical members of a movie audience, as the hope
for a better world is sheer nonsense.
    Goya darkness (the audience-starers) is, then, opposed in
The Day by Daumier caricatures (the artist-performers). In
addition *The Day* reflects the influence of certain Italian
artists, among them Salvator Rosa, Francesco Guardi, and
Monsu Desiderio, whom West calls "the painters of Decay
and Mystery" (p. 96). These painters are surrealistic in
tendency: the work of Rosa is intimately involved with destruction and pain; the work of Guardi and Desiderio is

full of images of falsity similar to those on a movie lot, where "there were bridges which bridged nothing, sculpture in trees, palaces that seemed of marble until a whole stone portico began to flap in the light breeze" (p. 96). These images of pain and falsity exist on every page of the novel, and they are typically associated with the performer-cheaters. Often the images of falsity are highly colorful and lend a phosphorescent air and a carnival atmosphere to the novel. This phosphorescent decadence West paints throughout his novel, and it is this mood which Tod Hackett desires to produce in "The Burning of Los Angeles." It is the contrast between the carnival atmosphere and the horrible reality that makes for a good part of the impact of the novel, for what it obviously suggests is a Babylon doomed to destruction. The sharp contrast also creates a nightmare world made out of the grotesque world of dreams, evoked by the sights in carnival mirrors that distort the human form into weird and magical shapes, realized in the sounds of some eternal bedlam, where the cries of the sufferers in their pain and misery drift out eerily into some eternal, uncaring fog.

In *The Day* the grotesqueness of man's creation is horrible in its falsity, but *The Day* also creates the feeling of some elaborate artifice in God's creation. This impression that God's creation is just as grotesque as that made by man is especially suggested in Chapter Eighteen of *The Day*. There Tod Hackett strolls through a Hollywood studio which is indicative of the deceit of Hollywood but also intimates the deceit of life itself. The deserts of sand dumped by a truck upon one set, the load of snow carried by another truck to another set, the picnic going on upon another set—all these paint the Hollywood falsity where men are "eating cardboard food in front of a cellophane waterfall" (p. 95), and they all hint of some bigger lie deluding man. This impression is strengthened by Tod's witnessing a production of the

battle of Waterloo. Ironically West weaves a comparison of
the actual Napoleonic error at Waterloo with the error of
the movie production of Waterloo. One was caused by the
classic mistake of Napoleon in which his cavalry was
trapped in a ditch, the other by the oversight of a producer
who does not recognize that Mont St. Jean is still unfinished,
its scaffolding still unsteady, its paint still wet. Both errors
end in the rout of the French. The Hollywood tragedy ends
when "the hill collapsed. The noise was terrific. . . . Lath
and scantling snapped as though they were brittle bones.
The whole hill folded like an enormous umbrella and covered Napoleon's army with painted cloth" (p. 100). The
final effect is that the actual Waterloo was a joke, just as the
Hollywood production is a farce. In the joke, which is wry
rather than funny, the true courage of the real Waterloo
becomes as comical as that of actors "carted off by the
stretcher-bearers, still clinging bravely to their claymores"
(p. 100).

The depiction of falsity and surrealistic grotesqueness in
The Day stems from still one other influence upon the novel,
for in some ways *The Day* owes more to West's writing of
screenplays than to any other source. In writing for the
screen West learned the cinematic advantages of writing in
short scenes or "shots." These pictorially dramatized, often
symbolized, a character or an event or an idea, and the
screen technique, unlike that of the stage, made it possible
to have numerous short scenes with swiftly changing set-
tings. The use of this roving, panoramic technique in *The
Day* effects extreme pictorialization, often highly symbolic,
as well as numerous short chapters. In most of the chapters
image upon image is flashed swiftly upon the reader's eye.
The sequence of the first chapter is typical: a colorful image
of cavalry and foot soldiers; a man in a cork hat cursing and

screaming at the chaotic movie "army"; an image of the army disappearing behind a Mississippi steamboat; a picture of a rapidly moving evening crowd with each member wearing a romantic garb that disguises his real occupation; a series of rapidly changing close-ups of middle-aged loiterers watching "with hatred" the "masqueraders"; and finally a series of swiftly changing images of a suburban residential section with all of the houses a violation of taste and logic, all pretending to be things they are not, such as Rhine castles or Samoan huts or Japanese temples. This swift succession of images reminds one of West's earlier desire to write a novel in the form of a comic strip, but in *The Day* the images flash so swiftly and are so fully permeated with falsity that the form seems more like that of rapidly unraveling celluloid. By this suggestive emulation of movie form, the real horror of the world of movies—the world of dreams and lies—is made fully manifest, not so much logically as subconsciously and permanently.

The influences of painting and screen writing upon *The Day* are a far cry from the literary echoes that dominate West's first novel and damage irreparably *A Cool Million*. Though *The Day* does not have the charm and high spirits of the brash and youthful experimentation of *Balso*, it has something far superior: the mark of a personality. That personality is not the reflection of a host of other literary names. Though the personality is Swiftian in its attitude toward man, it is unique in the fantastic extravagances with which it dramatizes its contempt for, and pity of, man and his follies. *The Day* completely lacks the smell of other books (except, perhaps, for *Balso Snell*) and is undoubtedly the best novel to come out of the Sargasso Sea called Hollywood. Its only real competitor is the imposing fragment of *The Last Tycoon* left by Scott Fitzgerald.

Once this has been said, it still must be added that *The Day* is not as perfect a book as *Miss Lonelyhearts*. One reason is that *The Day* is more ambitious, as is apparent textually in its greater cast of characters, greater complexity of plot and idea, and more subtle distinctions of thought and imagery. This greater ambitiousness, however, does not excuse the fact that the middle of *The Day* seems at times to be rambling, without effective direction, especially in the extended treatment of Earle Shoop and his Mexican companion. Nor does it alter the fact that the novel's insistence upon falsity everywhere eventually seems a little overdone, rather monotonous, and a bit irritating. Even more significant, though, is that the greater formal perfection of *Miss Lonelyhearts* rests on a more effective handling of viewpoint. In *The Day* there is some clumsiness in the shifts from the eyes of Tod Hackett to those of Homer Simpson, whereas in the earlier novel there is the constant development of the dramatic involvement of Miss Lonelyhearts in the story that he sees and lives. Or to put it more concretely, Miss Lonelyhearts' ambivalent attraction toward and repulsion from the grotesques he pities and detests at the same time is realized dramatically through West's choice of viewpoint. On the other hand, Tod Hackett, as an artist, is merely curious about the grotesques he sees, and he has no inward struggle over whether he must or must not lick the lepers around him. Ultimately this difference in viewpoint leads to a difference in the warmth of the novels, and at times in *The Day* there is the feeling that the sigh with which West views "the truly monstrous" (p. 4) is just a trifle cold, as if the fear engendered by the starers were slowly turning the pity of the author into hysteria, disgust, and even hatred. This may have been the effect that West intended, but more likely he wished to gain an effect similar to that of *Miss Lonelyhearts*. The fact that he did not is probably a weakness in his art, not a defect of his heart.

In January of 1939 Bennett Cerf wrote West suggesting that he might aid the sales of *The Day* by meeting some of the book sellers of the West Coast and asking them for preferential treatment of the novel. West replied to this idea curtly, stating that he was extremely poor at such activity and wouldn't know how to go about it.[43] Still, West desperately wanted the book to sell. When the first reviews began to appear, West felt that the bad ones were intended almost as a conspiracy to keep the book from selling. In May he wrote to Cerf, asking if there seemed any possibility that the book might sell five thousand copies; semi-humorously he added that he was praying at the Shrine of St. Francis of Vine Street and hoped that his intercession might boost sales.[44] There was reason for his prayers, for if the book failed, he realized he would have to stay in Hollywood until he could save enough money to write another "flop."[45] His prayers were not answered. The sales of *The Day* from May to June of 1939 totaled 1486. Bennett Cerf, in answer to West's assertion that he felt he had come to the end of a certain kind of writing, wrote:

> Maybe you've got the right angle for your next book. I must say that a number of people expressed their distaste for *Day of the Locust* to me in very emphatic terms. Women readers in particular don't seem to like it, and it is women who read most of the novels that are sold today.[46]

Today it seems strange that *The Day* should have sold so poorly, even though the critical reception, as usual with West's novels, was a mixed one. Some critics drew back in

horror at the world presented and indicted the novel because its morbidness was untrue to life. Such critics found
that West's images turned "intended tragedy . . . into
screwball grotesques, and groggy author West can barely
distinguish fantastic shadows from fantastic substance."[47]
Other critics mixed praise with blame. George Milburn compared the part of the novel where Tod Hackett is lost on a
movie lot to Stephen Dedalus' vision of hell, and then added:

> The worst fault of the book is that it follows the
> choppy, episodical technique of a movie scenario. It
> has that peculiar disorganization that most movies have.
> Maybe this was deliberate on the part of the author;
> if so, I think it was ill advised. . . .
>
> But when Mr. West really gives a scene all he's
> got, it is something that will stick in your memory for
> a while . . . the book ends on a . . . picture of an
> American Walpurgis Eve that must make anyone who
> reads it feel he was there, too, and remember it as
> vividly.[48]

F. H. Britten compared the novel to *Miss Lonelyhearts:*

> *The Day of the Locust* is superbly written. Less on
> the surrealist side than Mr. West's earlier *Miss
> Lonelyhearts* it is a more disciplined piece of writing;
> has a flexibility and a finish which the previous novel
> lacked. But by comparison with the other *The Day of
> the Locust* is emotionally inert. Perhaps because of Mr.
> West's bitter awareness of the futility of his materials
> . . . he shows none of that intensity of feeling, that
> idealistic vehemence which marked *Miss Lonelyhearts*
> . . . as a great book.[49]

Some critics admitted the power of parts of the novel but
objected to the method by which West treated his world.
These critics felt that West should have made his world
"less like the strongly highlighted scenes of a bad dream";

he should have had "more thorough characterization, more documentation—most of all, perhaps, a few ordinary people."[50] Other critics did not insist that West write sociological studies in the guise of fiction but were willing to judge his accomplishment on its own terms. Clifton Fadiman was such a critic. Though Fadiman's claim that West was "the ablest of our surrealist authors" irritated West because of its emphasis on surrealism, still Fadiman was perceptive. He compared West's world to a madhouse but granted its peculiar power, a world with "all the fascination of a nice bit of phosphorescent decay."[51] Edmund Wilson's treatment of the novel was even more astute. This lengthy study in the *New Republic* was probably the most important critical notice West received in his lifetime. It congratulated him on avoiding the artistic betrayal which was the fate of so many authors who had gone to Hollywood. Wilson then went on to note that West's novel

> deals with the nondescript characters on the edges of the Hollywood studios. . . . And these people have been painted as distinctly and polished up as brightly as the figures in Persian miniatures. Their speech has been distilled with a sense of the flavorsome and the characteristic which makes John O'Hara seem pedestrian. Mr. West has footed a precarious way and has not slipped at any point into relying on the Hollywood values in describing the Hollywood people. . . . But Mr. West has stalked and caught some fine specimens of these Hollywood lepidoptera and impaled them on fastidious pins. Here are Hollywood restaurants, apartment houses, funeral churches, brothels, evangelical temples, and movie sets—in this latter connection, an extremely amusing episode of a man getting nightmarishly lost in the Battle of Waterloo. Mr. West's surrealist beginnings have stood him in good stead on the Coast.

> The doings of these people are bizarre, but they
> are also sordid and senseless. Mr. West has caught
> the emptiness of Hollywood; and he is, as far as I
> know, the first writer to make the emptiness
> horrible. . . .
> . . . Nathanael West has survived to write another
> remarkable book—in its peculiar combination of
> amenity of surface and felicity of form and style with
> ugly subject and somber feeling, quite unlike—as *Miss
> Lonelyhearts* was—the books of anyone else.[52]

The sum of the reviews, however, left West once again dis-
couraged. To F. Scott Fitzgerald he wrote, somewhat inac-
curately, that the book had received 15 per cent good reviews, 25 per cent bad ones, and 60 per cent violent personal
attacks. Despite such reviews, West concluded, he planned
to write another novel.[53]

West lived on in Hollywood as artist and movie crafts-
man. Toward the end of his stay, he met Eileen McKenney,
the sister of Ruth McKenney. Born in Indiana in 1913,
Eileen had been raised in Ohio, largely under the care of her
sister, and in 1935 she and her sister came to New York.
There, in Greenwich Village, they lived through the adventures that Ruth romanticized in a number of short pieces
that she published in *The New Yorker* and which she ultimately converted into the witty play *My Sister Eileen.*

A witty, self-effacing woman, Eileen was sentimental and
emotional, outgoing, impulsive, and vital, alive in every part
of her being; and she herself might well have succeeded as
a writer (or at least so St. Clair McKelway and Charles A.
Pearce thought), but she failed "because she was too busy
living."[54] Of her, a friend recalls:

> What Ruth wrote [about Eileen] and *The New
> Yorker* printed with pride and success and we at
> Harcourt's made into a successful book was and still

is pretty damned good, but . . . the life itself was such
a marvelous, exciting and successful imitation of art
that it surpassed art.[55]

Despite these qualities, there was considerable insecurity
in Eileen—implied by the slight stutter which affected her
in moments of tension—and both she and Ruth suffered in
different ways from the feeling that their parents had abandoned and betrayed them (their mother had died in Eileen's
youth, and their father had remarried soon after). Eileen,
possibly because of her deep need for love, was especially
vulnerable in her relations with men. In 1935 she married
Morris Jacobs and soon became pregnant, but before her
child was born she had separated from her husband. With
her sister and her child, she moved to New Milford, Connecticut, and there the two women tried to cope not only
with a six-month-old baby but also with a large mansion de-
void of plumbing and electricity.

While in Connecticut, Eileen became emotionally en-
tangled with the writer St. Clair McKelway, who had a
summer home near New Milford. When he returned to
New York in the fall he rented an apartment there for her.
Truly in love with McKelway, she yet found it difficult to
accept being his mistress, and her role left her feeling entrapped and guilty. In 1939 she broke with McKelway and
came to Hollywood. Soon she took a job at the Walt Disney
studios, and her buoyant wit and charm immediately made
her popular. She dated often—most especially such men as
John O'Hara and Donald Friede—but an affair with a press
agent left her feeling full of self-revulsion and convinced
that she was betraying her young son. Though she retained
a mask of gaiety, she condemned herself for promiscuity and
began to drink a good bit. It was at this time, in October,
1939, that West met her at an intimate dinner—West and
Eileen were the only guests—arranged by the Lester Coles.

197

Their attraction toward each other was instantaneous—
though West left Eileen terrified, when he drove her home,
by his reckless driving—and on April 19, 1940, with S. J.
Perelman as best man, the two were married. The marriage
may show some new maturity that had come to West. Earlier he had evinced a paradoxical mixture of idealization and
contempt for women. West's idealism often led him to say
that he could never marry anyone who was not as fine a
woman as his sister Laura. As the Victorian who wanted
women to be purer creatures than men, he was repelled by
the sexual gambit on which much of Hollywood conversation depended, and even more he was disgusted by the sexual
irregularities and boastfulness of some of his colleagues. His
attitude toward the double standard was also Victorian: "affairs might be all right for husbands but not for wives. . . .
His attitude was rigid."[56] West's earlier attitude also showed
contempt for woman, a creature whom he often referred to
as merely a *saccus stercoris*. But all of these attitudes must
have been modified by West's courtship and marriage to
Eileen. No frail, etherealized, Victorian virgin, she was
"breezy, independent, and outspoken,"[57] and she would have
been appalled by any suggestion of contempt or even con-
descension.

Even before he met Eileen, West seemed to be struggling
to escape from the emotional tensions that, knowingly or
unknowingly, were partially responsible for his despair.
After the financial failure of *The Day* he wrote his publisher in apparent seriousness (though possibly in mocking
irony): "I have come to the end of my interest in a certain
kind of writing. I have a new book planned which I intend
to keep extremely simple and full of the milk of human
kindness, and I am not joking, I really mean it."[58] Such a
letter implies the desire for artistic change, and now, with
his love and compassion for his Irish beauty, West may have

gained some human release as well. That sense is plain in such comments of his friends as:

> I am trying to convey a relationship that had a valued factor of fun in it. Despite the serious nature of West's work, he was adept at small jokes and delighted by the average foolishness of life. Eileen was sunny. She was good for him.[59]

West not only fell in love with Eileen but also became deeply attached to young Thomas Patrick, her son by a previous marriage. Eileen's first reaction to West was given to her sister in a letter:

> I met a man named Nathanael West—they call him Pep—last night. . . . Tonight is when he's coming for dinner. . . . I just now called up Dorscher and told her to stir up something not out of a can, for two. I mean, that way he could see Johnny [Tom], and I'm not sure Pep has very much money or not; these damned Hollywood feeding holes are *expensive*. Or do you think he'll mock the homey touch? I don't know. . . . I feel breathless and queer. Don't laugh, dearest Chubb, but after all these years, I *think* I am in love.[60]

Shortly after Eileen and West were married, Ruth McKenney received another letter:

> We are love-nest hunting: something simple, with about five bathrooms, a large garden, and indirect lighting. . . . $25 a month, naturally. PLEASE SEND AIRMAIL ALL DETAILS ON HOW TO GET A SECOND MORTGAGE. Although Pep may sell some story to Warner's, in which case we will go fishing in Oregon and start his new book which, frankly, is going to be the most important American novel since Dreiser, Hemingway, et cetera. Isn't it NICE to be married? Aren't we LUCKY?[61]

Such schoolgirl prose, all fresh and bubbly and sunny, reveals the kind of personality one would expect West to
choose. As Miss Herbst comments, West loved hunting because in the hunt sophistication was lost and the primitive
equalities ruled under a fresh, open, unspoiled sky. Perhaps
in Eileen he found the same essential innocence, still there
despite her own sufferings, and that freshness, added to his
own compassion, may have drawn him toward Eileen.

West and Eileen spent their three-month honeymoon in
Oregon, where West devoted much of his time to hunting
and fishing and planning his new novel. A humorous bone
of contention between them was the fact that West's "family," his two dogs Danny and Julie, had established their
sleeping quarters on West's bed, and neither the dogs nor
West saw any great need to change such a compatible arrangement. Eventually Eileen accepted the "family"

> with amiable grace. On their Oregon honeymoon
> they had to shut Julie in the cabin alone one day
> when they went fishing, and the indignant pointer
> decorated the whole room with a crisscross of toilet
> paper. No one was more amused than Eileen.[62]

On his return from his honeymoon West and his secretary, Jo Conway, left RKO studios, where they had worked
continuously since 1938. They accepted a well-paid position
with Columbia Pictures, and in the fall of 1940 a windfall
came when Columbia bought *A Cool Million,* as well as an
adaptation of the same novel done by West and Boris Ingster. The additional money made life pleasant, and numerous social evenings followed. Not naturally gregarious, West
was quiet but enjoyed himself. Eileen proved an expansive
social hostess as she kidded her husband and vivaciously be-
witched his friends with anecdotes that were only slightly
rooted in fact. The light humor set off an imaginative and

vitally alive Irish personality; soon West's friends loved her and she them.

The last social evening for the Wests occurred on Friday, December 13. On this occasion Scott Fitzgerald was present, and though a sick man, to be dead in another week and a day, he was in a pleasant mood. Enlivened by Eileen's wit, the evening passed harmoniously. It was fitting that it should. Dark, moustached, suave in appearance, West made a striking contrast, physically, to the wan, yet boyish, classically perfect handsomeness of Fitzgerald. Still, beneath the surface they were two men who had found in life the same tragedy, a peculiarly American tragedy, beginning with the optimistic quest of the Puritans for a better world, continuing on through the determined pioneering of those who hopefully went Westerin' in the nineteenth century, and carrying forward into the twentieth century with the pathetic faith of those idealists who were confident that the war to end all wars would bring a rebirth of human aspiration and dignity. These were dreams, and Scott Fitzgerald had heard the mockery. In Jay Gatsby he had painted an unforgettable figure: the American who sees the green light of the future, beckoning, ever beckoning. More important, Fitzgerald saw that the green light, the Daisy toward which Gatsby yearned, could not escape the corruption of the past. Daisy was unworthy of her pursuer, but a dreamer, as Fitzgerald knew, must dream, and Gatsby was a man who

> believed in the green light, the orgiastic future that
> year by year recedes before us. It eluded us then,
> but that's another matter—tomorrow we will run
> faster, stretch out our arms farther. . . . And one fine
> morning—[63]

Like Gatsby, we die. Fitzgerald saw the mockery. Deep in his bones, Nathanael West felt it. He had written about nothing else.

The evening ended, and a few days later West and Eileen set out on another trip, this time a brief one to northern Mexico. They were returning to Hollywood on December 22, 1940, in their heavy station wagon, when West failed to see a stop sign at an intersection near El Centro, California. The road was wet from an earlier rain, and his car plowed into a smaller sedan. Eileen died on the way to the hospital. West died shortly after arriving there. Only the fine hunting dog that was with them managed to step free from the wreckage.

The eventual death certificate gave the cause of death for both Eileen and West as skull fractures. A friend of West, Charles Katz, made the arrangements by which West's body was shipped to New York for burial. In Mount Zion Cemetery, Queens, Nathanael West was buried.

Conclusion

IN THE HOME into which the Wests had recently moved, at
12706 Magnolia Boulevard, much was still undone. Cartons
of household furnishings, newly purchased, were still un-
opened. Christmas presents, recently wrapped, waited to be
opened. A letter to the Perelmans, still unfinished, rested in
the typewriter.

The things left undone mattered only to a few people, for
West was practically unknown. The report of his death in
the *New York Times* gave West almost no recognition: his
name was misspelled, his age was incorrect, only three of

his novels were mentioned and two of these were given incorrect titles, Eileen was featured in the headline of the story, and the facts of Eileen's life received much more space than those of West's. The final irony is that the story appeared on the amusements and movie page.[1]

Since the time of his death, however, West has become known to the literary world. In April, 1946, Marcel Sibon's translation of *Miss Lonelyhearts* appeared in France and caused considerable stir there. Philippe Soupault's introduction to the edition noted:

Nathanael West is probably . . . the writer of his generation who has most willingly accepted being known as an American. He has not looked for excuses, he has not been willing to appeal to the enchantments of landscapes, to local color, or to the delusions of the subconscious. He is as straightforward as an arrow and as direct as a scalpel. At the same time that his contemporaries, the writers of the lost generation, never hesitated to say too much, West never desired to go far enough. When one spoke to him, or when he wrote, he gave the impression that he imparted only what he believed, not the essential, but the most significant. . . .

Thus West has proposed to the men of his time—and this is, in my opinion, what gives his work all its importance—to be dupes of nothing. Now, in the United States, more than in any other country, one risks letting himself be fooled ceaselessly by the deceptions of a happy civilization, but one which is built on appearances. There exists a sort of command for happiness. It is, moreover, written into the Constitution of the United States. He who is unhappy is suspect. Almost all the American novelists, even if they do not acknowledge it, have started from this principle, that one is born to be happy. Nathanael West has flatly denied this principle.*

Since 1946 various editions of *Miss Lonelyhearts*, *A Cool Million*, and *The Day of the Locust* have appeared in England and America, and the American paperback editions of *Miss Lonelyhearts* and *The Day* have sold in the hundreds of thousands. The publication of West's *Complete Works* in 1957 brought awesome critical acclaim. The review in *The New Yorker* stated that the book "contains some of the best writing that has been produced by an American in this century"; in treating "the big, significant things". . . West wrote "to greater effect, in my opinion, than Fitzgerald, who lacked West's capacity for intelligent self criticism, or even Hemingway, whose view of life seems to me rather more limited than West's."[3] An initial scholarly bibliography by William White covered eighteen pages and was soon followed by a lengthy supplement devoted to writing about

---

* My translation from the French text:
Nathanaël West est probablement . . . l'écrivain de sa génération . . . qui a accepté le plus volontiers de se savoir américain. Il n'a pas cherché d'excuses, il n'a pas voulu faire appel aux prestiges des paysages, à la couleur locale, ni aux mirages du subconscient. Il est direct comme une flèche et franc comme le scalpel. Alors que ses contemporains, les écrivains de la génération perdue, n'hésitèrent jamais à trop dire, West n'en voulut jamais dire assez. Quand on lui parlait ou quand il écrivait, on gardait l'impression qu'il ne livrait que ce qu'il croyait, non pas l'essentiel, mais le plus significatif. . . .
Ainsi, West a proposé aux hommes de son temps—et c'est, à mon avis, ce qui donne à son oeuvre toute sa valeur—de n'être dupes de rien. Or, aux Etats-Unis, plus que dans aucun autre pays, on risque de se laisser prendre sans cesse aux ruses d'une civilisation heureuse mais qui est construite sur les apparences. Il existe une sorte de consigne du bonheur. Elle est, d'ailleurs, inscrite dans la Constitution des Etats-Unis. Qui est malheureux est suspect. Presque tous les romanciers américains, même s'ils ne l'avouent pas, sont partis de ce principe, qu'on naît pour être heureux. Nathanaël West a refusé nettement ce principe.[2]

West's art. In late 1957 Howard Teichmann's play *Miss Lonelyhearts,* based on West's novel, appeared on Broadway; in 1959 the movie *Lonelyhearts* was produced, with some artistic pretensions, by Dore Schary; and since the present volume (in an earlier edition) was published in 1961, three books and one lengthy monograph have appeared. It would seem that the cult of Westians—for the passionate few who ultimately preserve the name of a writer have always admired West—is broadening to formidable proportions. Why?

No easy answer can be given. Certainly the universe of West, like that of Hemingway, is a limited one, and it repels rather than attracts. Its gloom is even deeper and the hopelessness more profound than the despair of the sad young men of the twenties who proclaimed, a little self-pityingly, their courage and stoicism in a world they never made. In West's world the normality of such a creature as Betty stands out because it is so rare and because it is so based in blindness. The anti-Christ figure of Shrike dominates this world, and he shouts that love is dead, screams that the only miracle of our time is man's ability to walk on his own water. It is a universe of Darwinistic competition: animal struggles with animal (we all eat each other in one way or another), actor conflicts with audience, dream opposes fact, and spirit struggles with flesh.

The consequences of such a competitive world are grotesqueness and violence. In their grotesqueness, West's characters are more pathetic than tragic. In their entrapment they are similar to the dogs, birds, lambs, flies, lizards, and cocks to which West compares them, but they are unlike the ensnared quail in *The Day* who sings sweetly, with neither anxiety nor hope. Instead, theirs is a more bitter lament, for they are entrapped between, always between, the animal and the spiritual. In *Balso Snell,* B. Hamlet Darwin contemplates the depths of this dilemma: "Terrible indeed was the competition in which his hearers spent their lives, a competition that demanded their being more than animals" (p. 55). Frustration and then violence result from this unfair competition. Therefore not only grotesques like John Raskolnikov Gilson, Miss Lonelyhearts, Lemuel Pitkin, Homer Simpson, and Faye Greener parade through the world of West; violence also stalks the action and the imagery. This violence largely lacks motivation, for West believed violence in America was so common as to need, in art, no justification or explanation. But though individual acts of violence need no lengthy artistic motivations, the commonness of American violence does need some explanation. For West, the implied cause for the omnipresence of American violence is the fact that mass man has deep within him a rage against the trick that life plays upon man. So much does life promise, so little does it give. Mass man senses this deception, rages against it, and commits violence because of it.

Truly West's universe is a limited one, but as the novelist himself pointed out, to introduce the normal into it would be to destroy its very fabric, to make mockery of the nightmare whole. Though limited, it is a valid universe; to deny its existence is to deny the existence, in all their horror, of nightmares. But nightmares do exist, despite some critics who insist on "healthiness" as the basic essential for a truly American literature. A major vein of American creative writing asserts the horrors that some authors have perceived. Often these writers were troubled by the same nightmare that perturbed West: the dual nature of man and the resultant quest. Melville, for instance, is obsessed, in one form or another, with "chronometricals," or heavenly time, as opposed to "horologicals," or earthly time; and when Pierre tries to live by chronometrical time and ideals, he is soon destroyed by a world incapable of rising beyond expediency and "horological" ideals. Twain constantly rails at man, who is merely animal but who creates his own misery by his invention of some higher "moral nature" at which to aim. Hemingway envisions peace in the "high, cold, dry" country of Switzerland, a world seemingly of "peace" and "service," but the death of Catherine in this apparently spiritual world makes Lt. Henry aware that there is really no more peace in Switzerland than in the chaos of the retreat from Caporetto. All these writers are aware of the nightmare in which man dreams of a life of peace, a life of the spirit, but is foiled by the basic pragmatic facts: life is struggle and man is flesh. Man's dangling forever in the nightmare between the dream and the fact constantly tormented Eugene O'Neill. In *The Hairy Ape*, the hero Yank observes the gorilla in a cage at the end of the play; talking to the gorilla, Yank gropes for truth:

> It's dis way, what I'm drivin' at. Youse can sit and
> dope dream in de past, green woods, de jungle and de
> rest of it. . . . I ain't on oith and I ain't in Heaven,
> get me? I'm in de middle tryin' to separate 'em, takin'
> all de woist punches from bot' of 'em. Maybe dat's
> what dey call hell, huh?[4]

And, of course, the torment of dangling is neither a strictly American nor a purely twentieth-century phenomenon. One senses it, despite the final optimism and the cold reason, in Alexander Pope; for him, man is a creature who

> . . . hangs between; in doubt to act or rest;
> In doubt to deem himself a God, or Beast;
> In doubt his Mind or Body to prefer;
> Born but to die, and reas'ning but to err. . . .

The struggle is perhaps most powerfully expressed in the eternal tension that drives Dostoevsky's grotesques on to acts both of incomparable saintliness and haunting deviltry.

In these terms all men are really marginal creatures, forever dangling. This fundamental psychological truth about man Jung expresses when he points out that life is energy and energy is conflict:

> Everything human is relative, because everything
> depends on a condition of inner antithesis; for every-
> thing subsists as a phenomenon of energy. Energy
> depends necessarily upon a pre-existing antithesis,
> without which there could be no energy. There must
> always be present height and depth, heat and cold,
> etc., in order that the process of equalization—which
> is energy—can take place. All life is energy and there-
> fore depends on forces held in opposition.[5]

From this, it follows that the libido, or psychic energy, is always, to some degree, in conflict, constantly questing and never finding its object permanently. Men, some more than others, have the universal problem of finding harmony and balance and peace, but though they seek them, men have no chance, while alive, of becoming free of tension. Things always are becoming, they never are: the universe is controlled by the Heraclitean principle, so often cited in Jung.

The fact of flux—the sun rises and sets, man wakes and sleeps, the moon goes through its phases, youth begets age and age begets youth—is, if not the perfect archetypal idea, as close to it as it is possible to come. Test it by Jung's clarification:

> I have often been asked whence come these archetypes
> or primordial images. . . . It seems to me that their
> origin can be explained in no other way than by
> regarding them as the deposits of the oft-repeated
> experiences of humanity. A common, yet, at the same
> time, most impressive experience is the daily apparent
> movement of the sun. We certainly cannot discover
> anything about it in the unconscious, in so far as

the physical processes known to us are concerned,
but we do find the sun myth there in all its innumerable
modifications. It is this myth that forms the sun
archetype, and not the physical process. The same can
be said of the phases of the moon. The archetype is
a disposition to produce over and over again the same,
or similar mythical conceptions.[6]

In using the concept of the dangling man, then, West is
first of all expressing a psychological truth. More important
for his art, he is dramatizing an archetypal idea which has
the power to move the reader excessively. Though it is possible that West's awareness of the tragicalness of man's marginal nature was intensified because of its close similarity to
his own bicultural status, how he gained such perception is
really irrelevant. The only valid appraisal of his nightmares
is the test of their congruousness and their power. West's
writing stands such tests. To use the word of Henry James,
West's world is *done*, not *done* in any realistic or natural-
istic sense, but still *done*. Most of all, it is realized in surrealistic conceits. These, more than any other single thing, make
for the horrid, nightmare quality of West's universe. The
conceits demonstrate man's role as a clown in a foolish
dream-play called life, and the poor art of the Creator and
Director of the dream-play seems evident in the fact that
the machinery creaks and the still-life background is just
as phony as the death rattles of the actors. In this world of
conceits the animal appetites of man become a chauffeur
"dressed in ugly, ready made clothing. His shoes, soiled from
walking about in the streets of a great city, are covered with
animal ordure and chewing gum" (p. 29, *Balso Snell*). Christ
becomes a newspaper advice-to-the-lovelorn columnist or
a bright fly tantalizing this world of fish. The Horatio Alger
hero becomes an innocent roaming in a world of confidence
men, and he dies to ensure the birth of American fascism.

Love becomes a vending machine, a place of deposit. Life becomes a fraud devised by some super Hollywood producer.

These conceits, pictorially, symbolically, and dramatically, help to create a world of irreconcilable conflict, where life is not to be taken seriously but is really a terrible prank played by some malevolent prankster. In a world where even the continued existence, to say nothing of the meaning and importance, of the human race is open to question, West's world of conflict and dreams has the ring of truth for even the most common of common men.

In a significant way the influence of West's art and vision is also evident in the writings of a number of contemporary writers. At times, as in his story "Me and Miss Mandible," Donald Barthelme uses experimental techniques which in their violation of the common-sense world seem to draw their inspiration from *The Dream Life of Balso Snell*. Without doubt Terry Southern's use of surrealistic distortions and transformations in his novel *Candy*, as well as his emphasis upon the fleshly appetites of man, draws upon West's first novel for aspects of its conception. In addition the black humor of Joseph Heller's *Catch-22*, where man has entrapped himself by the political, military, and social lies he has invented, probably owes a considerable debt to West's frightening ironies and conceits. But more than anyone else, those contemporary American writers who have exploited the character of the suffering man owe a debt to West, one probably greater even than to Dostoevsky, for the artistic manipulation of their narratives. Bernard Malamud's *The Assistant,* Normal Mailer's *The Deer Park*, and Kurt Vonnegut's *God Bless You, Mr. Rosewater* bear Westian marks in their depiction of men suffering for the agonies of their fellows. Likewise, Flannery O'Connor, in her novel *Wise Blood*, has depicted—though with a more orthodox religious intent than West would have conceived —a world of violence and shadows inhabited by grotesques. This world is strongly reminiscent of that of West, and is made even more so by the inclusion of a fanatic who is doomed, in spite of himself, to deep religious fervor and an ironic martyrdom.

No writer, however, reveals the influence of West more fully than Edward Lewis Wallant (whose artistic growth was cut short by his tragic death in 1962 at the age of 36). In all of his novels—*The Human Season, The Pawnbroker, The Tenants of Moonbloom,* and *The Children at the Gate* —Wallant dramatizes the kinds of characters with whom West was so obsessed (and whom William James would have categorized as morbid-minded in their religious probings). But in *The Tenants* and *The Children*, both of them novels of considerable merit, Wallant has especially drawn upon the central dramatic conceit of *Miss Lonelyhearts.* Where West, however, has Miss Lonelyhearts undergo his religious experience because of the letters he receives from the tormented of the universe, the major characters of *The Tenants* and *The Children* receive the impetus for their ordeals from slightly different reasons: the protagonist of *The Tenants* sees the ugliness and the agony in the lives of the slum apartment tenants from whom he must collect rents; the protagonist of *The Children*, a young cynic who denies all save the flesh, sees the pain of the innocent victims in the hospital where he comes to take small orders for the pharmacy in which he works. Major characters in both novels, one the rent collector and the other a Jewish orderly, agonize as fully as Miss Lonelyhearts does over the doomed whom they cannot aid. In both *The Tenants* and *The Children* Wallant's characters experience, as does Miss Lonelyhearts, the torment which is life by seeing realized before them the torment which life actually is. In *The Children*, which, like all of Wallant's novels, is written in stark Westian sentences filled with shadows and implications (as, for instance, in the hysterical laughter of the clownish, suffering, Jewish orderly, so like the laughter of the Greeners in *The Day of the Locust*), Wallant especially contrasts the concepts of the material and the spiritual, and the climax of the novel, in which the Christ-like orderly is impaled upon an iron fence-rail, is the kind that West himself would have appreciated.

Such writers as these, added to the growing audience which West's art commands, imply the artistic truth of West's vision. Limited though it is, its despair cries out from the heart with the honesty, the seriousness, and the power to assure that it will not soon be forgotten. For more and more readers the Quest of West's heroes and the constant frustration of that Quest are comparable to their own hopes and frustrations.

Notes

1. Walter J. Degnan, Principal of De Witt Clinton High School, to James F. Light, November 6, 1957.

2. James R. Strawbridge, Recorder of Tufts University, to James F. Light, November 15, 1960.

3. The facts concerning the confusion between two Nathan Weinsteins are from letters and documents from James R. Strawbridge, Recorder of Tufts University, dated November 22, 1957, November 1, 1960, and November 15, 1960; from Milton E. Noble, Recorder of Brown University, dated September 21, 1960, and October 20, 1960; and from Kimball S. Elkins,

Senior Assistant in the Harvard University Archives, dated October 11, 1960, and October 21, 1960. Although the records do not bluntly state that West was given the credits earned at Harvard and Tufts by the Boston Nathan Weinstein, no other explanation seems possible. Mr. Strawbridge notes, November 9, 1960: "I am pleased to have an explanation of the difficulty we have been in regarding Weinstein-West. I have read with interest your manuscript explanation and have also reviewed the record again to be sure we were correct. I find one technical error [on whether West entered Tufts as a candidate for the B.A. or B.S. degree]. . . . I find that I can concur with the rest of your manuscript as far as the records at Tufts can be interpreted."

4. Ira S. Robbins, once a camp counselor at Camp Paradox, to James F. Light, October 23, 1957.

5. John Sanford, "Nathanael West," *The Screen Writer* (December, 1946), p. 12.

6. *Ibid.*

7. Philip Lukin to James F. Light, December 12, 1957. I might note here that my debt to Mr. Lukin extends beyond any acknowledgment through quotation marks. His contributions permeate much of the factual treatment of West's college years.

8. Jeremiah Mahoney to James F. Light, February 20, 1958.

9. Quentin Reynolds, from the original manuscript of "When 'Pep' was a Ghost," *Brown Alumni Monthly* (December, 1957). This portion of the manuscript was omitted from the published version. The original manuscript is in the possession of Mr. Reynolds.

10. Reynolds, "When 'Pep' was a Ghost," p. 8.

11. Mahoney to Light, February 20, 1958.

12. *Ibid.*

13. Frank O. Hough to James F. Light, March 4, 1958.

14. Reynolds to Light, November, 1957.

15. F. Scott Fitzgerald, "Sleeping and Waking," in *The Crack Up,* ed. Edmund Wilson (New York, n.d.), p. 66.

16. Quoted in Lillian Ross, "How Do You Like It Now, Gentlemen?", *The New Yorker* (May 13, 1950), pp. 42–43.

17. Lukin to Light, December 12, 1957.

18. Mahoney to Light, February 20, 1958.

19. *Ibid.*

20. Lukin to Light, December 12, 1957.

21. *Ibid.*

22. Mahoney to Light, February 20, 1958.

23. Lukin to Light, February 20, 1958.

24. Reynolds to Light, November, 1957.

25. *Ibid.*

26. Hough to Light, March 4, 1958.

27. *Ibid.*

28. Lukin to Light, December 12, 1957.

29. Reynolds to Light, November, 1957.

30. Lukin to Light, December 12, 1957.

31. Hough to Light, March 4, 1958.

32. Mahoney to Light, January 24, 1958.

33. Everett V. Stonequist, "The Marginal Character of the Jews," in *Jews in a Gentile World,* ed. Isacque Graeber and Steuart Henderson Britt (New York, 1942), p. 307.

34. Lukin to Light, December 12, 1957.

35. William A. Dyer, Jr., to James F. Light, March 16, 1958.

36. Hough to Light, April 13, 1958.

37. *Ibid.*

38. Lukin to Light, February 20, 1958.

39. Mahoney to Light, February 20, 1958.

40. Mahoney to Light, March 10, 1958.

41. Hough to Light, April 13, 1958.

42. I. J. Kapstein to James F. Light, August 23, 1952.

43. Percy Marks, *The Plastic Age* (New York, 1924), p. 225.

44. Lukin to Light, May 16, 1958.

45. Hough to Light, April 13, 1958.

46. John Monk to James F. Light, February 2, 1958.

47. Arthur Machen, *The Hill of Dreams* (New York, 1923), p. 243.

48. Mahoney to Light, February 20, 1958.

49. Kapstein, *op. cit.*

50. Mahoney to Light, February 20, 1958.

51. Lukin to Light, November 12, 1959.

52. Monk, *op. cit.*

53. Nathan von Wallenstein-Weinstein, "Death," *Casements* (June, 1924), p. 15.

54. Nathan von Wallenstein-Weinstein, "Euripides—A Playwright," *Casements* (July, 1923), unpaginated.

55. Lukin to Light, April 11, 1959.

56. Reynolds, "When 'Pep' was a Ghost," p. 9.

57. *Liber Brunensis,* Brown College Yearbook (Providence, 1924), unpaginated.

58. Mahoney to Light, February 20, 1958.

CHAPTER TWO

1. John Sanford to James F. Light, August 8, 1958.

2. *Ibid.*

3. *Ibid.*

4. *Ibid.*

5. A. J. Liebling, "Shed a Tear for Mr. West," *New York World Telegram* (June 24, 1931), p. 11.

6. Nathanael West, "L'Affaire Beano," an unpublished short story quoted in Richard Gehman's Introduction to Nathanael West, *The Day of the Locust,* New Directions' New Classics Series (New York, 1950), p. xiv.

7. Translation quoted in Marcel Raymond, *From Baudelaire to Surrealism* (New York, 1950), p. 270.

8. The French is from *Lettres de guerre* (Paris: Au San Pareil, 1919), p. 9, and the passage defines Dada humor as *"un sens . . . de l'inutilité theatrale (et sans joie) detout, quand on sait."*

9. Translation quoted in Raymond, p. 286.

10. J. K. Huysmans, *Against the Grain,* trans. John Howard (New York, 1922), pp. 106–7.

11. Wallace Fowlie, *Age of Surrealism* (New York, 1950), pp. 24–25.

12. Professor I. J. Kapstein, of Brown University, to James F. Light, August 23, 1952.

13. Norman Podhoretz, "A Particular Kind of Joking," *The New Yorker* (May 18, 1957), p. 144.

14. Liebling, *loc. cit.*

15. Hans Arp, "Notes from a Diary," trans. Eugene Jolas, *Transition Workshop,* ed. Eugene Jolas (New York, 1949), p. 334.

16. *Ibid.*

17. Tristan Tzara, "Dada Manifesto 1918," *The Dada Painters and Poets,* ed. Robert Motherwell (New York, 1951), pp. 78–80.

18. Liebling, *loc. cit.*

19. *Ibid.*

CHAPTER THREE

1. John Sanford to James F. Light, April 11, 1959.

2. Jeremiah Mahoney to James F. Light, March 10, 1958.

3. Dr. Saul Jarcho to James F. Light, September 20, 1957.

4. Sanford to Light, April 11, 1959.

5. *Ibid.*

6. *Ibid.*

7. Quentin Reynolds, from the original manuscript of "When 'Pep' was a Ghost."

8. James T. Farrell to Richard Gehman, January 29, 1947.

9. Edmund Wilson to Cyril Schneider, April 30, 1952.

10. *Ibid.*

11. Sidney Jarcho to James F. Light, August 16, 1957.

12. *Ibid.*

13. Dr. Jarcho to Light, September 20, 1957.

14. John Sanford, "Nathanael West," *The Screen Writer* (December, 1946), p. 13.

15. Sanford to Light, April 11, 1959.

16. *Ibid.*

17. *Ibid.*

18. *Ibid.*

19. William Carlos Williams, *The Autobiography* (New York, 1951), pp. 301–2.

20. Nathanael West to William Carlos Williams, October 10, 1931. The letter is in the Williams collection held by the Lockwood Memorial Library of the University of Buffalo.

21. Josephine Herbst to James F. Light, October 22, 1952.

22. Nathanael West to Josephine Herbst, undated.

23. Nathan Asch to James F. Light, November, 1952.

24. *Ibid.*

25. Sanford to Light, August 8, 1958.

26. Nathanael West, "Some Notes on *Miss Lonelyhearts*," *Contempo* (May 15, 1933), p. 2.

27. *Ibid.*

28. *Ibid.*

29. Nathanael West, "Some Notes on Violence," *Contact* (October, 1932), p. 132.

30. John Sanford, "Nathanael West," *op. cit.*

31. Information in a letter quoted in an unpublished paper by Richard Gehman, "Miss Lonelyhearts and the Surrealists."

32. Quoted in Rene Fuellop-Miller, *Fyodor Dostoevsky* (New York, 1950), p. 56.

33. J. K. Huysmans, *Là Bas,* trans. Keene Wallis (Evanston and New York, 1958), p. 101.

34. *Ibid.*

35. *Ibid.*

36. *Ibid.*

37. West's indebtedness to Baudelaire, and specifically to the prose poem "Anywhere Out of This World," is treated at some length in Marc L. Ratner's " 'Anywhere Out of This World': Baudelaire and Nathanael West," *American Literature* (January, 1960), pp. 456–63.

38. West, "Some Notes on *Miss Lonelyhearts*," p. 2.

39. *Ibid.*, p. 1.

40. *Ibid.*, p. 2.

41. James T. Farrell, *Studs Lonigan,* from the author's Introduction, Modern Library (New York, 1938), pp. vii–viii.

42. *Boston Transcript Book Review* (July 26, 1933), p. 2.

43. William Troy, "Four Newer Novelists," *The Nation,* (June 14, 1933), p. 673.

44. *Harrison's Reports* (August 26, 1933), p. 4.

45. T. C. Wilson, "American Humor," *The Saturday Review,* (May 13, 1933), p. 589.

46. "Miss Lonelyhearts," *New York Times Book Review* (April 23, 1933), p. 6.

47. Angel Flores, "Miss Lonelyhearts in the Haunted Castle," *Contempo* (July 25, 1933), p. 1.

48. Josephine Herbst, *"Miss Lonelyhearts:* an Allegory," *Contempo* (July 25, 1933), p. 4.

49. William Carlos Williams, "Sordid? Good God!" *Contempo* (July 25, 1933), p. 5.

50. Nathanael West to Josephine Herbst, May 31, 1932.

CHAPTER FOUR

1. Dr. Saul Jarcho to James F. Light, September 20, 1957.

2. Nathanael West, "Business Deal," *Americana* (October, 1933), p. 14.

3. *Ibid.,* p. 15.

4. Nathanael West to Josephine Herbst, March 4, 1932.

5. Malcolm Cowley to Richard Gehman, February 21, 1947.

6. John Sanford, "Nathanael West," *The Screen Writer* (December, 1946), p. 11.

7. *Ibid.,* p. 13.

8. Mrs. Richard Pratt to James F. Light, November 20, 1952.

9. Charles and Mary Beard, *America in Midpassage* (New York, 1939), I, 65–66.

10. Dixon Wecter, *The Age of the Great Depression* (New York, 1948), p. 39.

11. Quoted in Charles and Mary Beard, *op. cit.*, I, 100.

12. Quoted in Charles and Mary Beard, *op. cit.*, I, 100.

13. Quoted in Charles and Mary Beard, *op. cit.*, I, 101.

14. Quoted in Charles and Mary Beard, *op. cit.*, I, 101.

15. Reinhold Niebuhr, "Catastrophe or Social Control?" *Harper's Magazine* (June, 1932), p. 118.

16. Quoted in an NBC Television Documentary: "Life in the Thirties."

17. *Ibid.*

18. Nathanael West, "Christmass Poem," *Contempo* (February 21, 1933), p. 4.

19. Edward Newhouse to James F. Light, July 31, 1952.

20. James T. Farrell to Richard Gehman, January 29, 1947.

21. *Ibid.*

22. Nathanael West to Josephine Herbst, March 24, 1932.

23. "Editorial," *Americana* (November, 1932), front-page cover.

24. *Ibid.*

25. Gilbert Seldes, "Editorial," *Americana* (December, 1932), front-page cover.

26. Nathanael West to Jack Conroy, quoted in Richard Gehman's Introduction to Nathanael West, *The Day of the Locust*, New Classics (New York, 1950), p. x.

27. Robert M. Coates to Cyril Schneider, June 6, 1952.

28. Newhouse to Light, July 31, 1952.

29. Lewis Gannett, "A Cool Million," *New York Herald Tribune*, book section (June 21, 1934), p. 19.

30. "A Cool Million," *New York Post* (June 23, 1934), p. 7.

31. Fred T. Marsh, "A Cool Million," *New York Times Book Review* (July 1, 1934), p. 6.

32. "A Gallery of Novels," *New Republic* (July 18, 1934), p. 271.

33. I. J. Kapstein to James F. Light, August 23, 1952.

CHAPTER FIVE

1. John Sanford to James F. Light, August 8, 1958.

2. Wells Root to Richard Gehman. This letter was written around 1947 and is in Mr. Gehman's possession.

3. See J. G. Fraser, *The Golden Bough* (London, 1913), Vol. II, "The Scapegoat." The most pertinent chapters are "Public Scape-Goats," "On Scapegoats in General," and "Human Scape-goats in Classical Antiquity."

4. Everett V. Stonequist, "The Marginal Character of the Jews," in *Jews in a Gentile World*, ed. Isacque Graeber and Steuart Henderson Britt (New York, 1942), p. 297.

5. Will Herberg, *Protestant, Catholic, Jew* (New York, 1956), p. 31.

6. Herman Hesse, *Steppenwolf*, trans. Basil Creighton (New York, 1929), p. 28.

7. Saul Bellow, *Henderson the Rain King* (New York, 1959), p. 329.

CHAPTER SIX

1. Robert M. Coates to Cyril Schneider, June 6, 1952.

2. Jo Conway to James F. Light, January 15, 1958.

3. Frank Nugent [Review of *The President's Mystery*], *New York Times* (October 19, 1936), p. 22.

4. Douglas W. Churchill, "Rumors in Hollywood," *New York Times* (October 4, 1936), section x, p. 5.

5. Frank Nugent, *op. cit.*

6. Meyer Levin, "The Candid Cameraman," *Esquire* (December, 1936), p. 134.

7. *Ibid.*, pp. 134, 136.

8. Frank Nugent [Review of *Five Came Back*], *New York Times* (July 5, 1939), p. 20.

9. Wells Root to Richard Gehman. Quoted in Gehman's Introduction to Nathanael West, *The Day of the Locust*, New Classics (New York, 1950), pp. xviii–xix.

10. *Ibid.*

11. *Spirit of Culver*, screenplay by Nathanael West and Whitney Bolton. A copy of the shooting typescript is in the New York Public Library.

12. Whitney Bolton to James F. Light, September 20, 1957.

13. Wells Root to James F. Light, July 6, 1959.

14. *Ibid.*

15. *Ibid.*

16. *Ibid.*

17. William Faulkner to Cyril Schneider, July, 1954.

18. Stuart McGowan to James F. Light, February 26, 1958.

19. Jo Conway, *op. cit.*

20. *Ibid.*

21. Brooks Atkinson [Review of *Good Hunting*], *New York Times* (November 22, 1938), p. 26.

22. Leo C. Rosten, *Hollywood* (New York, 1941), p. 308.

23. Henry Hart, ed., *American Writers Congress* (New York, 1935), p. 10.

24. Jo Conway, *op. cit.*

25. Whitney Bolton, *op. cit.*

26. James T. Farrell to Cyril Schneider, March 25, 1952.

27. Nathanael West to Malcolm Cowley, May 11, 1939.

28. Whitney Bolton, *op. cit.*

29. Robert Coates, *op. cit.*

30. James T. Farrell, *op. cit.*

31. Allan Seager to Cyril Schneider, April 15, 1952.

32. Josephine Herbst to James F. Light, October 22, 1952.

33. Nathanael West to George Milburn. Quoted in Gehman's Introduction to *The Day*, p. xxii.

34. Nathanael West to Saxe Cummins, January 13, 1939.

35. Nathanael West to George Milburn, April 6, 1939.

36. Nathanael West to Edmund Wilson. Quoted in Gehman's Introduction to *The Day*, p. xviii.

37. Robert Coates, *op. cit.*

38. *Ibid.*

39. Nathanael West to Saxe Cummins, January 26, 1939.

40. Trans. by Stanley Kunitz, *An Anthology of French Poetry from Nerval to Valéry in English Translation*, ed. Angel Flores (New York, 1958), p. 18.

41. Nathanael West to Jack Conroy. Quoted in Gehman's Introduction to *The Day*, pp. ix–x.

42. Nathanael West, "Soft Soap for the Barber," *New Republic* (November, 1934), p. 23.

43. Nathanael West to Bennett Cerf, January 13, 1939.

44. West to Cerf, May 29, 1939.

45. West to Cerf, January 13, 1939.

46. Cerf to West, June 16, 1939.

47. "Truly Monstrous," *Time* (June 19, 1939), p. 84.

48. George Milburn, "The Hollywood Nobody Knows," *Saturday Review* (May 20, 1939), pp. 14–15.

49. F. H. Britten, *Books* (May 21, 1939), p. 7.

50. Louis Salomon, "The Day of the Locust," *The Nation* (July 15, 1939), pp. 78–79.

51. Clifton Fadiman, "The Day of the Locust," *The New Yorker* (May 20, 1939), p. 79.

52. The original article was entitled "Hollywood Dance of Death" and appeared in *New Republic* (July 26, 1939), pp. 339–40. I have quoted from the reprinted revision entitled "Postscript," which appeared in *Classics and Commercials* (New York, 1950), pp. 53–55.

53. Nathanael West to F. Scott Fitzgerald, June 30, 1939. The letter is in the possession of Princeton University Library.

54. Charles A. Pearce to James F. Light, June 8, 1959.

55. *Ibid.*

56. Josephine Herbst, *op. cit.*

57. Root to Light, July 6, 1959.

58. West to Cerf, June 13, 1939.

59. Root to Light, July 6, 1959.

60. Eileen McKenney to Ruth McKenney, quoted in Ruth McKenney's *Love Story* (New York, 1950), pp. 175–76.

61. *Ibid.*, p. 176.

62. Root to Light, July 6, 1959.

63. F. Scott Fitzgerald, *The Great Gatsby* (New York, 1925), p. 218.

CHAPTER SEVEN

1. *New York Times* (December 23, 1940), p. 23. For a full discussion of the history of West's critical reputation see William

White, "IIow Forgotten Was Nathanael West?" *American Book Collector* (December, 1957), pp. 13–17.

2. Nathanael West, *Mademoiselle Cœur Brisé*, trans. by Marcelle Sibon and with an intro. by Philippe Soupault (Paris, 1946), pp. 11–12.

3. Norman Podhoretz, "A Particular Kind of Joking," *The New Yorker* (May 18, 1957), p. 156.

4. Eugene O'Neill, *The Hairy Ape, Anna Christie, The First Man* (New York, 1922), p. 85.

5. C. G. Jung, *Two Essays in Analytical Psychology*, trans. H. G. and C. F. Baynes (New York, 1928), p. 79.

6. *Ibid.*

Index

73, 81–82; vacation in Adirondacks, 75–77; co-editor of *Contact*, 78–79; leaves the Sutton Hotel, 81; end of engagement to Miss Shepard, 82; publishing problems of *Miss Lonelyhearts*, 82; reaction to reviews of *Miss Lonelyhearts*, 106–10; works in Hollywood for Twentieth Century-Fox, 111–13; returns to East, 113; residence in Bucks County, Pa., 116–19; reaction to depression, 123–26; political ideas, 123–27; association with *Americana* magazine, 125–27; reaction to reviews of *A Cool Million*, 138–40; hired as screen writer by Republic studios, 154; screenplay writings, 111–13, 154–60; liberal activities in Hollywood, 165–67; revulsion from Hollywood vulgarism

and grotesqueness, 167–70; reaction to reviews of *The Day of the Locust*, 192–96; courtship of and marriage to Eileen McKenney, 196–201; death, 202. Works listed by title.
"Western Union Boy," 144–45
Weston, Jessie L., xvii, xix, xxii, 97
White, William, 205
Whitman, Walt, 128
Willard, Daniel, 120
Williams, William Carlos, 68, 78, 110
Wilson, Colin, 56
Wilson, Edmund, 71, 74–75, 142, 169, 195–96
Winslow, Thyra Samter, 68
Winters, Yvor, 78
Wise Blood, 211
Wouk, Herman, 149
Wylie, Philip, 70

A NOTE ON MANUFACTURE

In 1462 THE RHENISH TOWN OF MAINZ, workplace of Johann Gutenberg, espoused the cause of the loser in a struggle between rival archbishops. The victorious Adolph von Nassau sacked the wealthy city, had it stripped of imperial privilege, and drove many of its citizens into exile. Among their effects, some carried away knowledge of the decade-old techniques of casting and printing from movable metal types, opening the era of the peripatetic scholar-printer whose apparition, the itinerant journeyman, still lingers in dusty jobbing-shops and the offices of little country weeklies.

The text of this book was set on the Linotype in a face called JANSON. Having in mind the wandering proclivities of the early masters, it is interesting to note that the type was cut in Amsterdam by a Hungarian named Nicholas Kis, *circa* 1690. It was erroneously named for the Dutch punch-cutter Anton Janson who had been employed in Leipzig where the original matrices were discovered years later.

Constantly seeking freedom from arbitrary restraint, leadership in the printing arts had passed from Christophe Plantin and the shadow of Philip II into Holland, even as the bloody Farnese ravished the borders. In the seventeeth century the sea-people of the northern states provided the liberty, knowledge, and wealth which underlay the productions of the Elzevirs and the sturdy and excellent types of Christoffel van Dijk and Dirk Voskens of which school JANSON is such a worthy representative.

This book was composed, printed, and bound by KINGSPORT PRESS, INC., Kingsport, Tennessee. The typography and binding designs are by GUY FLEMING.